LOUISIANA TRAIL RIDERS

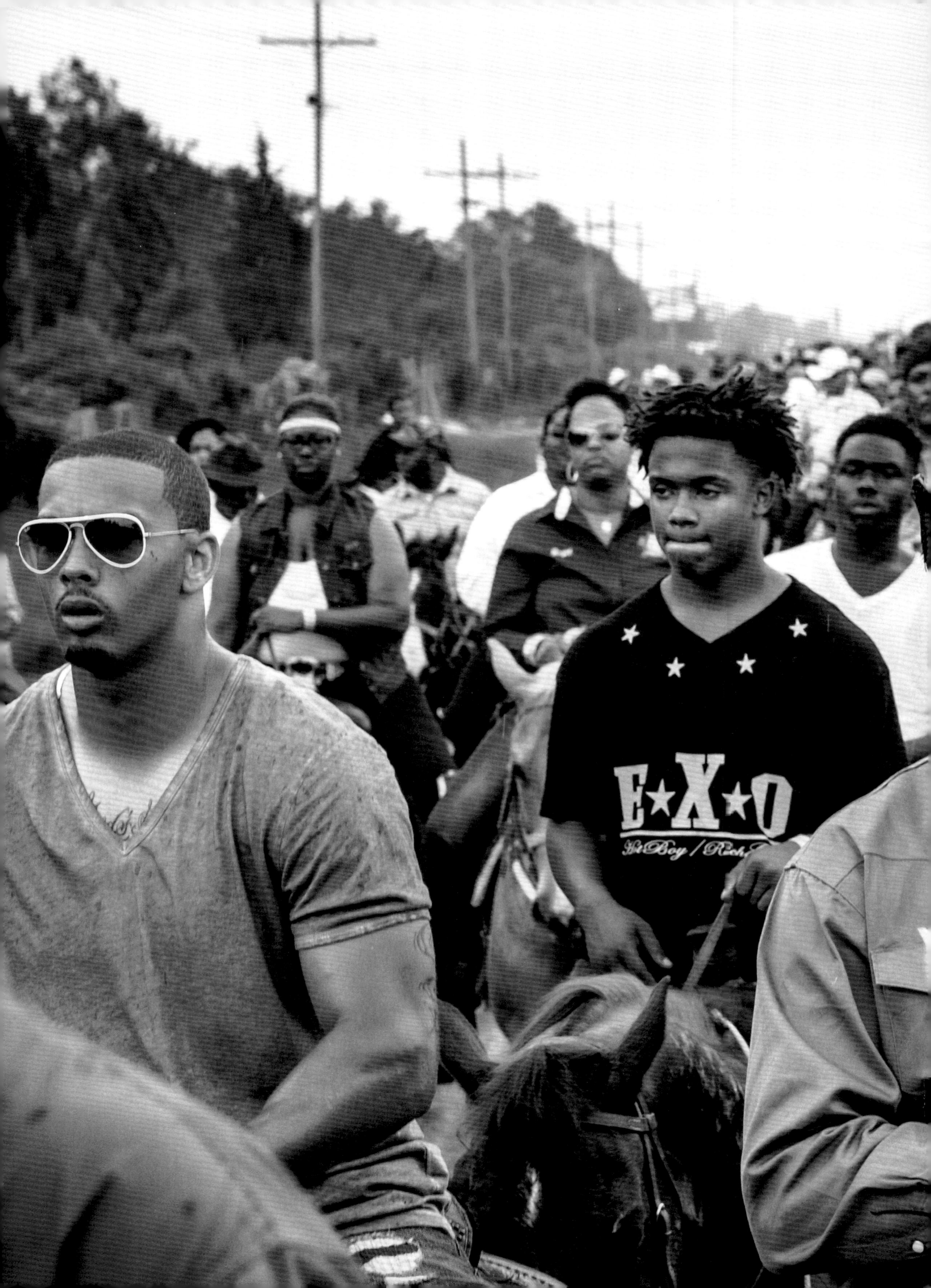
E★X★O

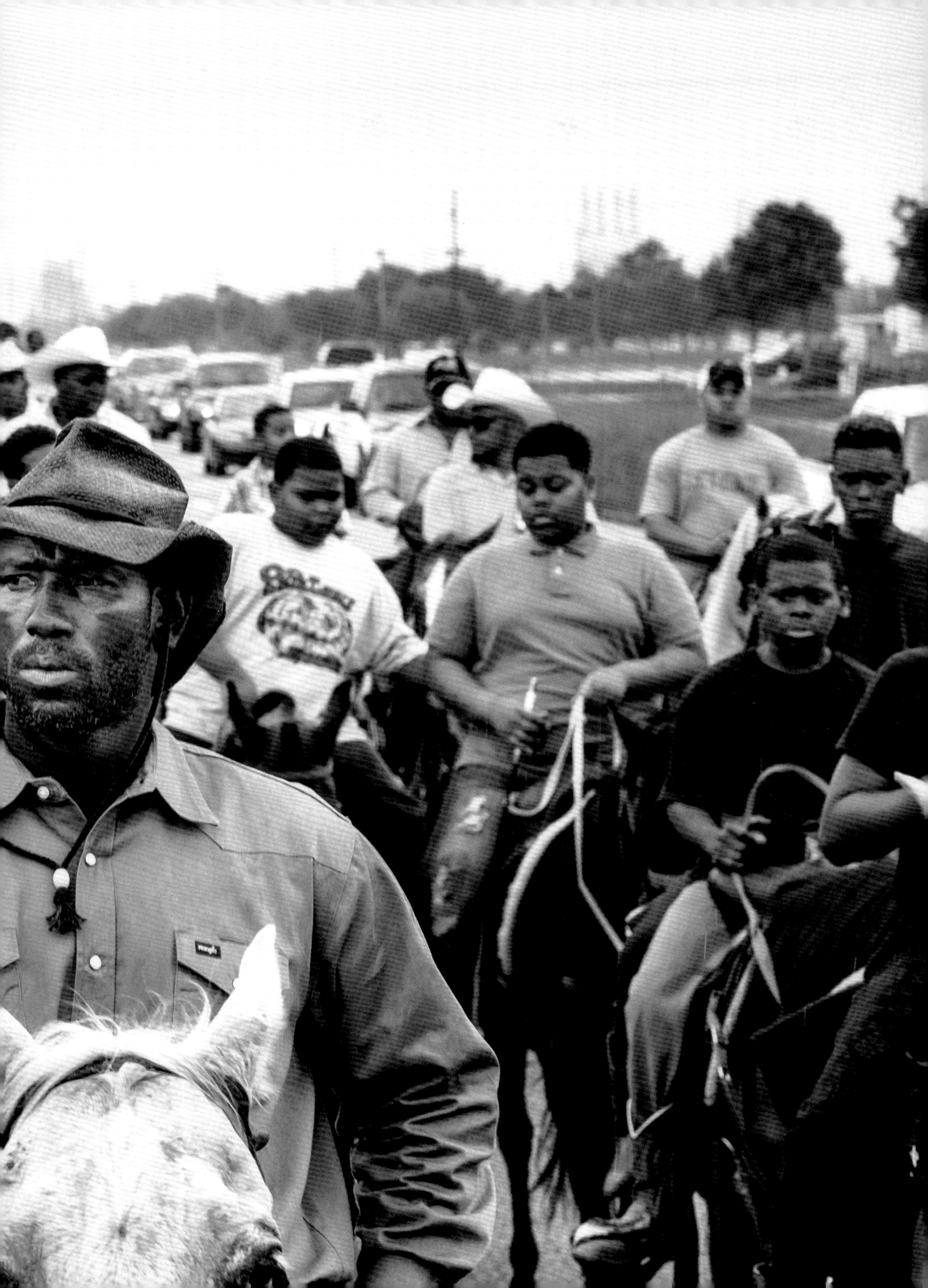

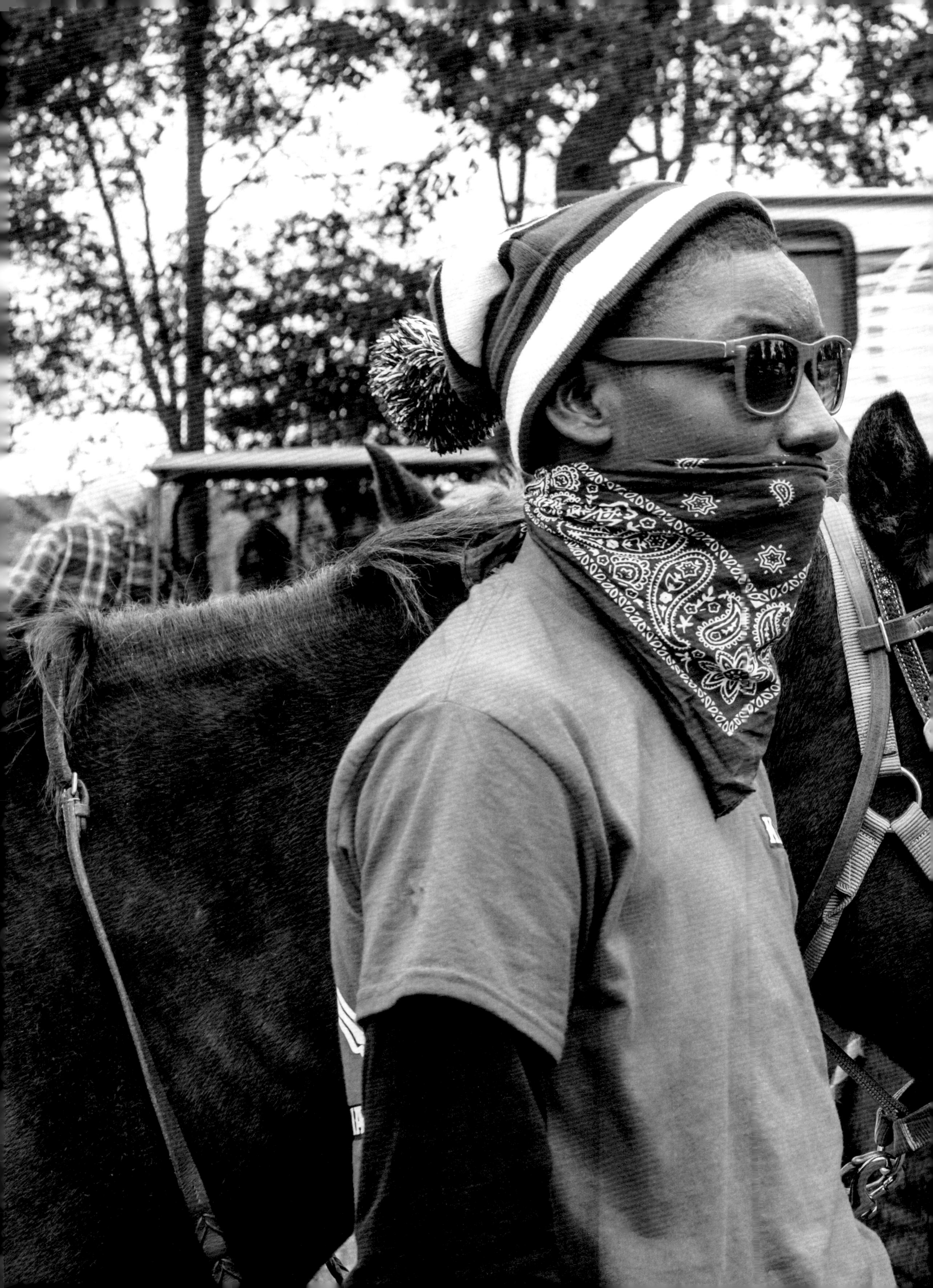

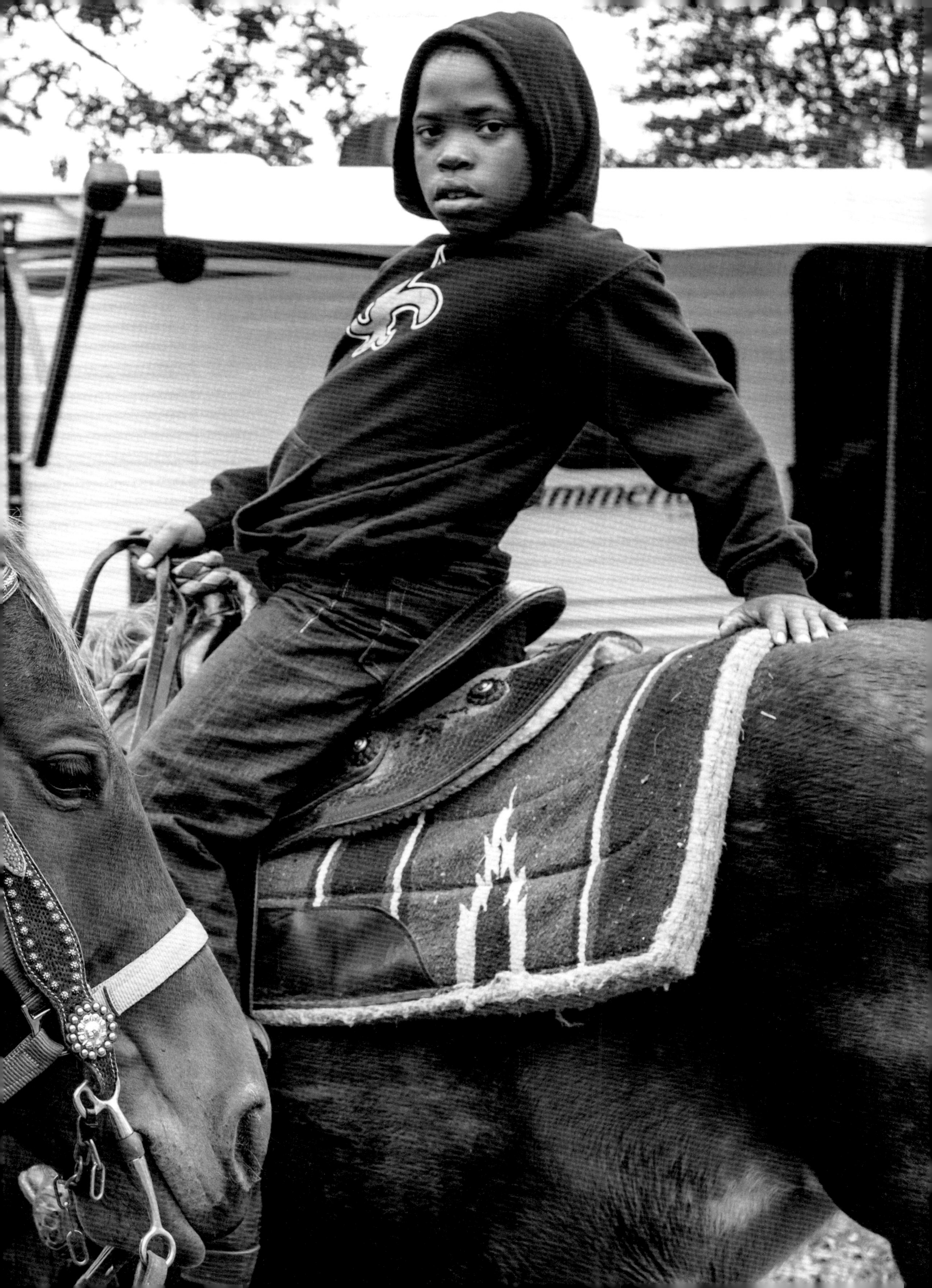

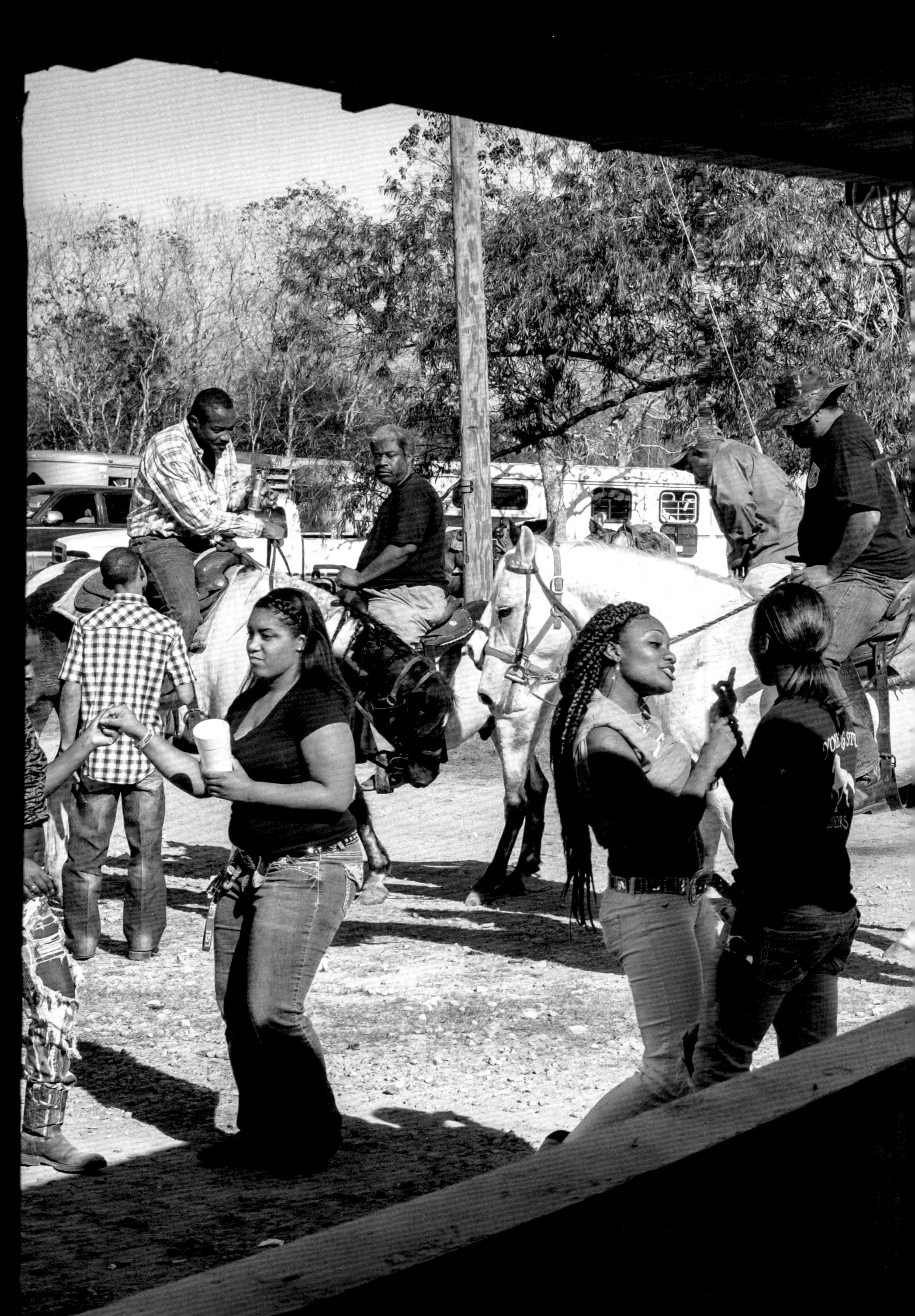

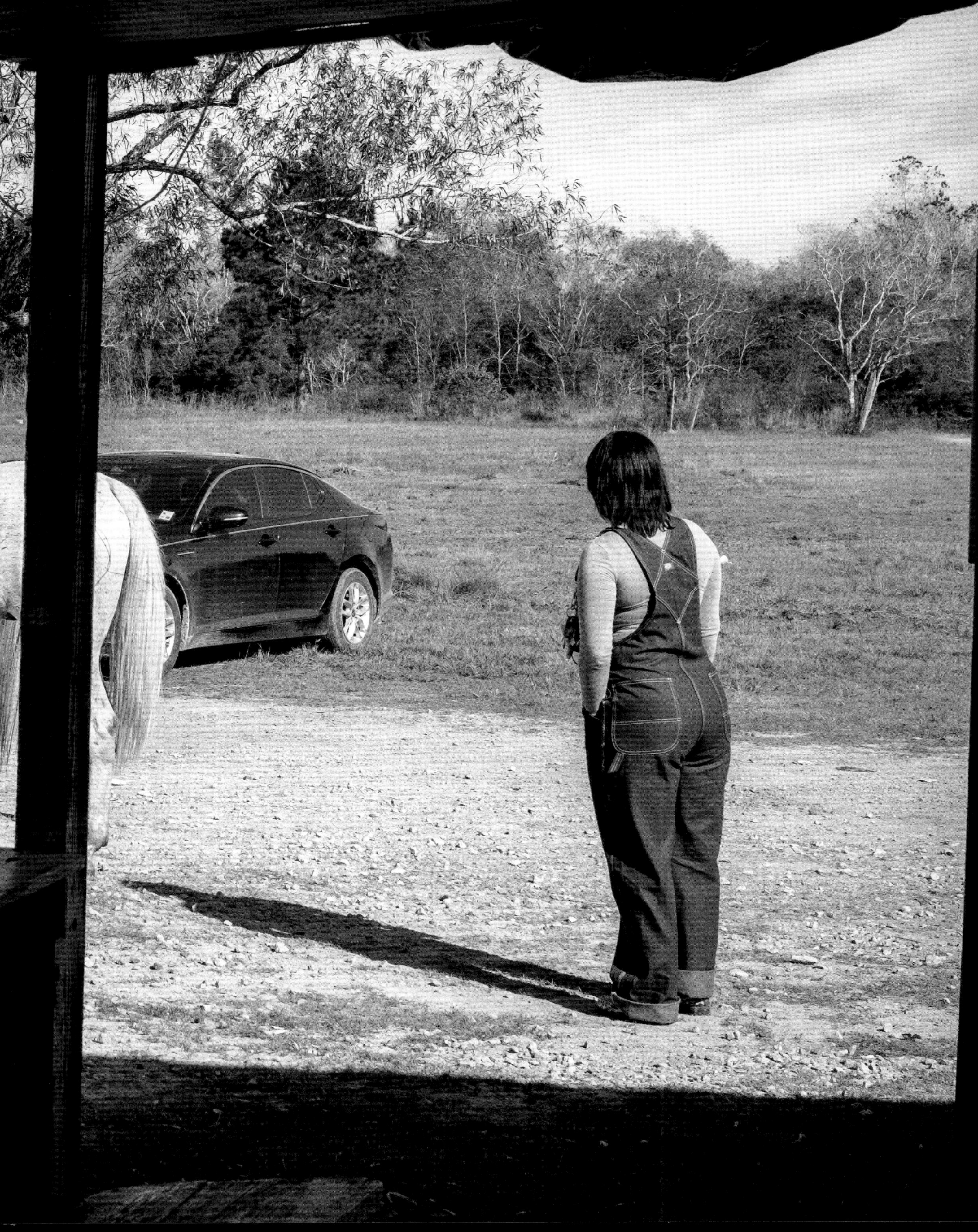

LOUISIANA TRAIL RIDERS

JEREMIAH ARIAZ

2018
UNIVERSITY OF LOUISIANA AT LAFAYETTE PRESS

Introduction

Jeremiah Ariaz

While riding my motorcycle on Highway 77 along Bayou Grosse Tete, I encountered a group of nearly fifty people on horseback. They commanded the two-lane road, and I pulled over for them to pass. I retrieved my camera from the saddlebag of my bike and took a few photographs as they rode by. People waved, hollered, lifted beer bottles, or tilted hats, availing themselves to the camera. A gentleman at the end of the procession motioned to me, encouraging me to join them. I was captivated by the passing riders and immediately aware of the rare opportunity I had been granted. I turned my motorcycle around and began to follow, occasionally pulling ahead to photograph the loose procession of riders. The ride concluded several miles down the road in a large open field. I took off my helmet and jacket and mingled amongst the riders. Music was playing, jambalaya was offered, riders demonstrated their equestrian skills, and a small crowd placed bets on two racing horses. It was an overcast day in March, and the sun was beginning to set. I made a few photographs but mostly struck up conversations, inquiring about the scene I had stumbled into. I was handed a hand-written flier for the next ride with a phone number to call for directions. So began nearly five years of riding and making photographs with Louisiana trail riding clubs.

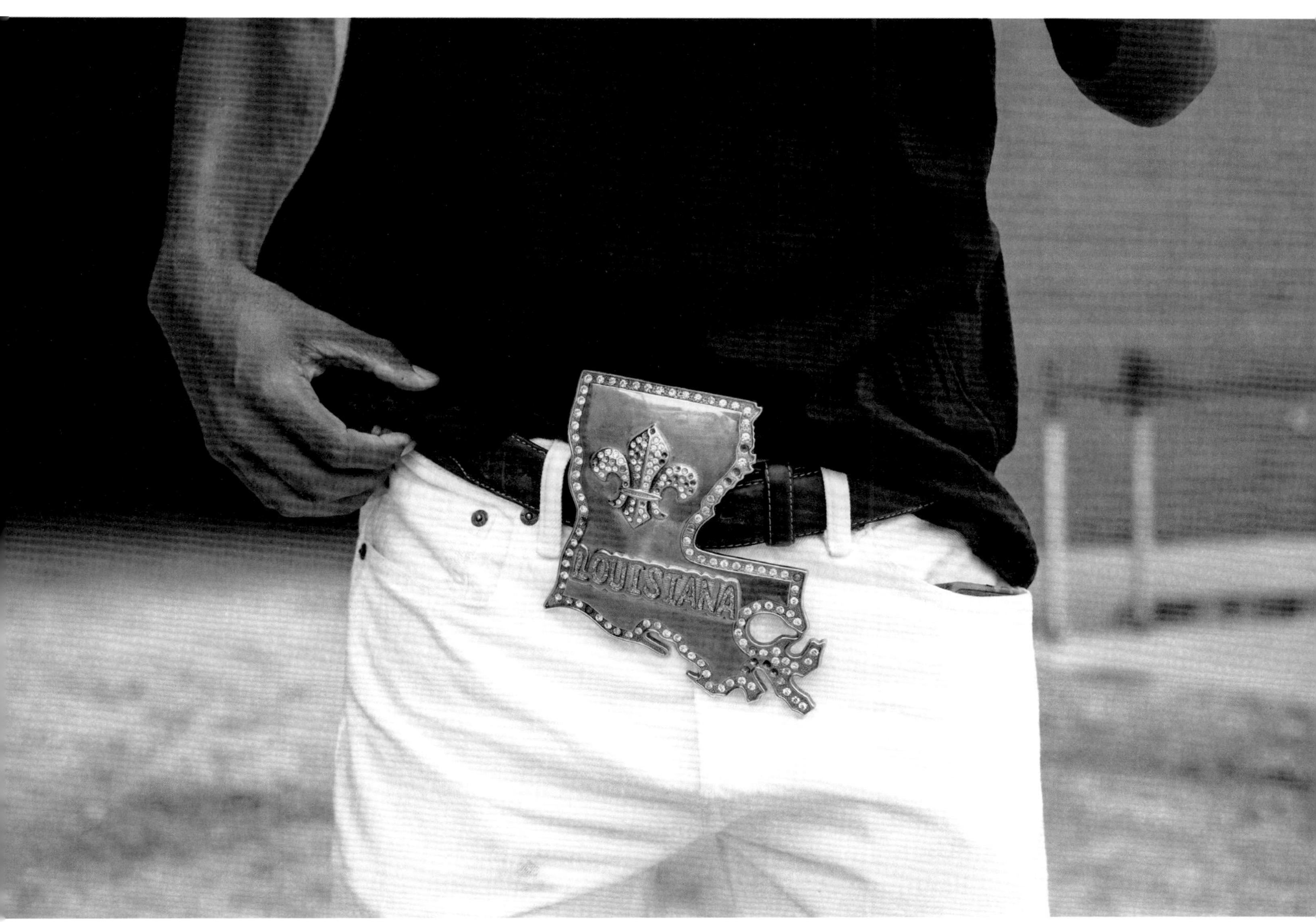
LOUISIANA

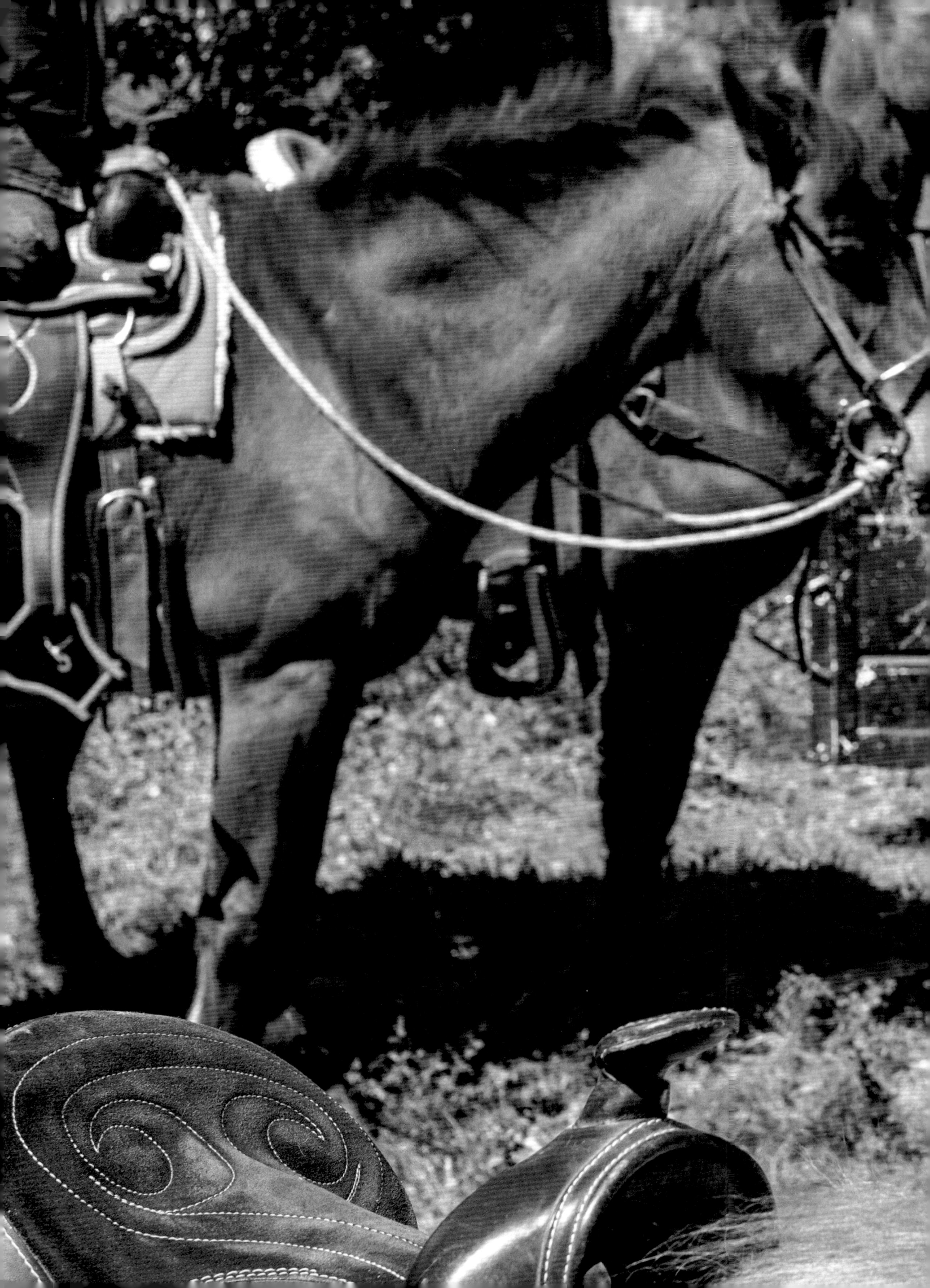

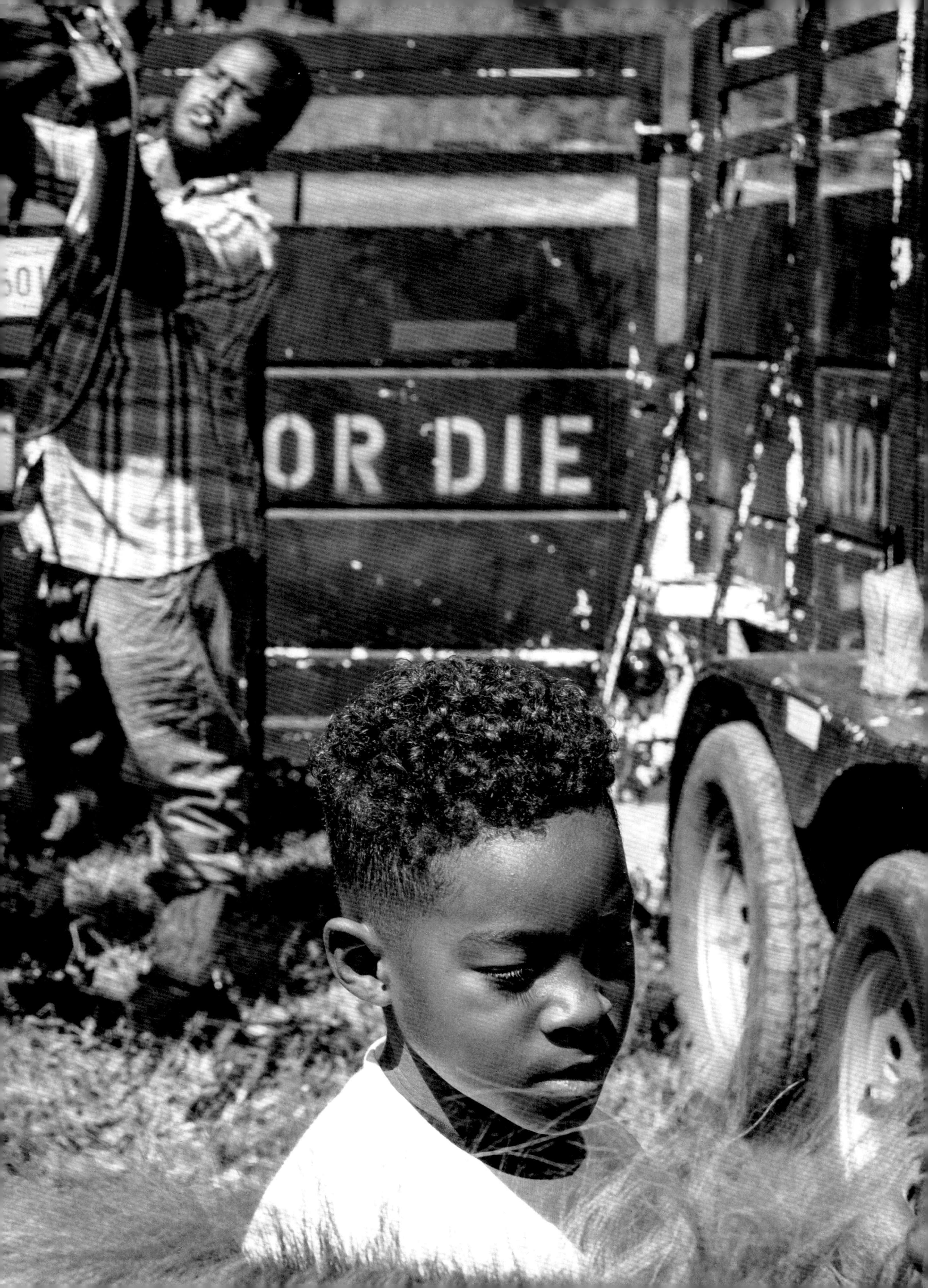
OR DIE

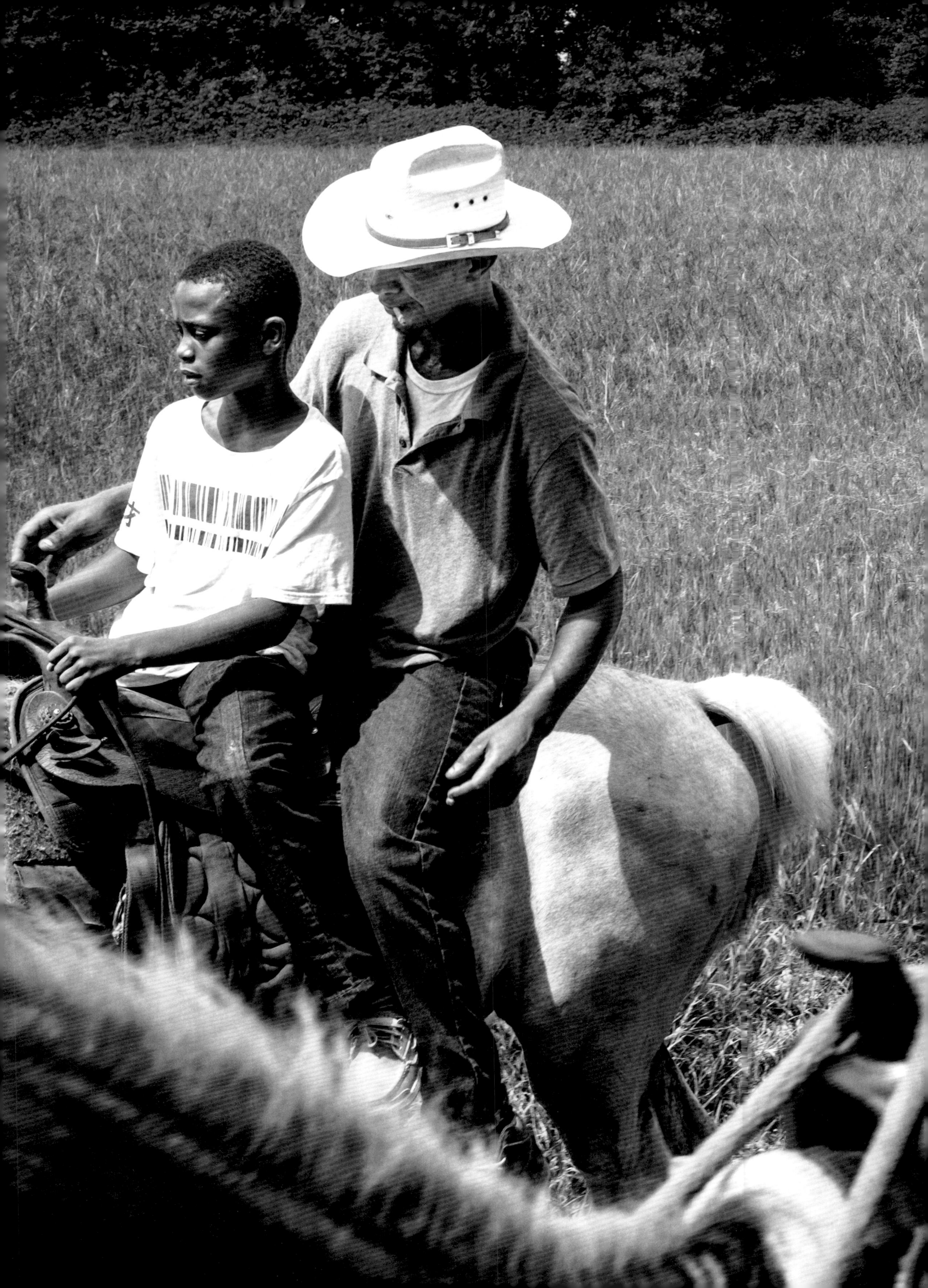

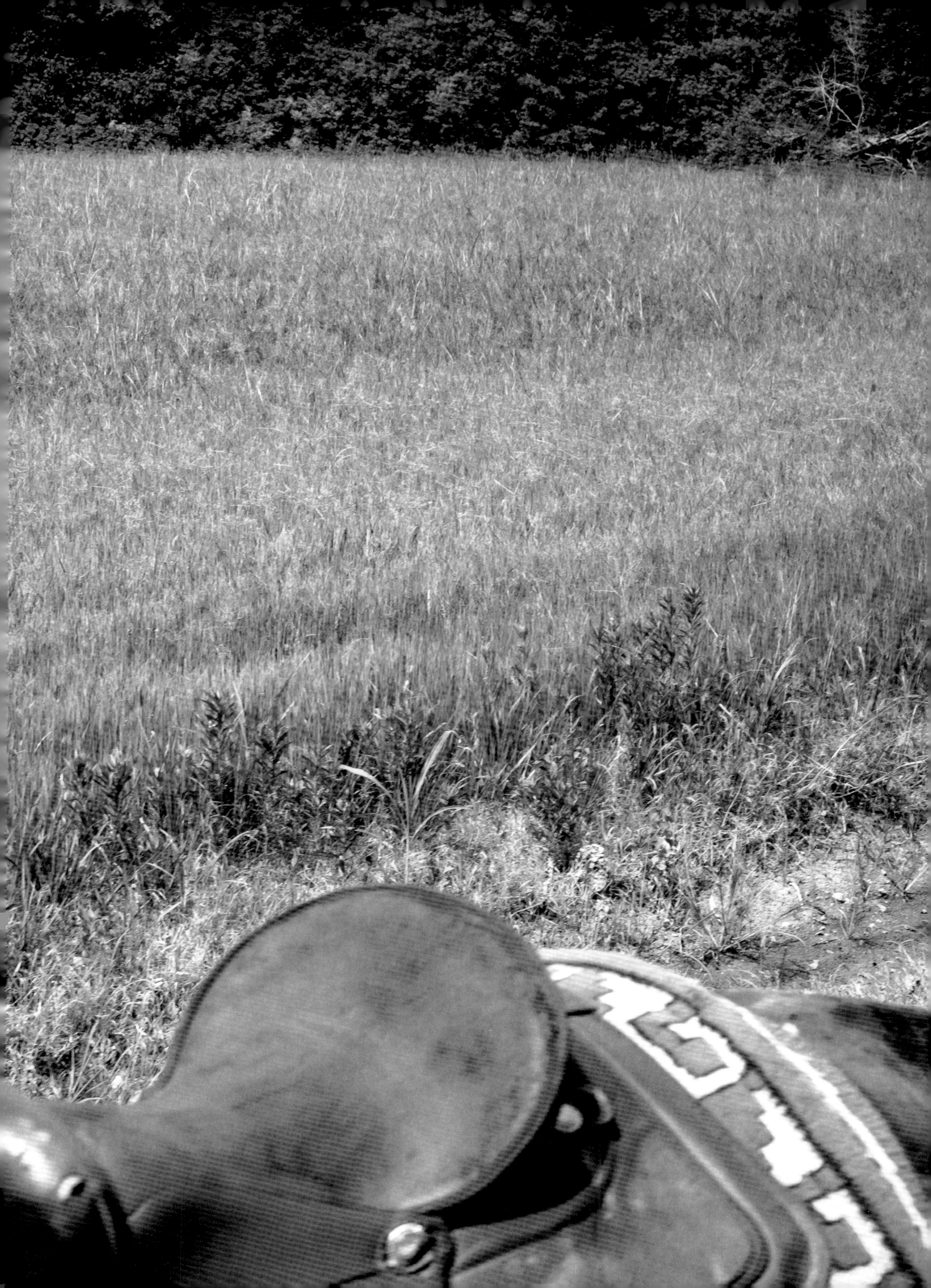

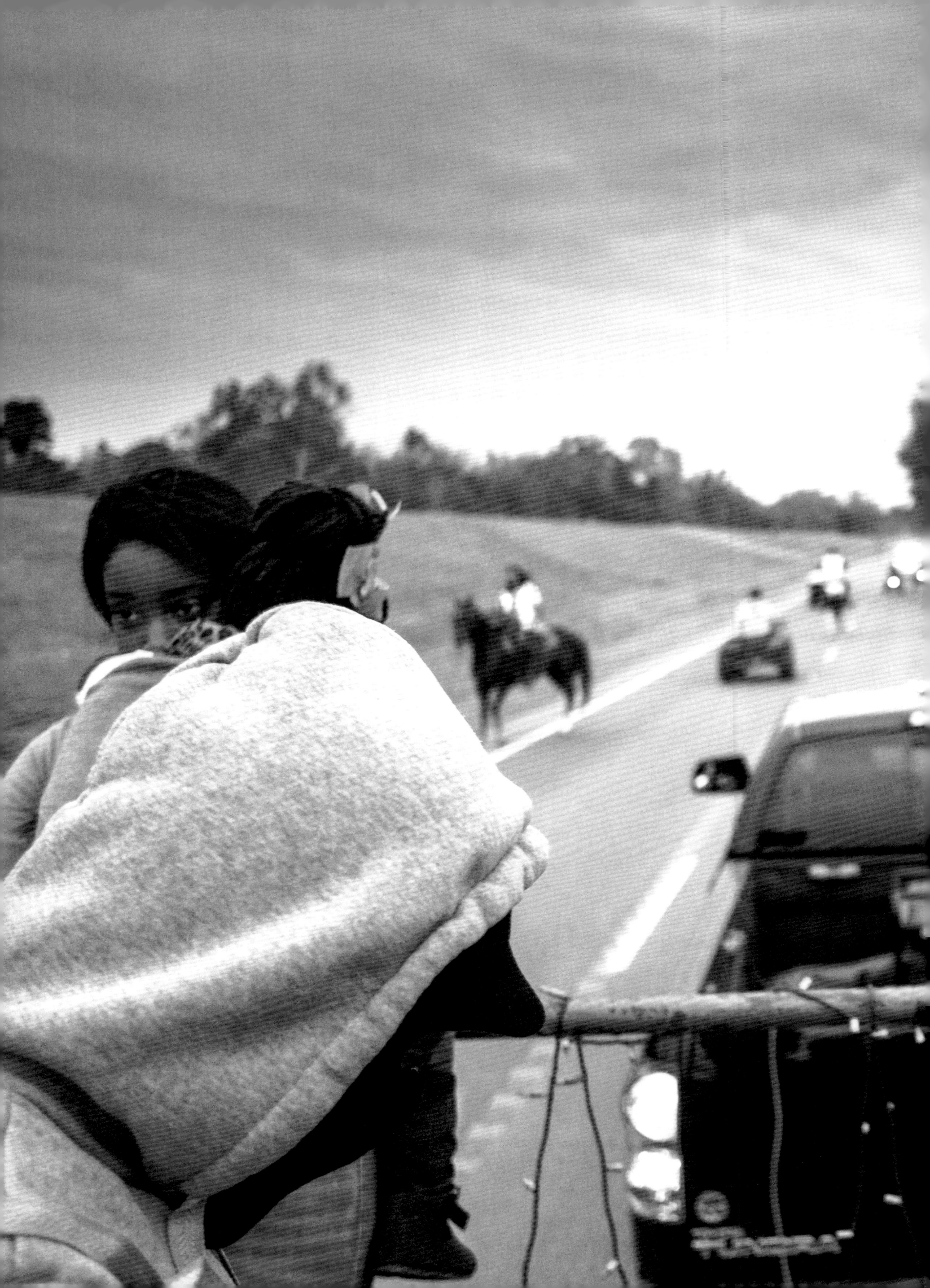

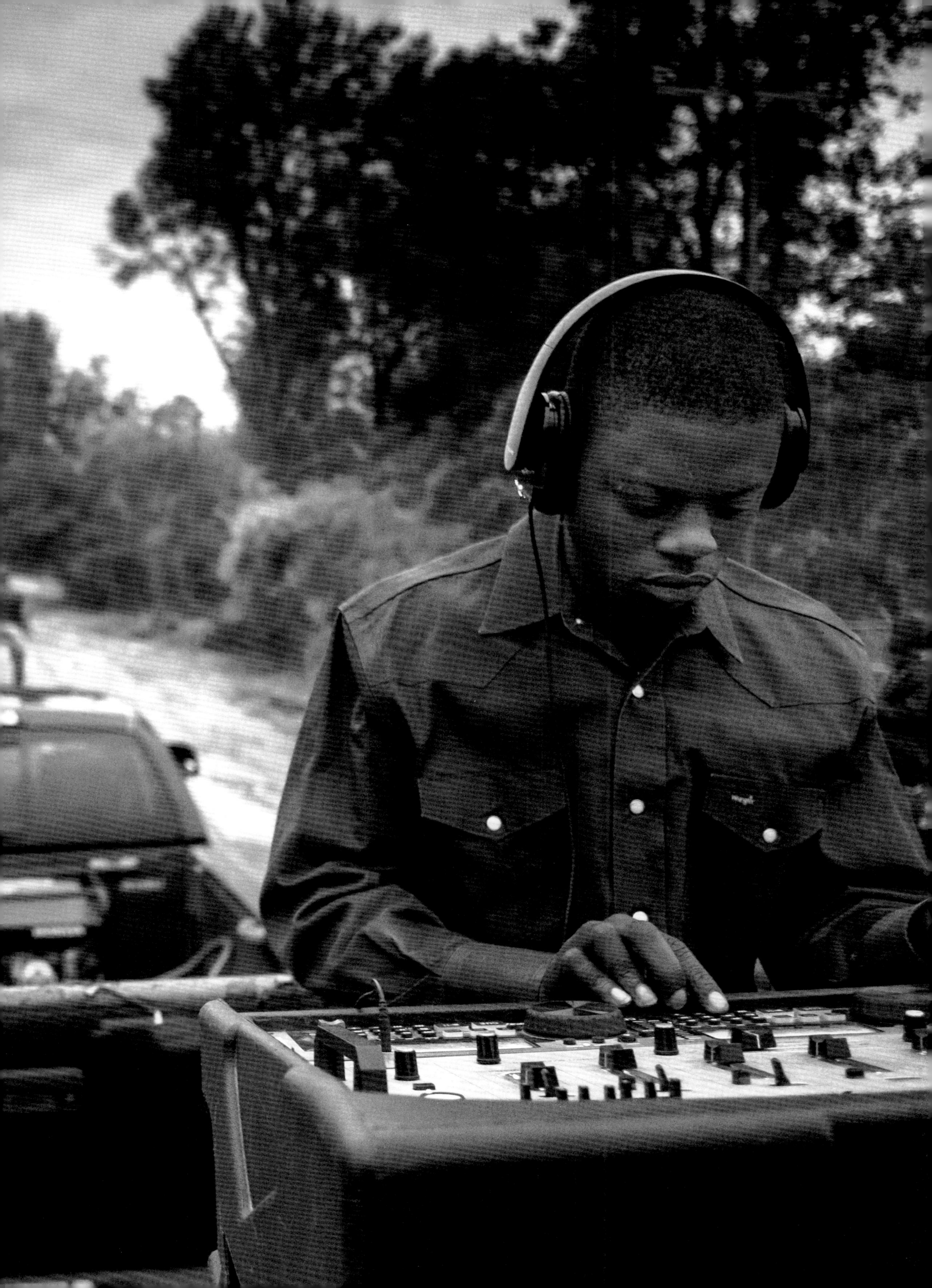

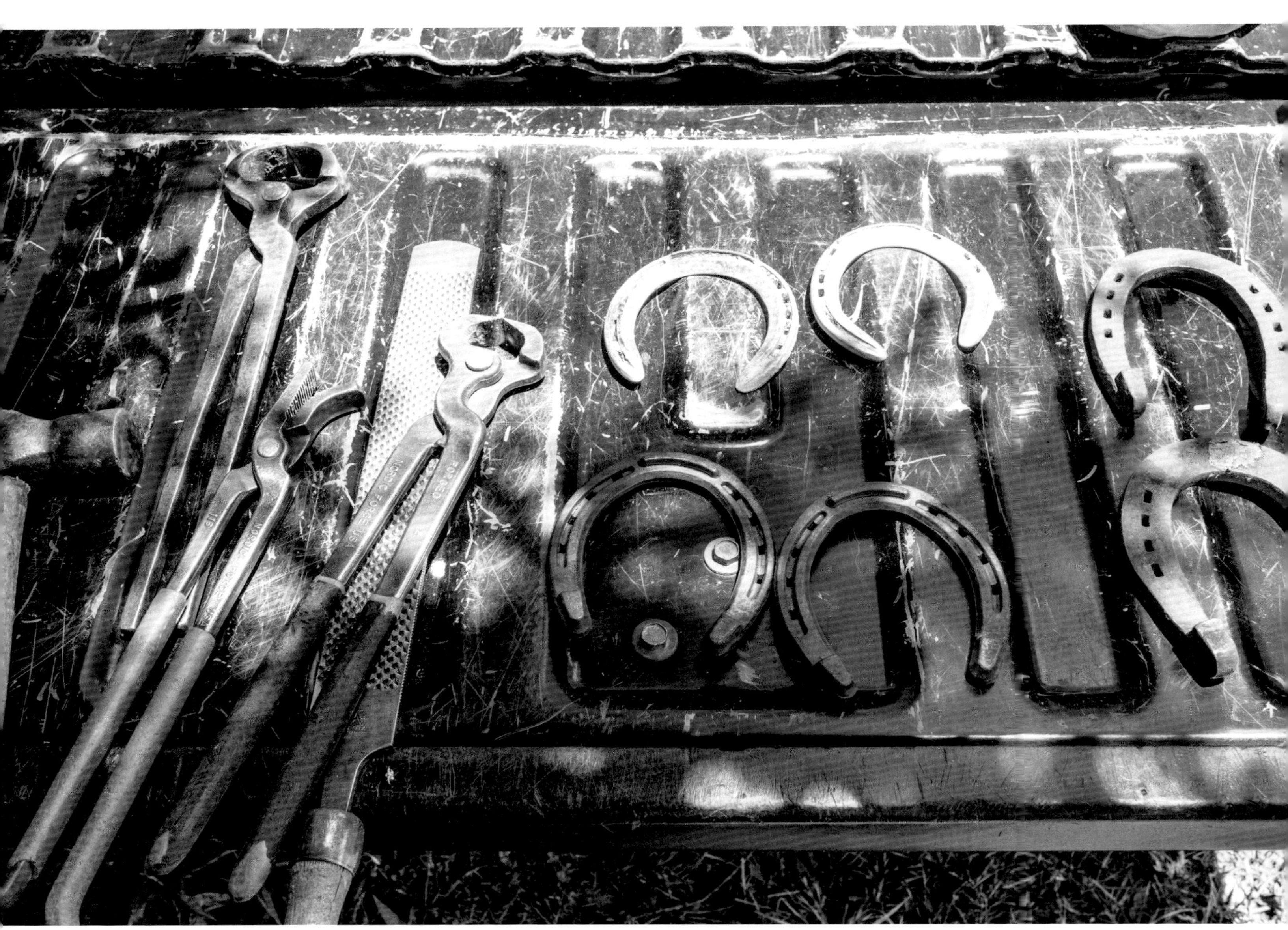

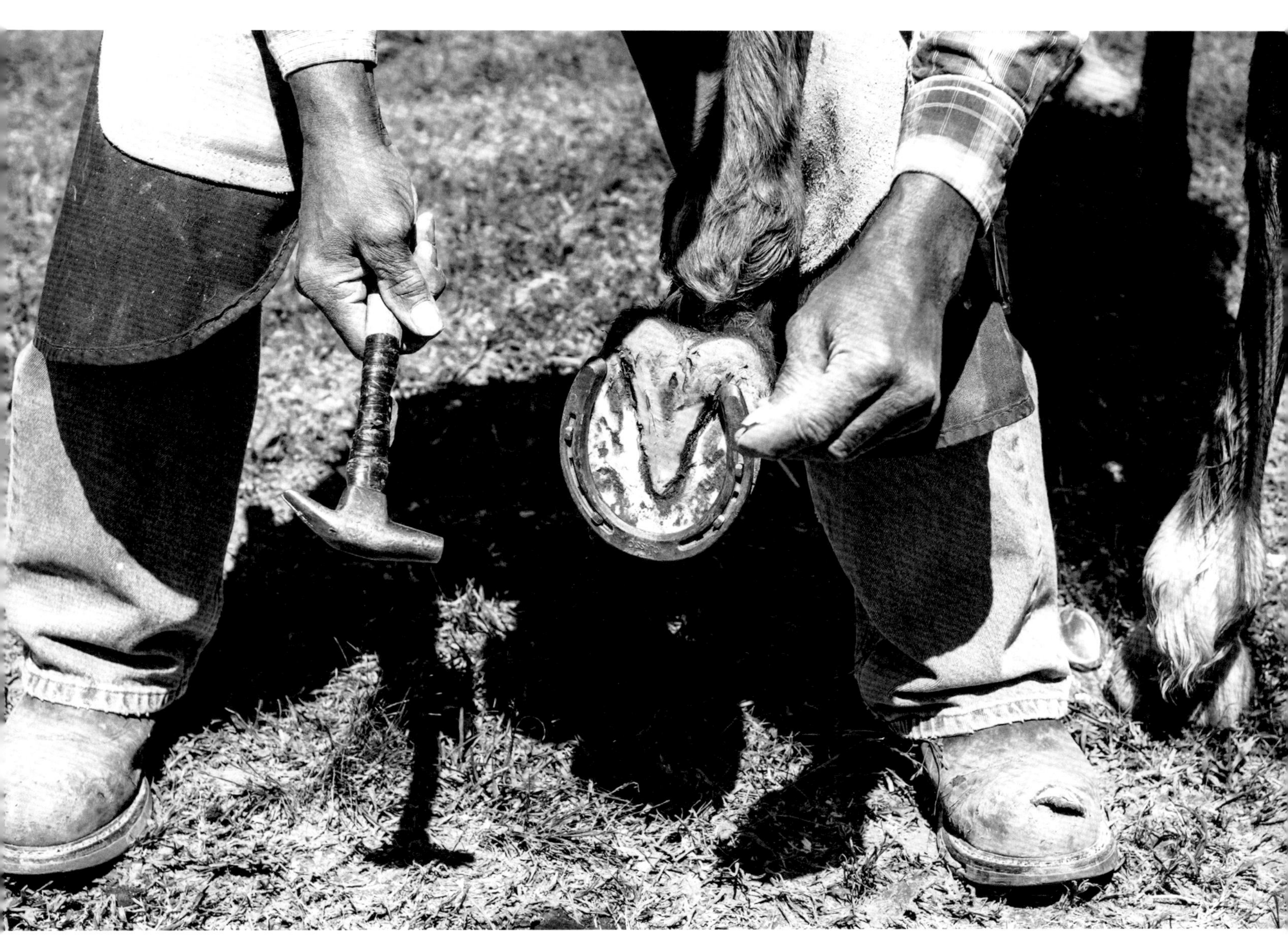

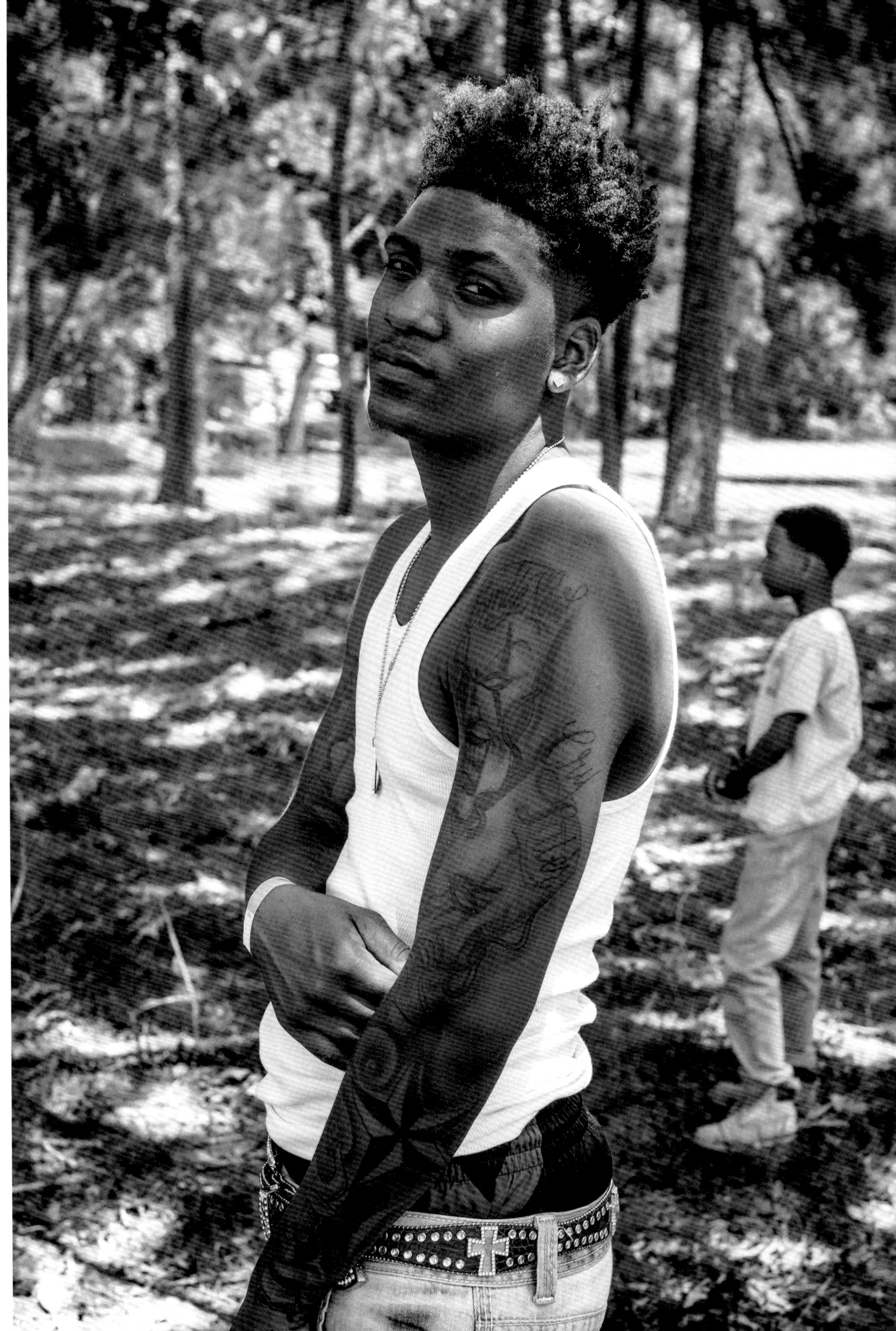

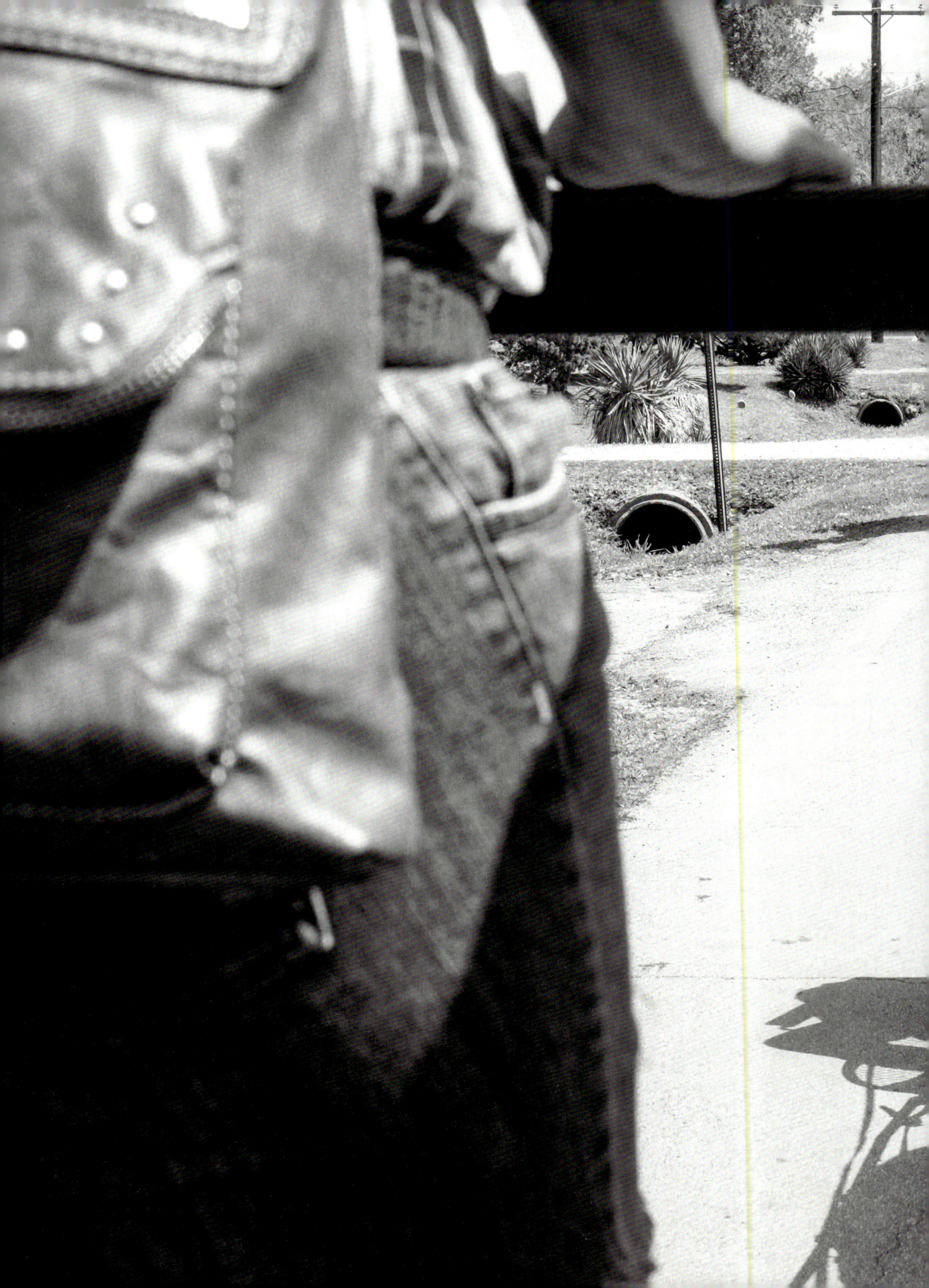

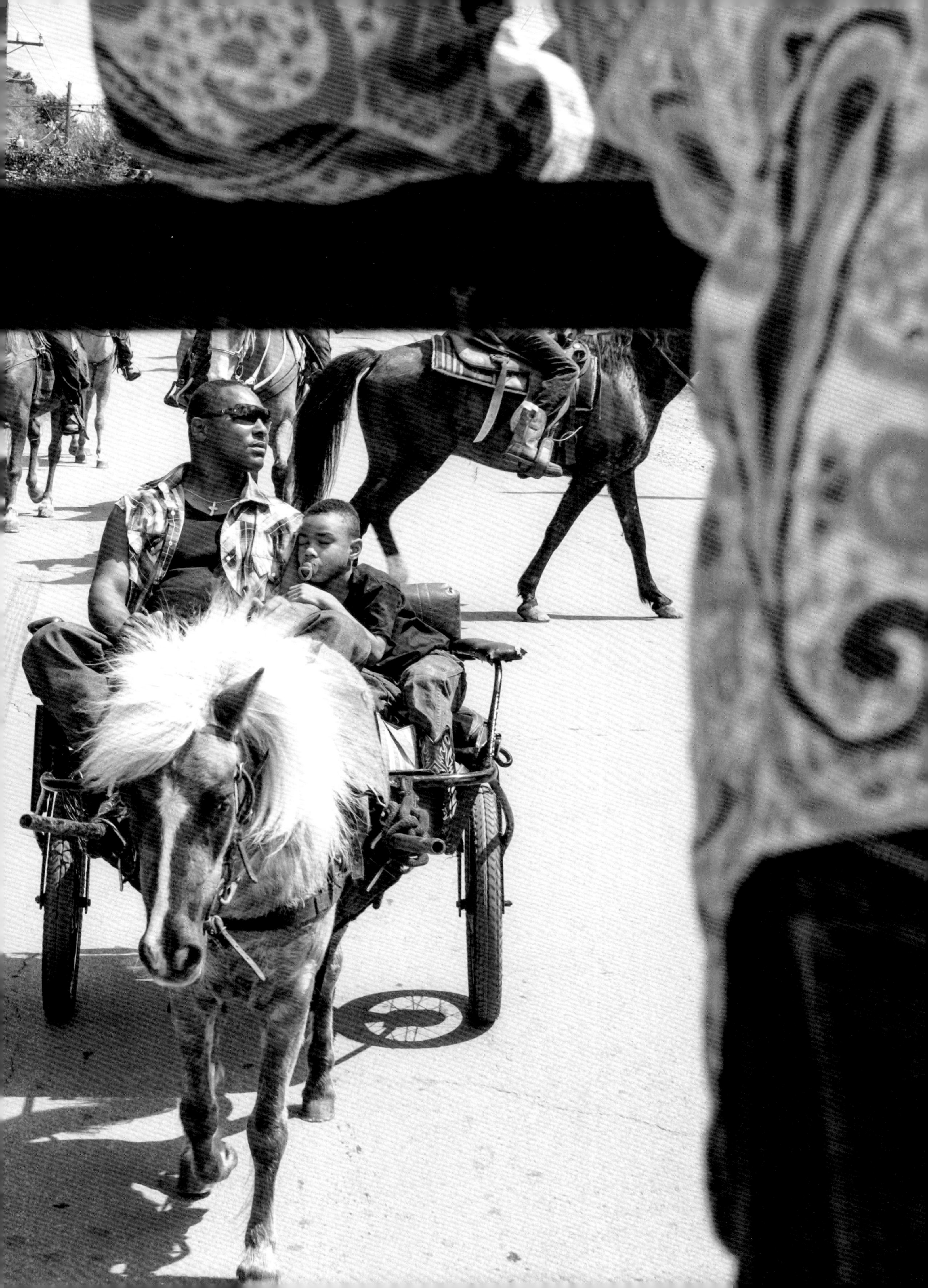

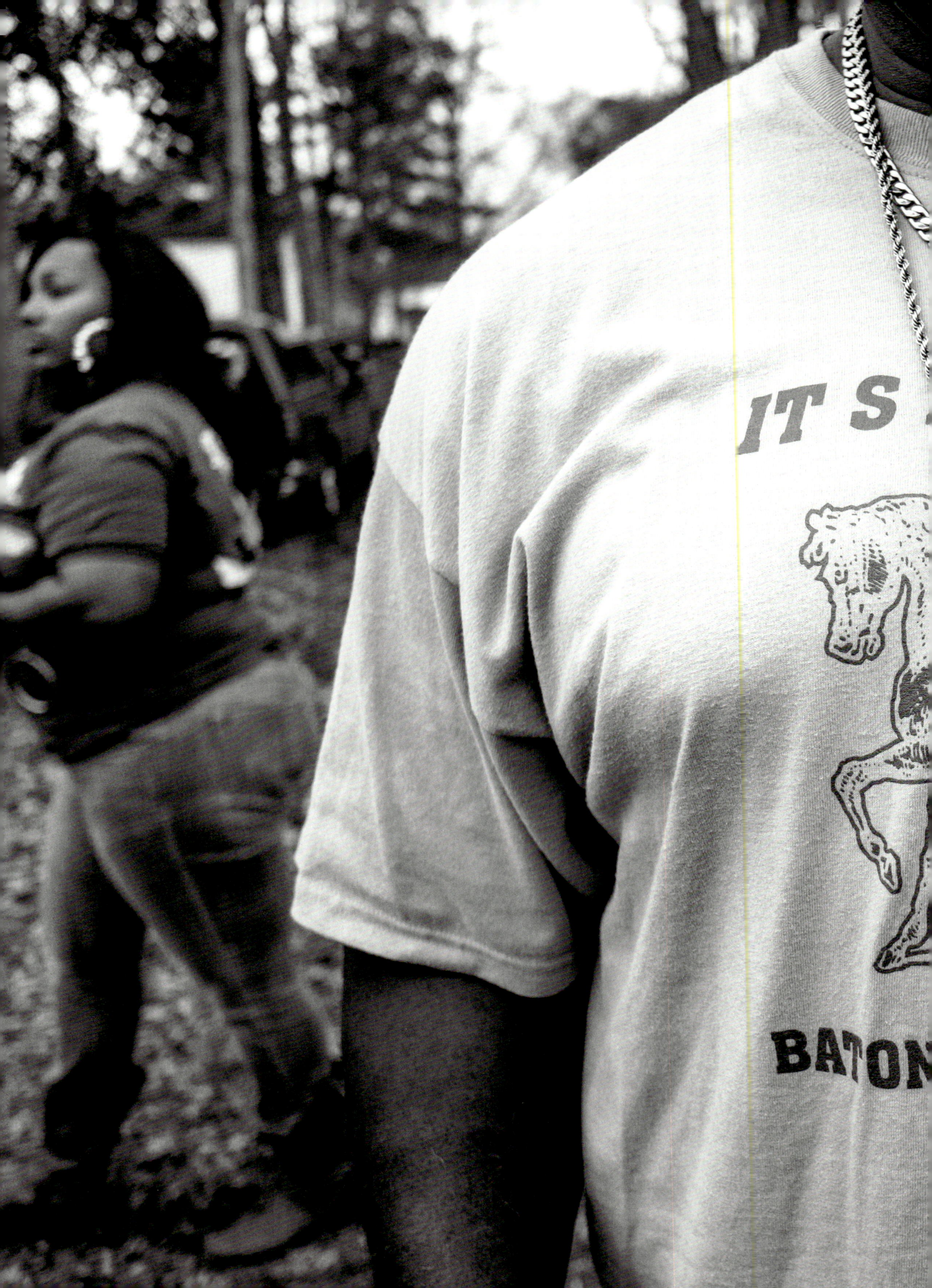
IT S
BATON

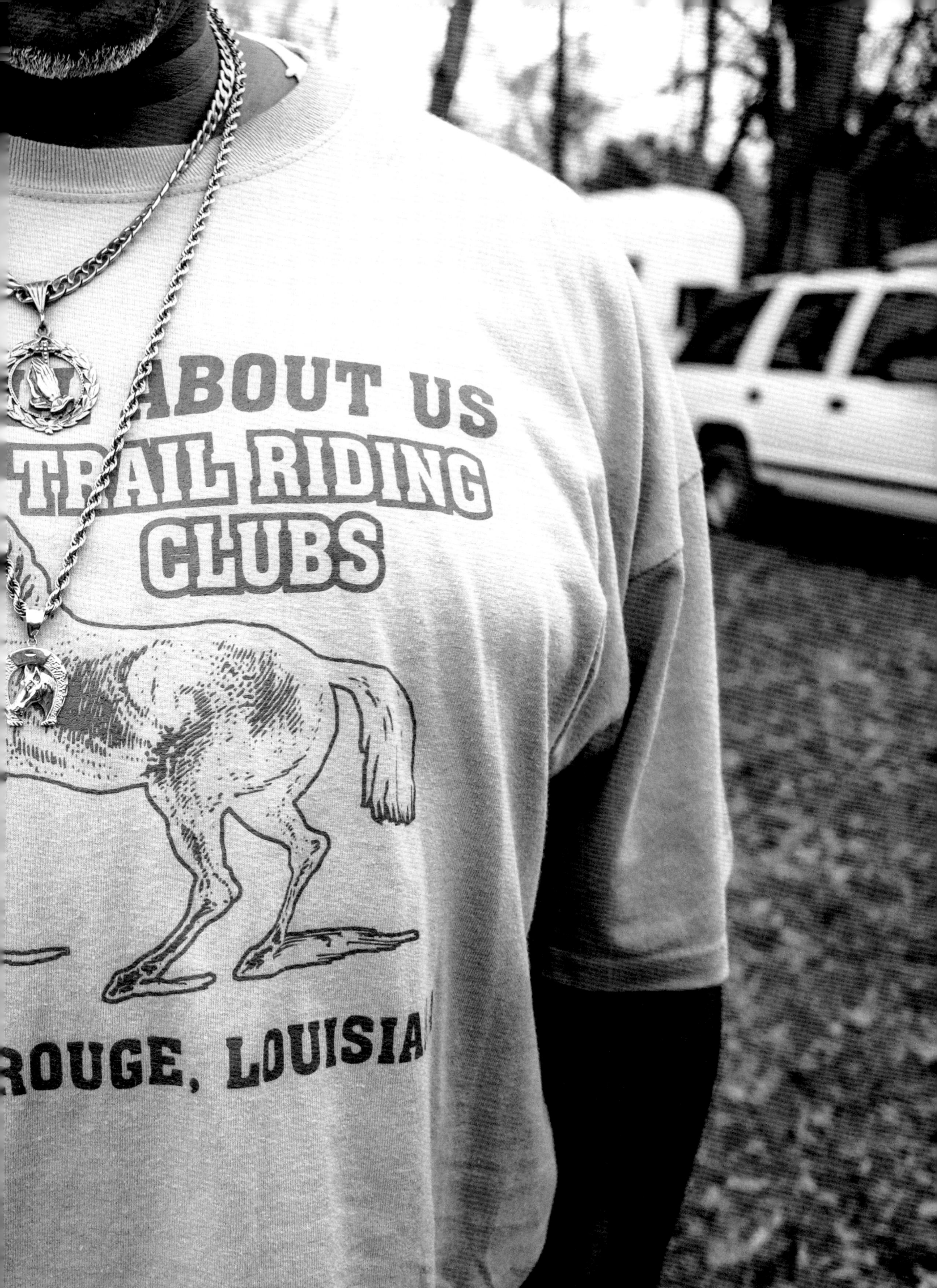

ABOUT US
TRAIL RIDING
CLUBS
ROUGE, LOUISIA

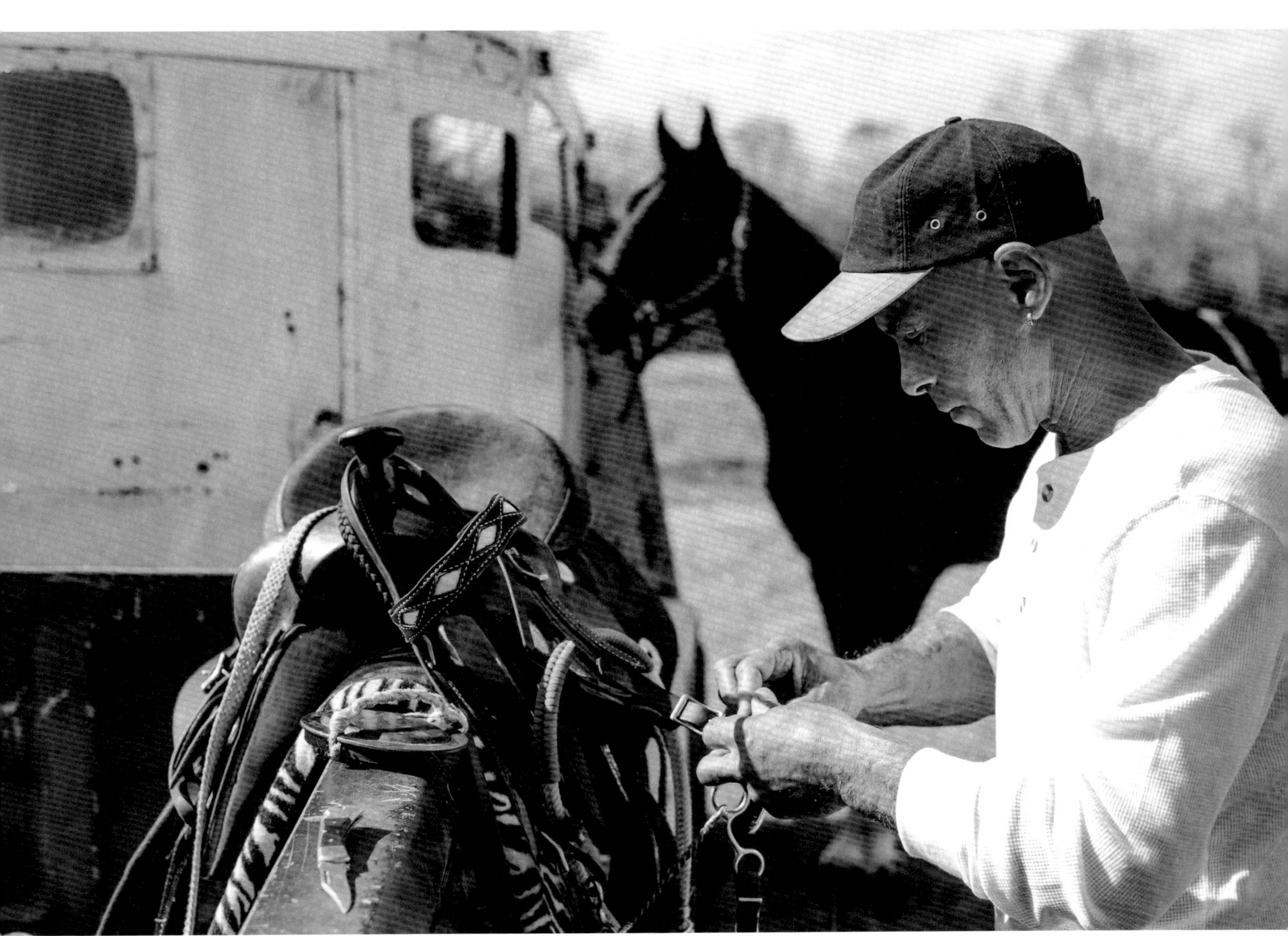

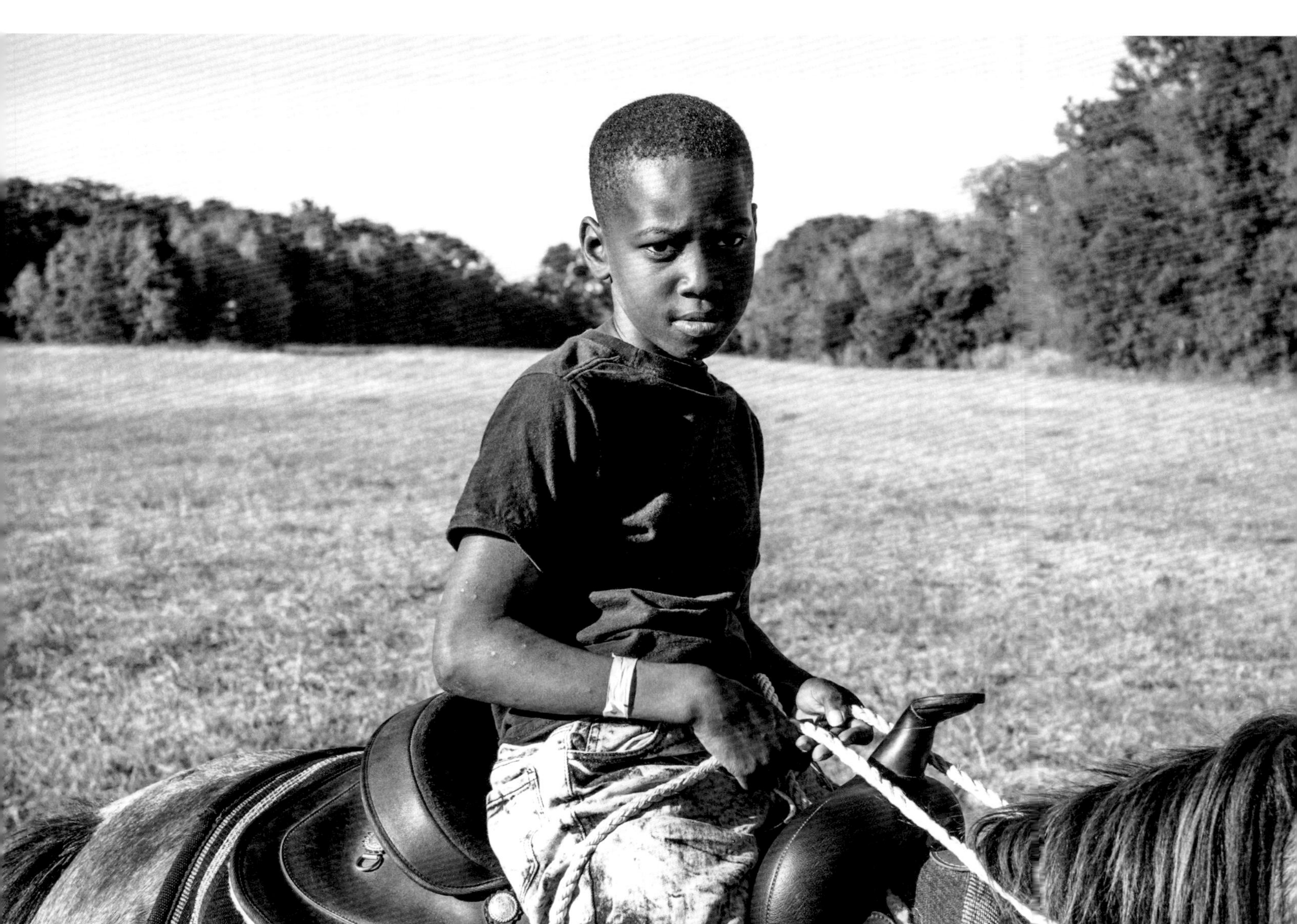

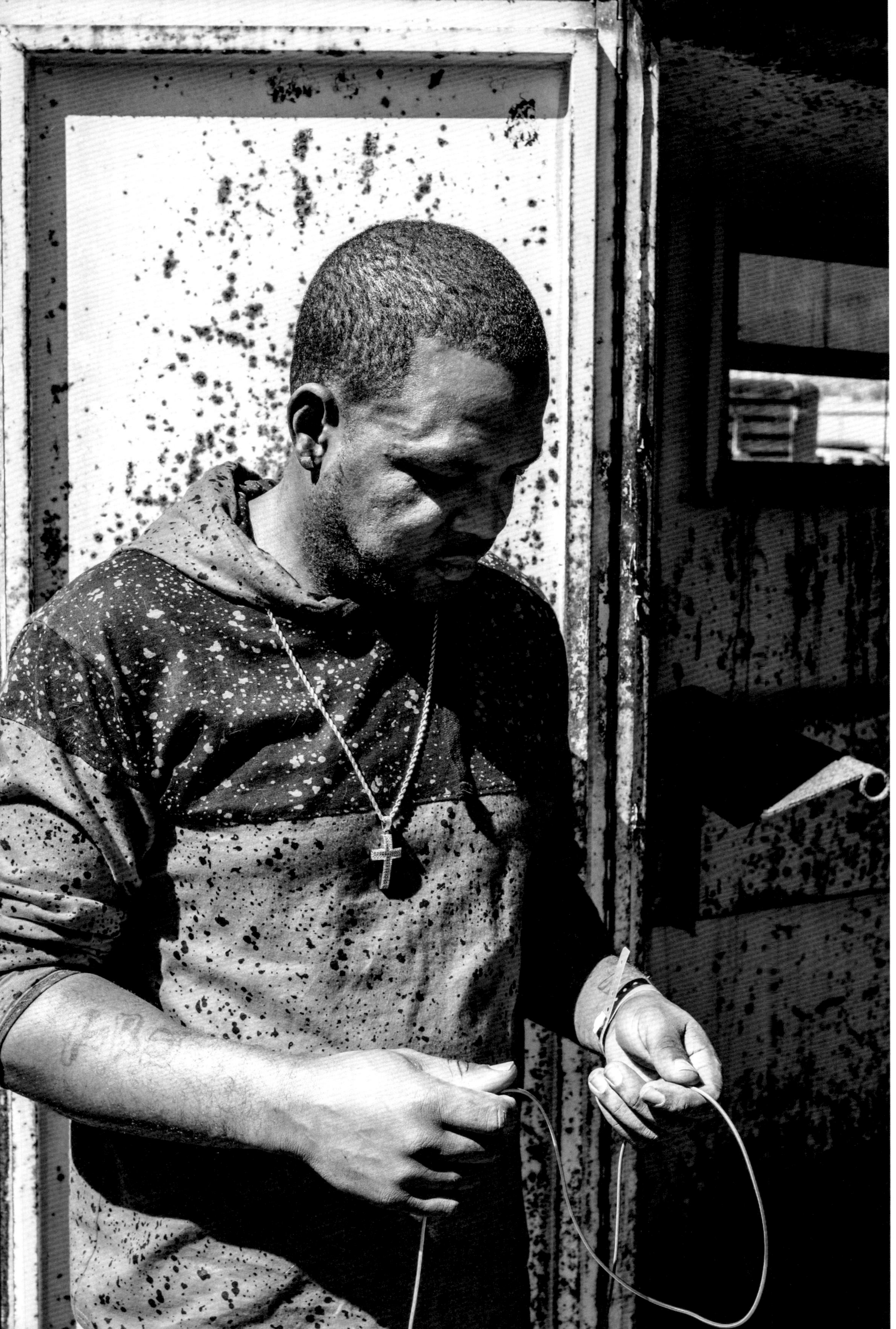

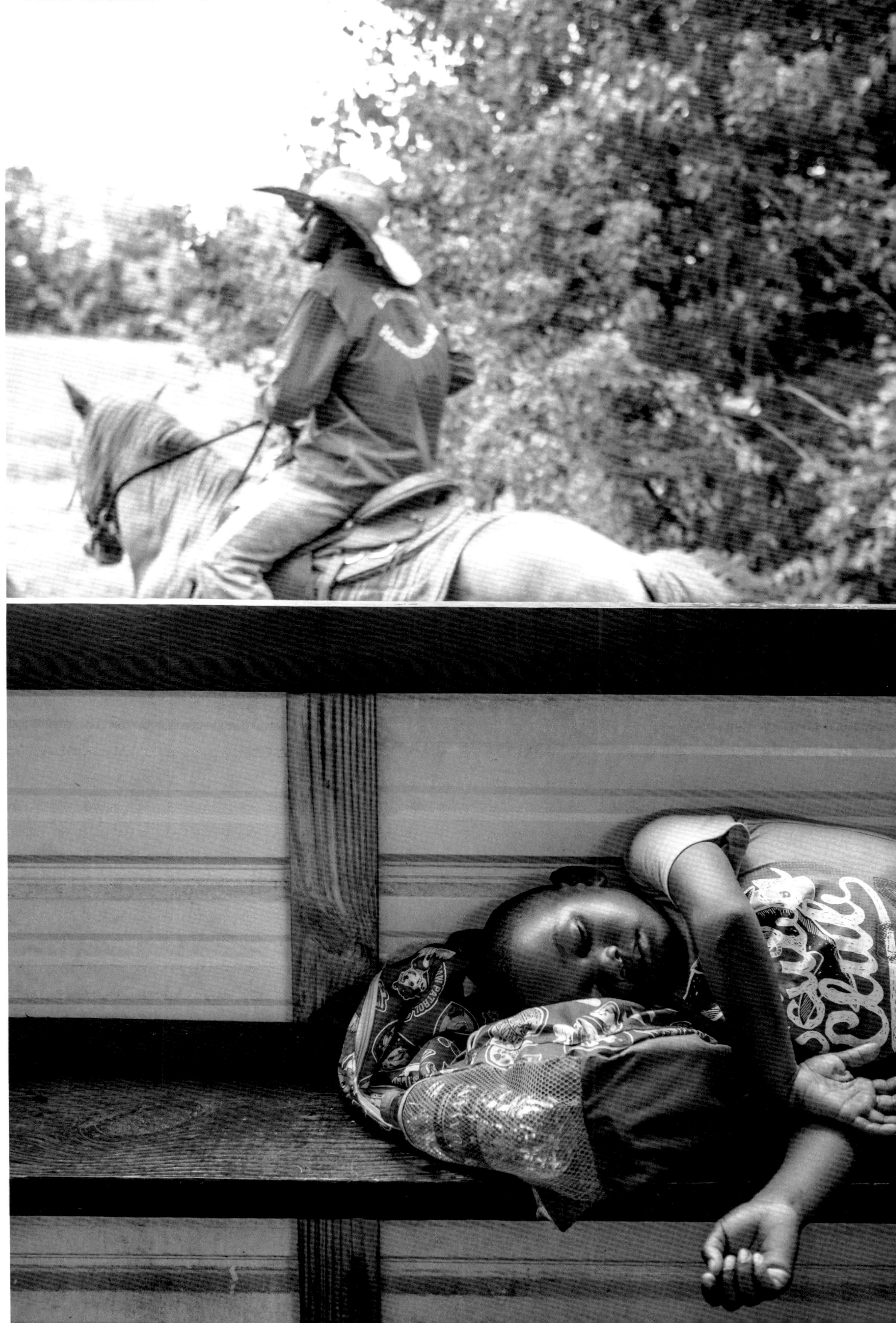

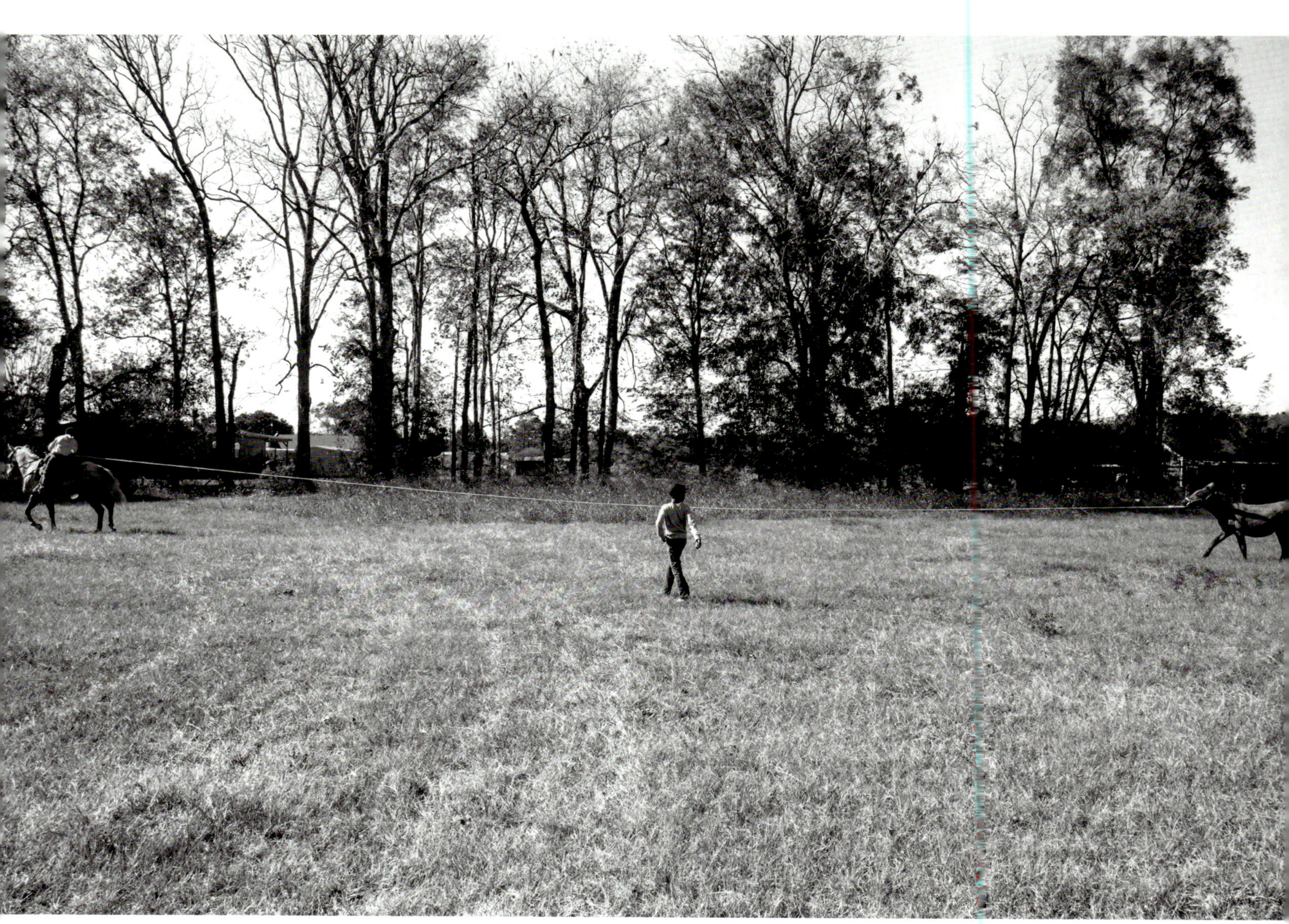

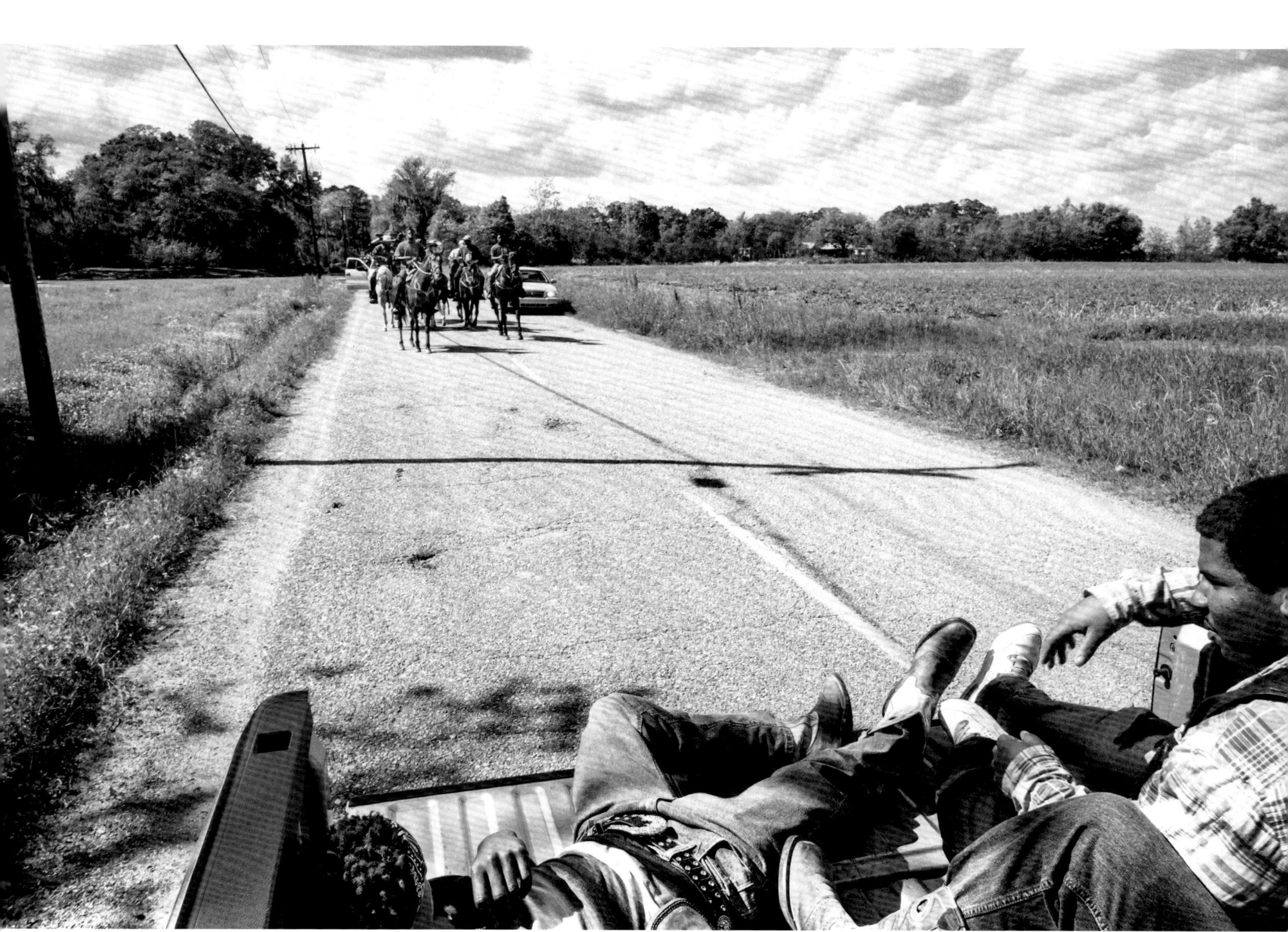

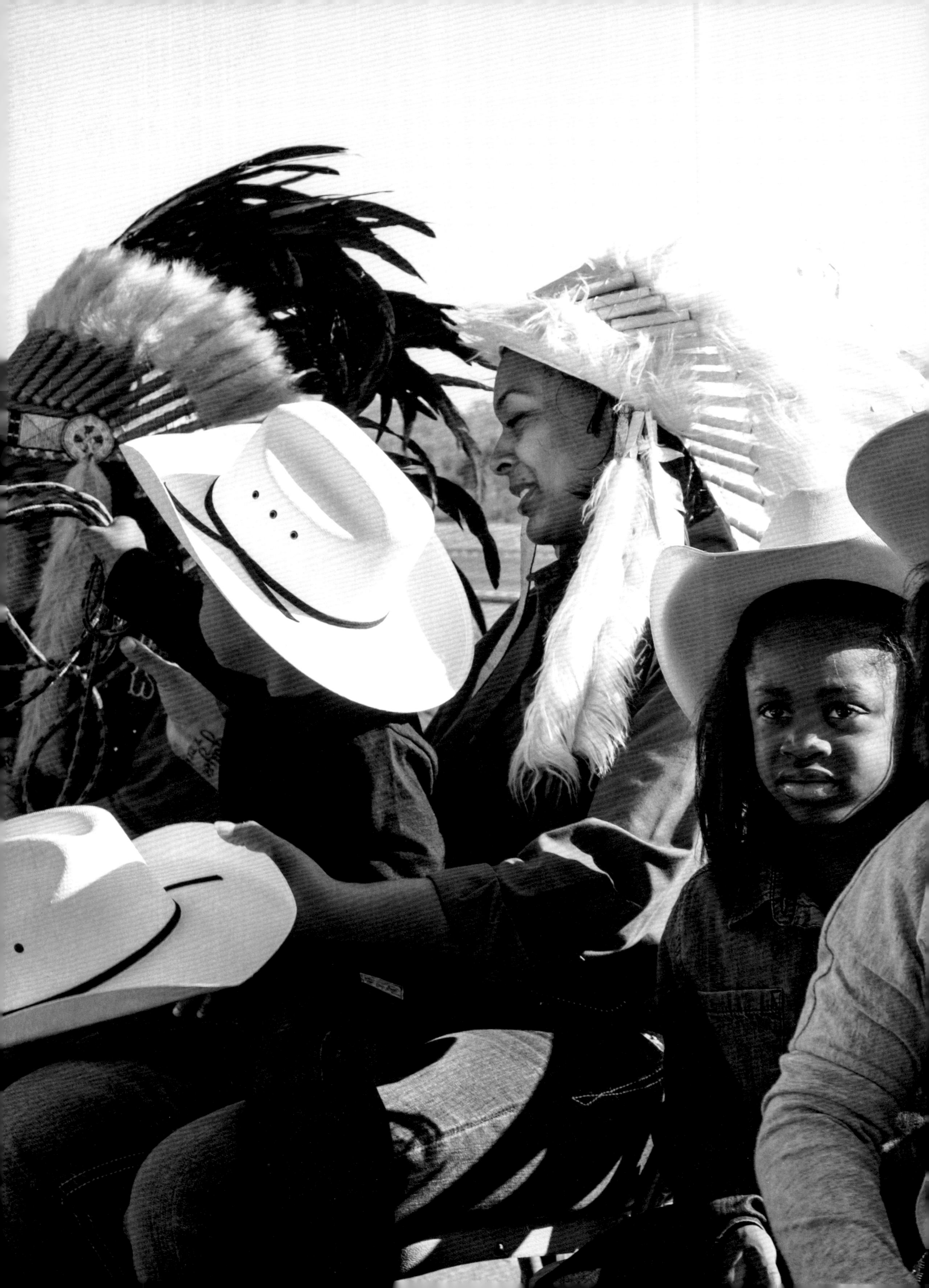

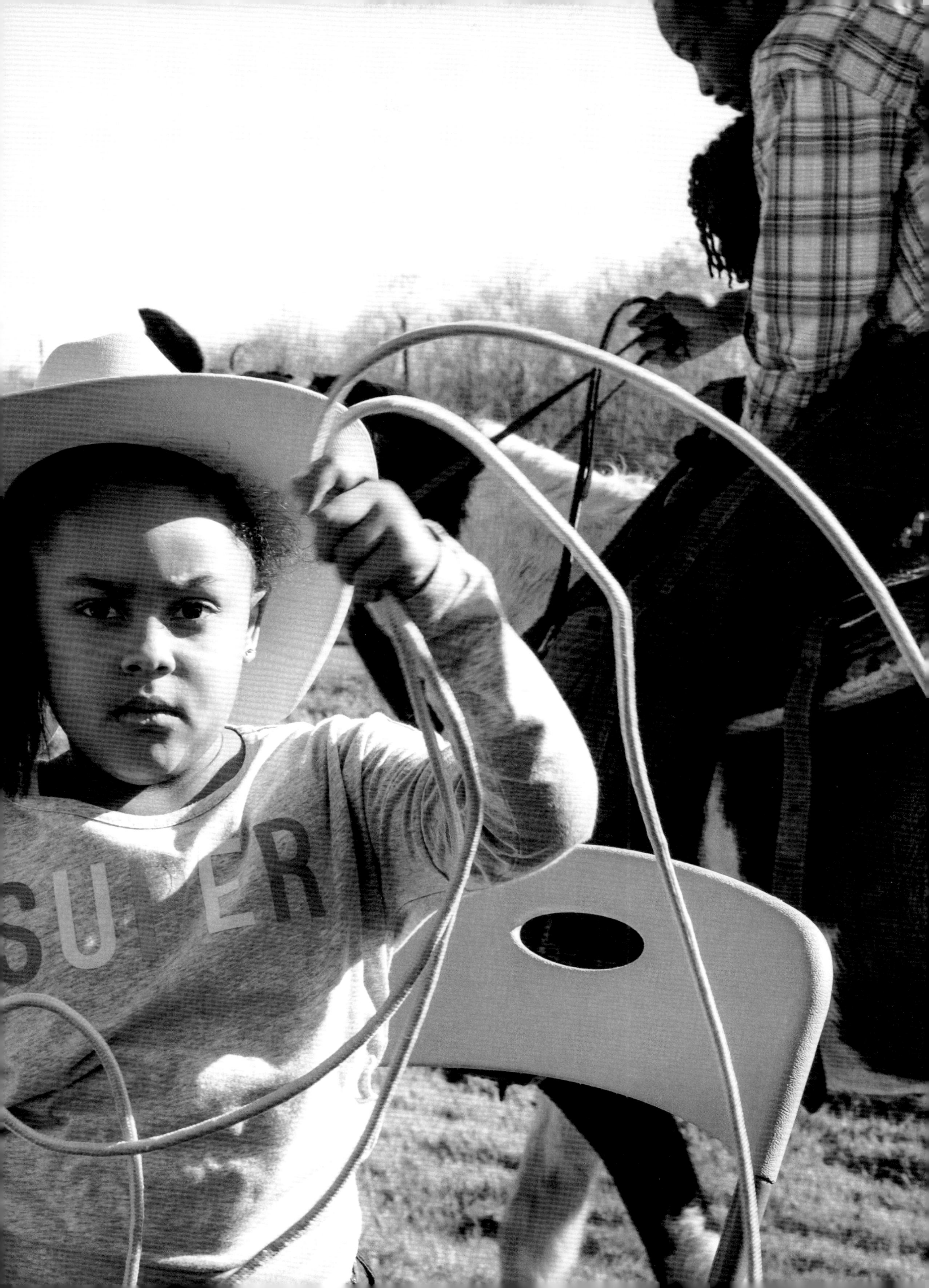

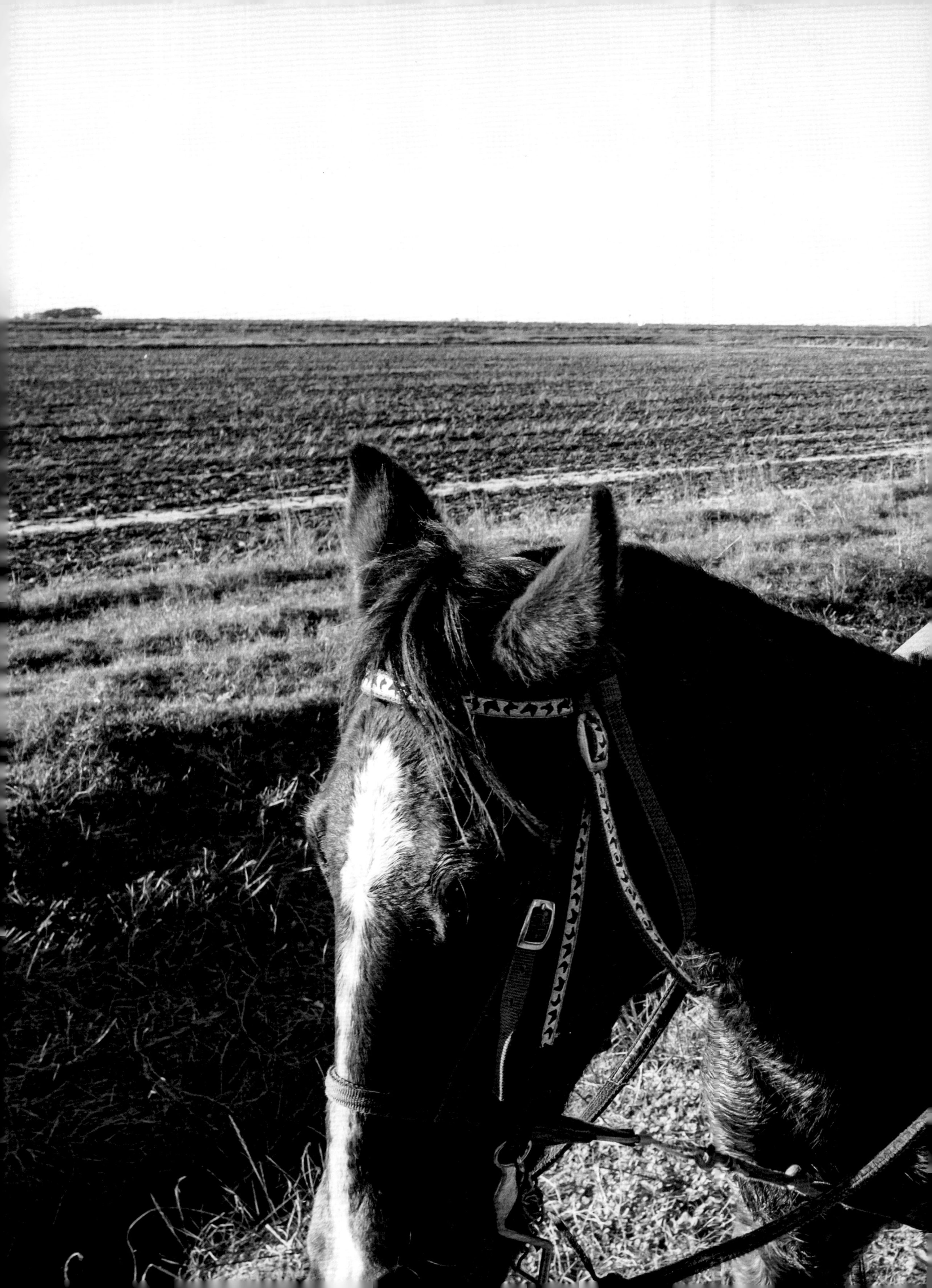

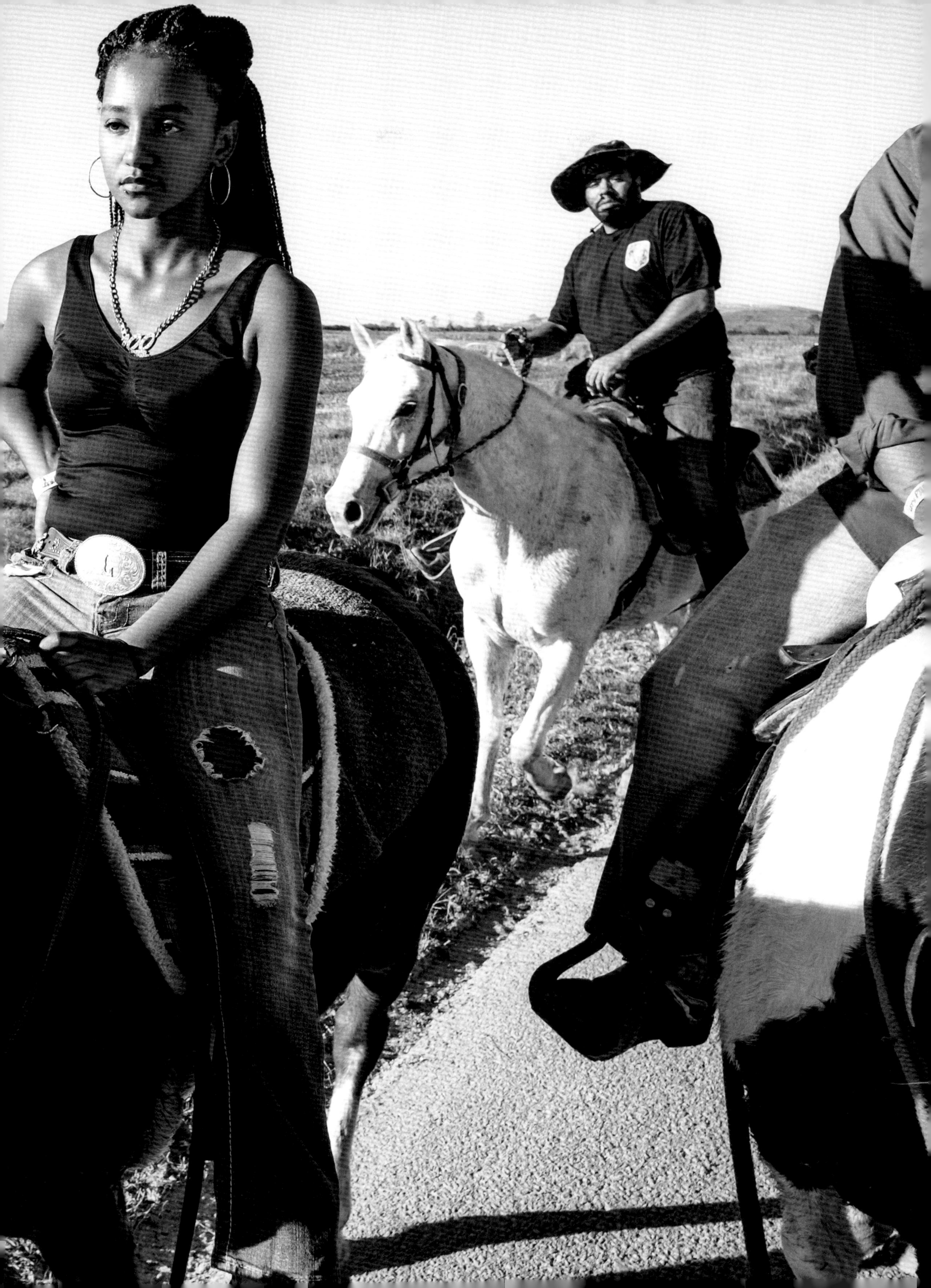

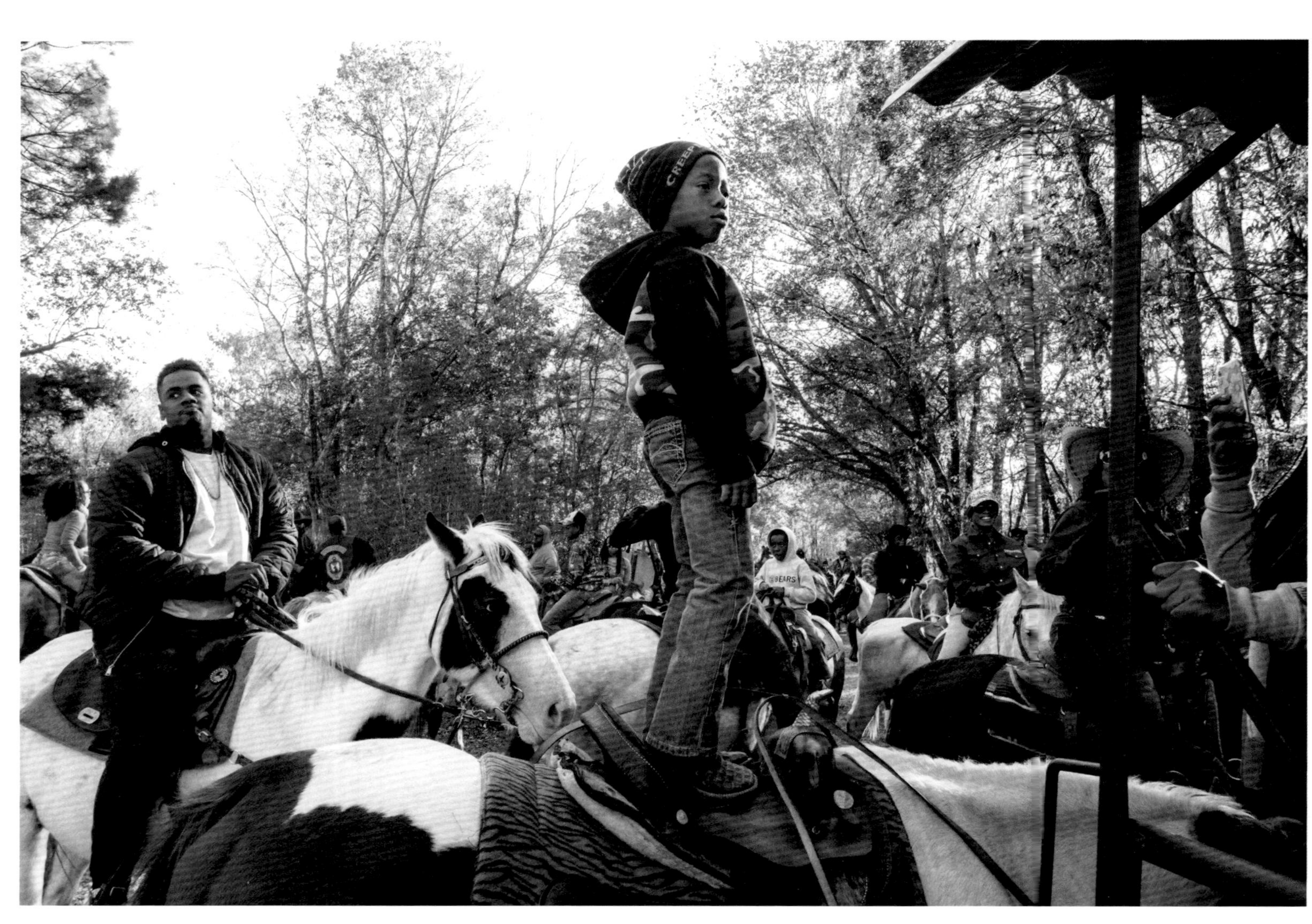

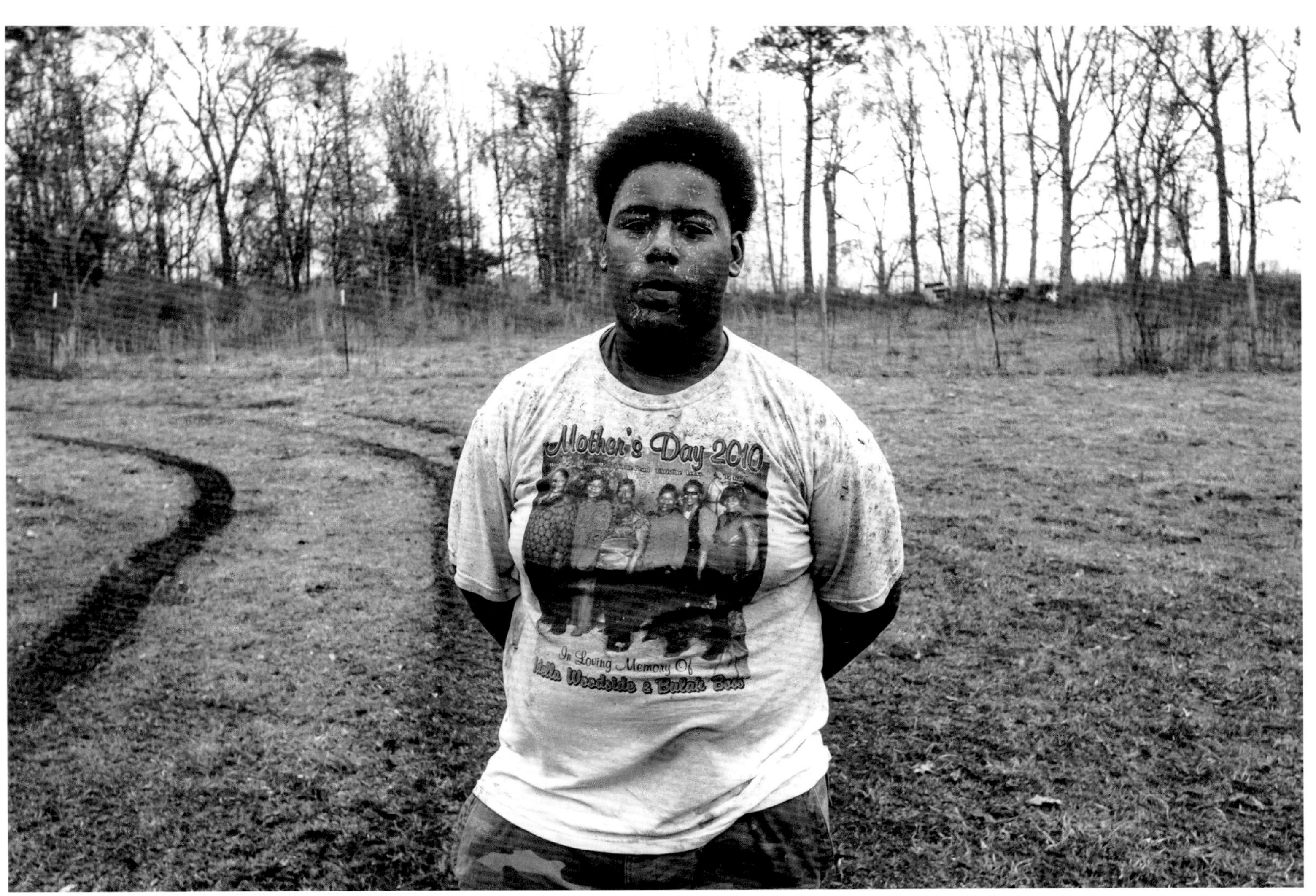
Mother's Day 2010
In Loving Memory Of

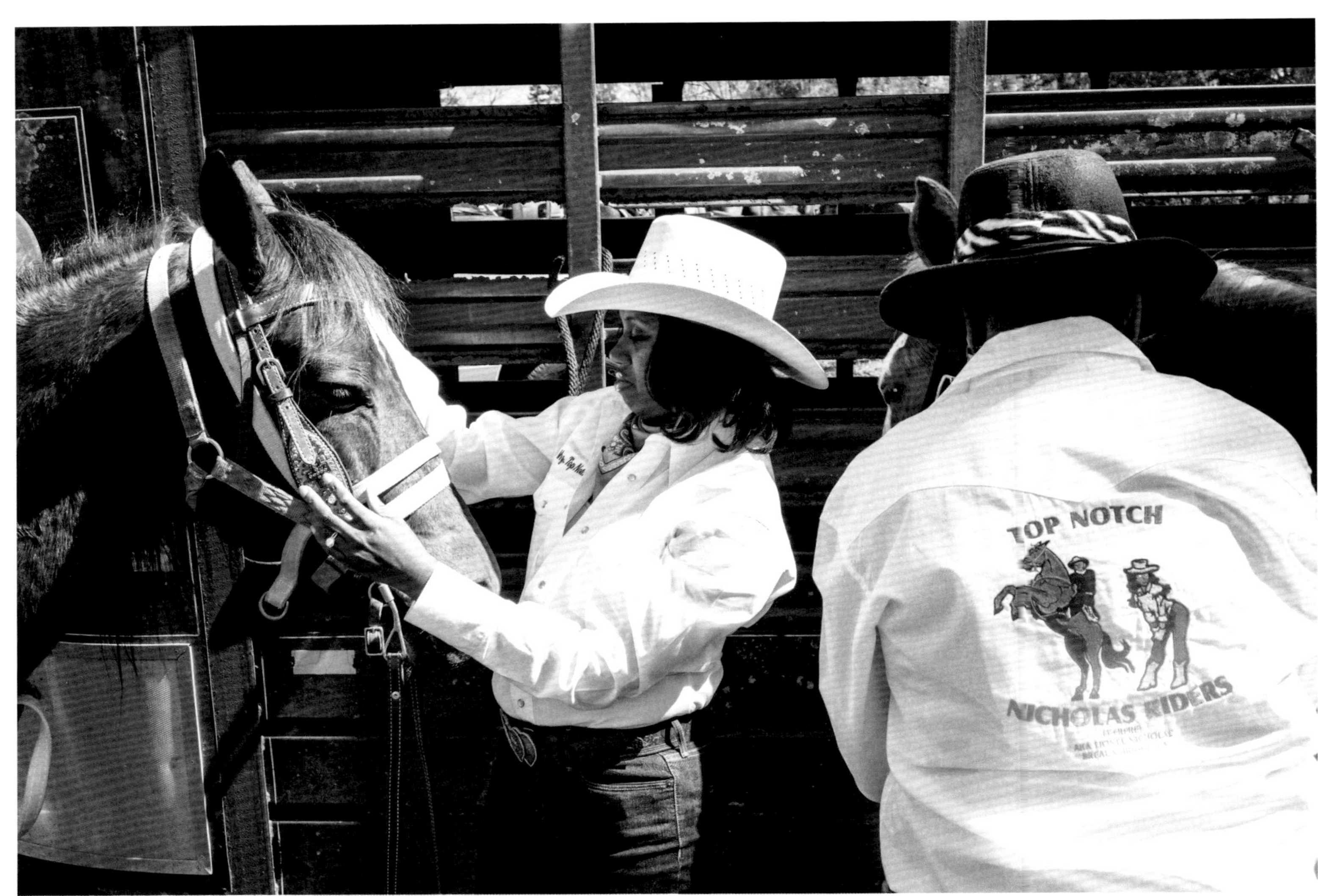
TOP NOTCH
NICHOLAS RIDERS

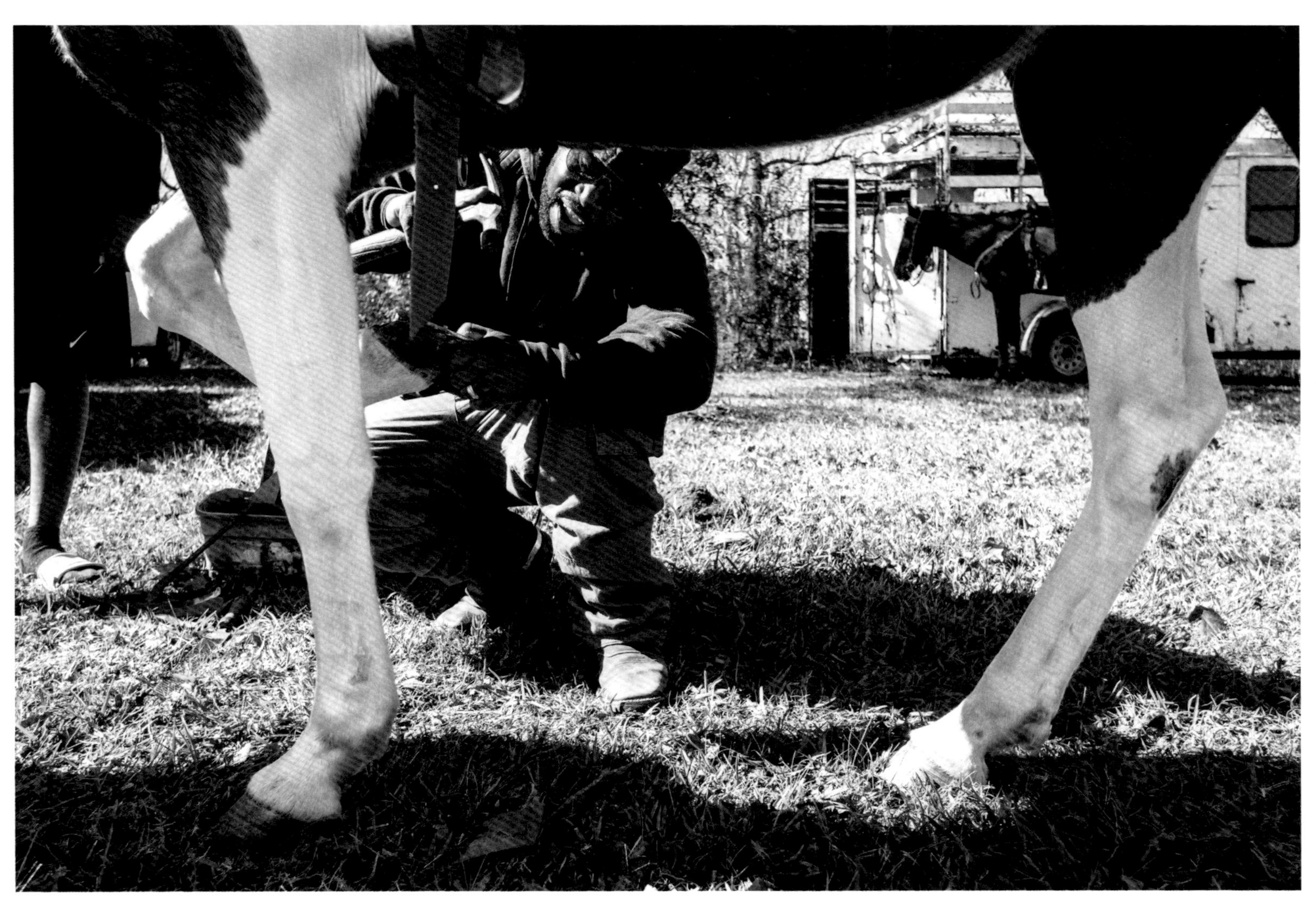

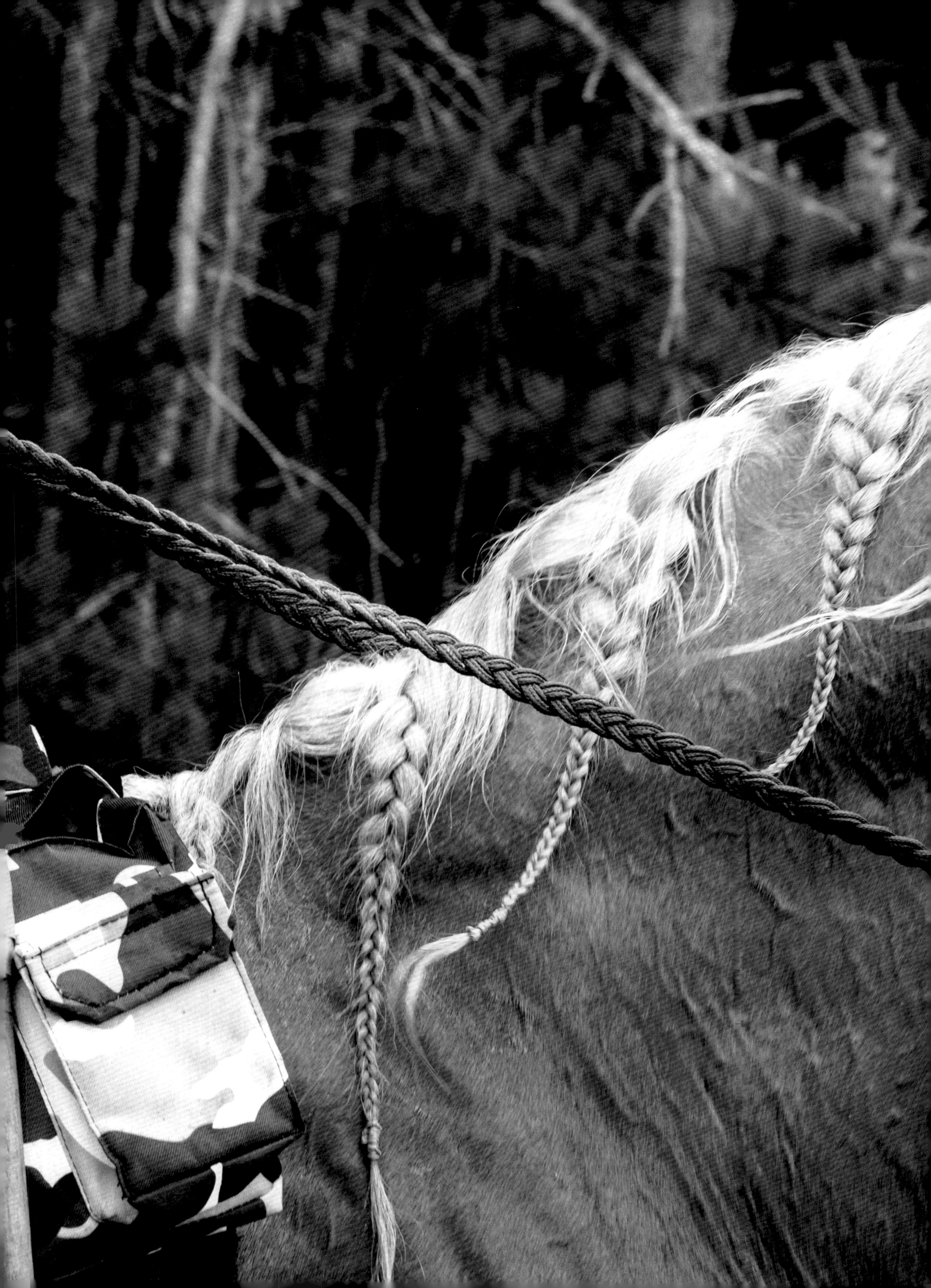

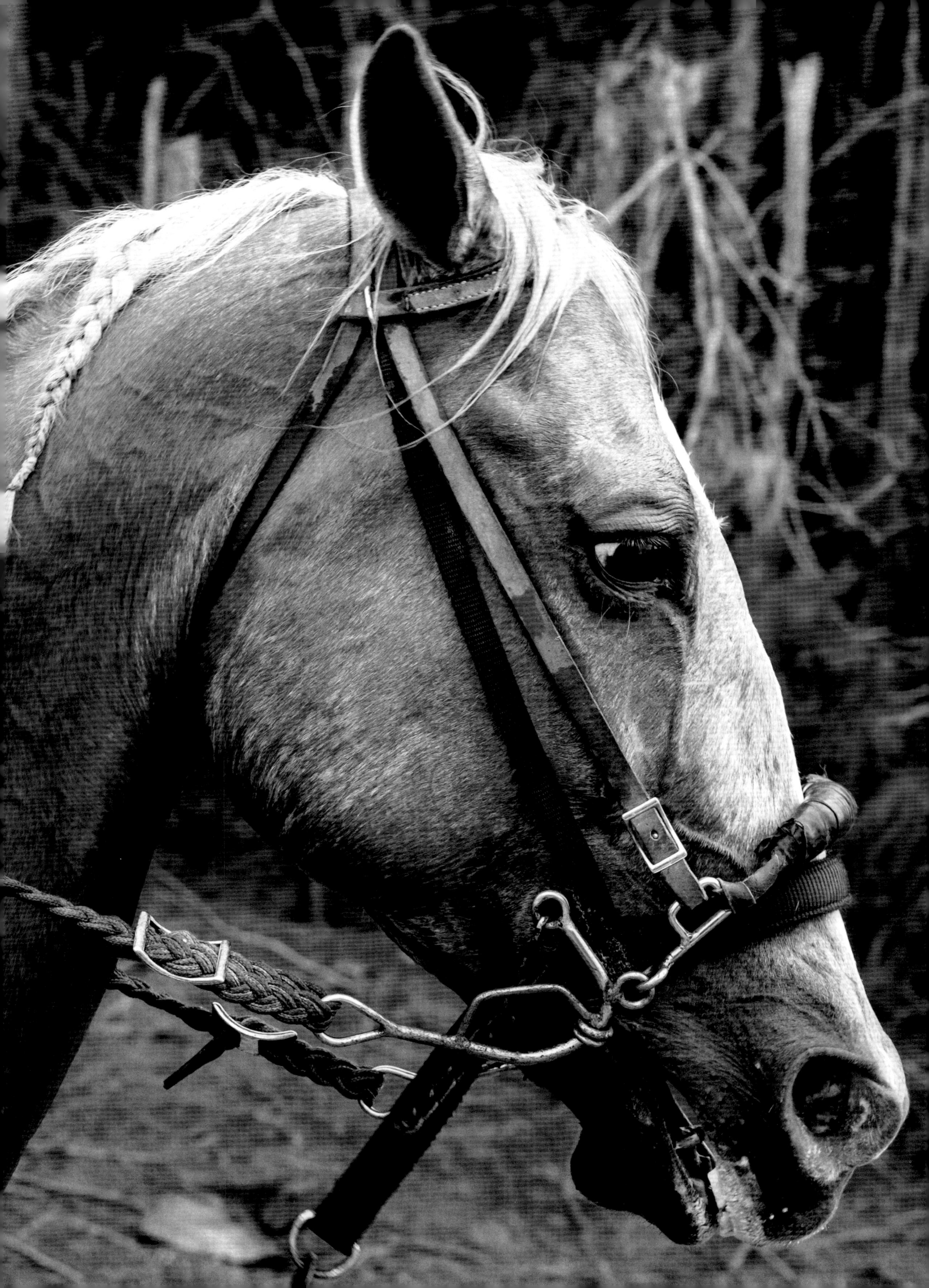

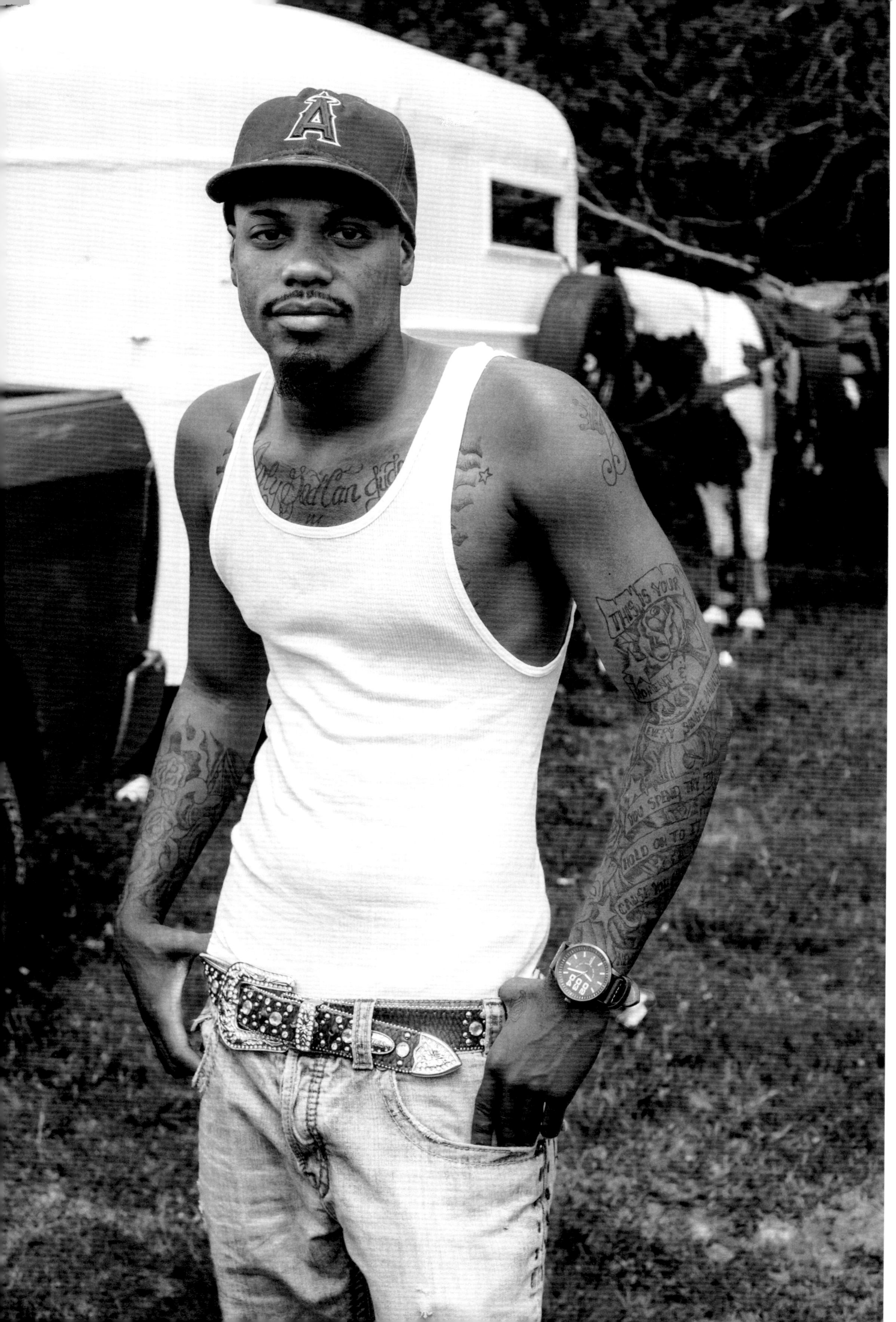
THIS IS YOUR

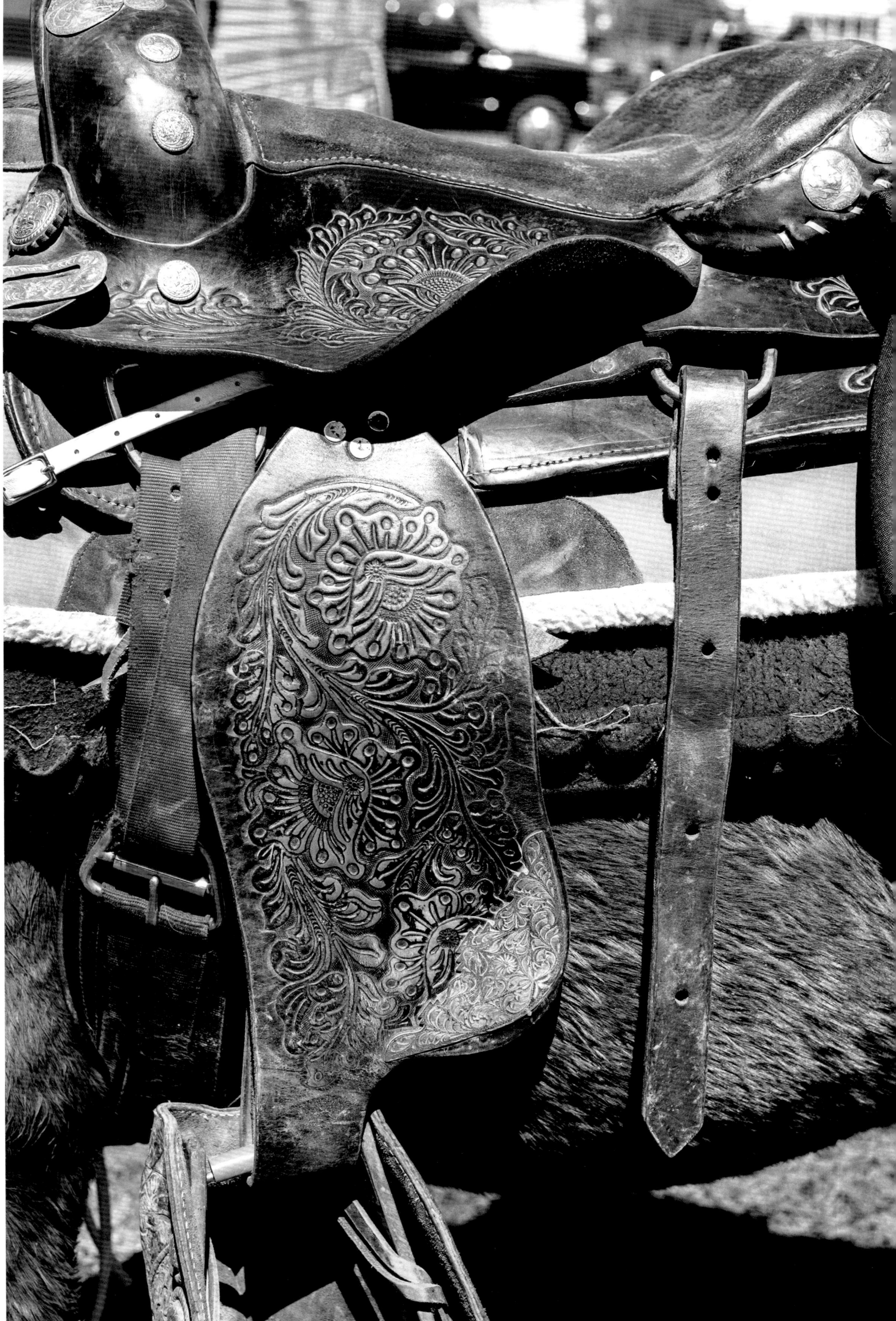

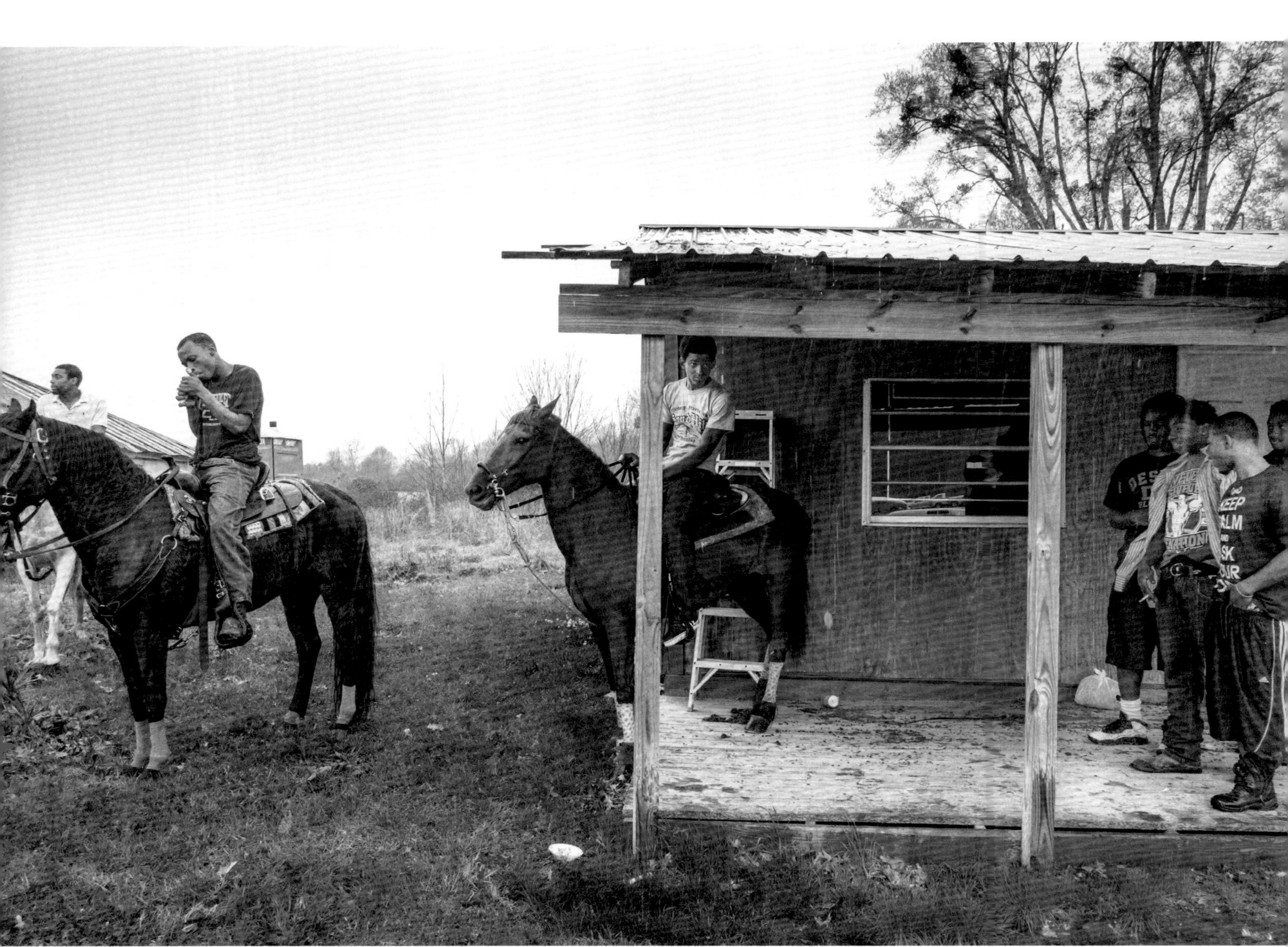

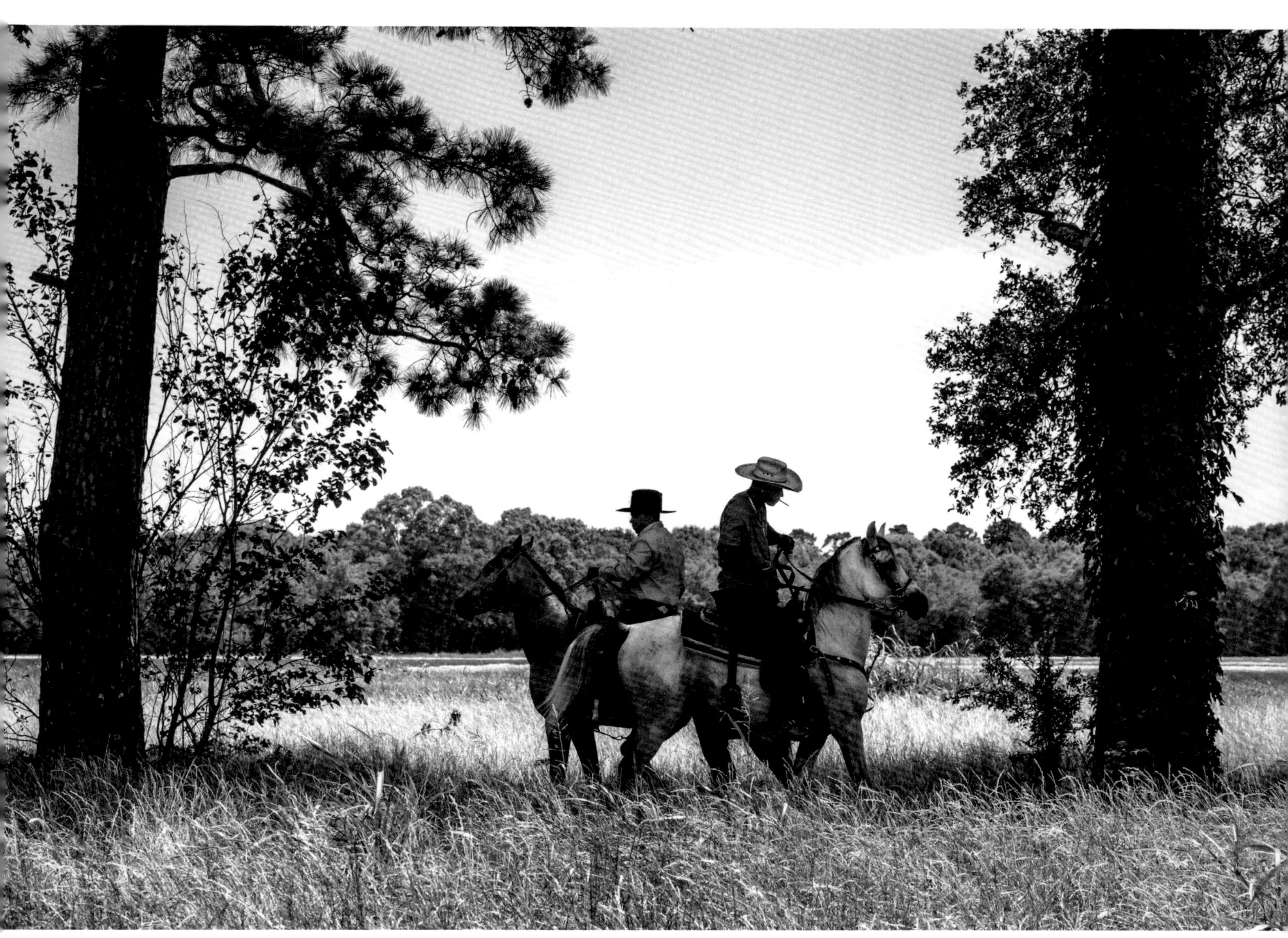

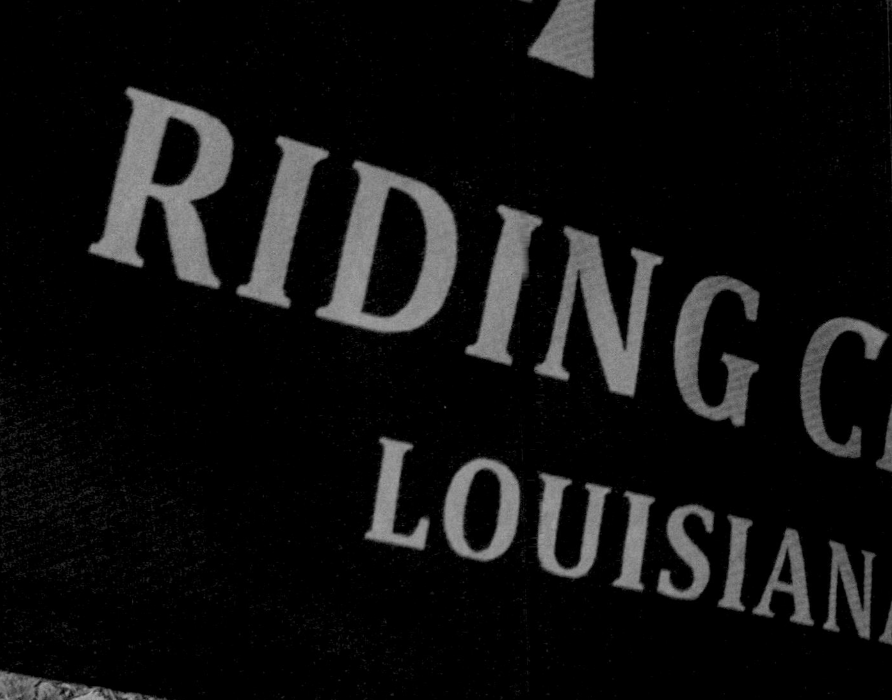
RIDING
LOUISIANA

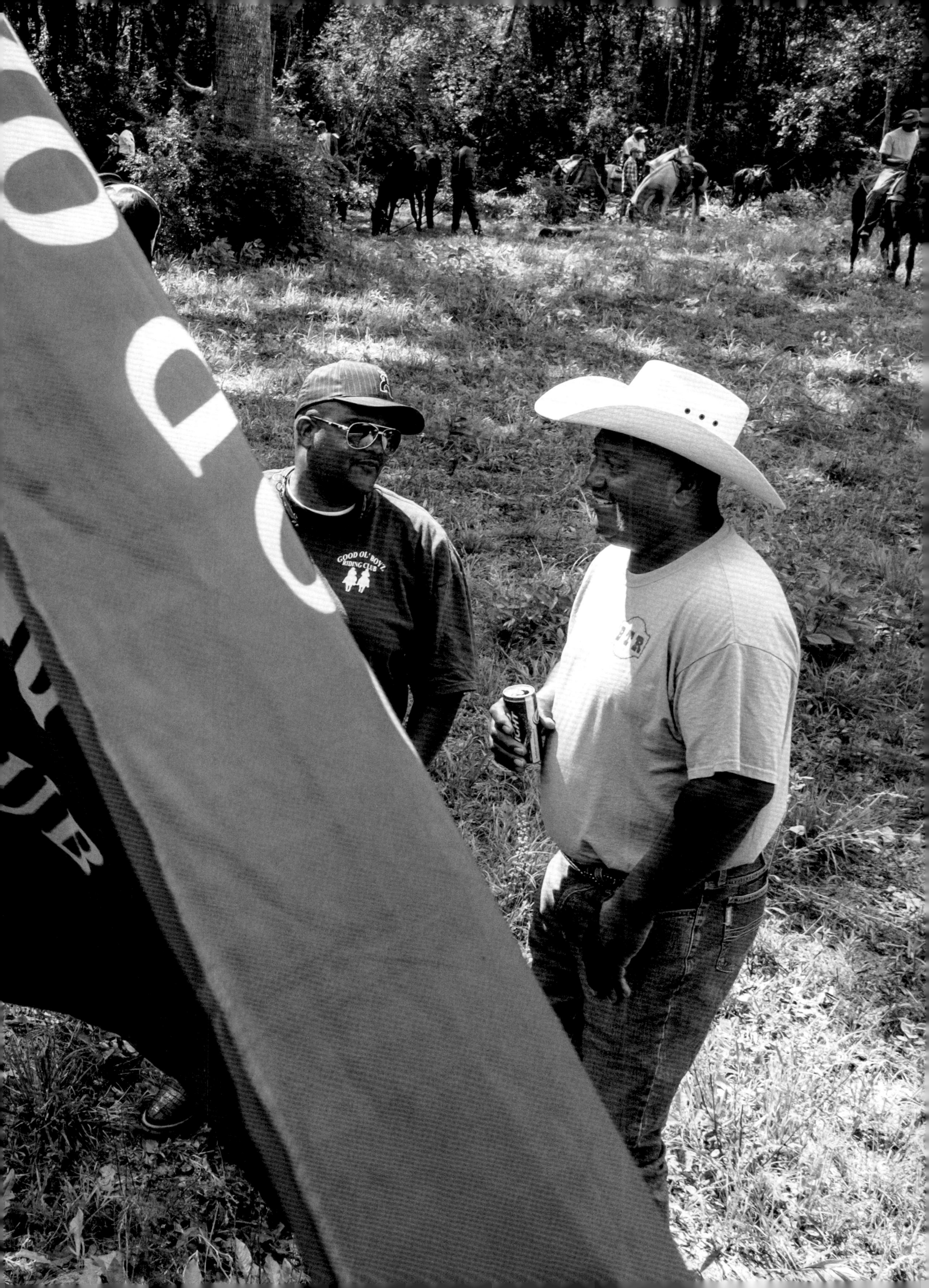
GOOD OL' BOYZ
RIDING CLUB

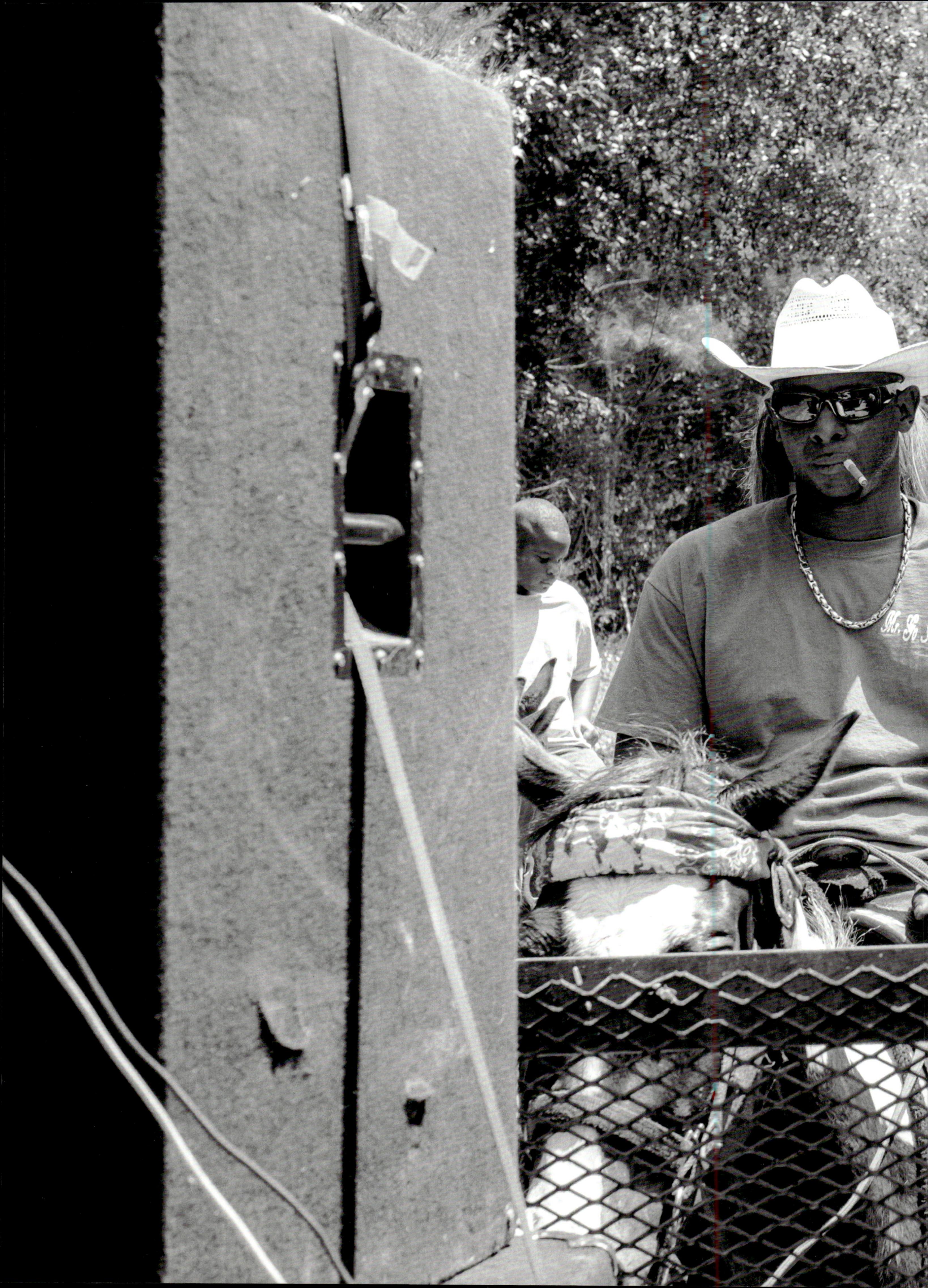

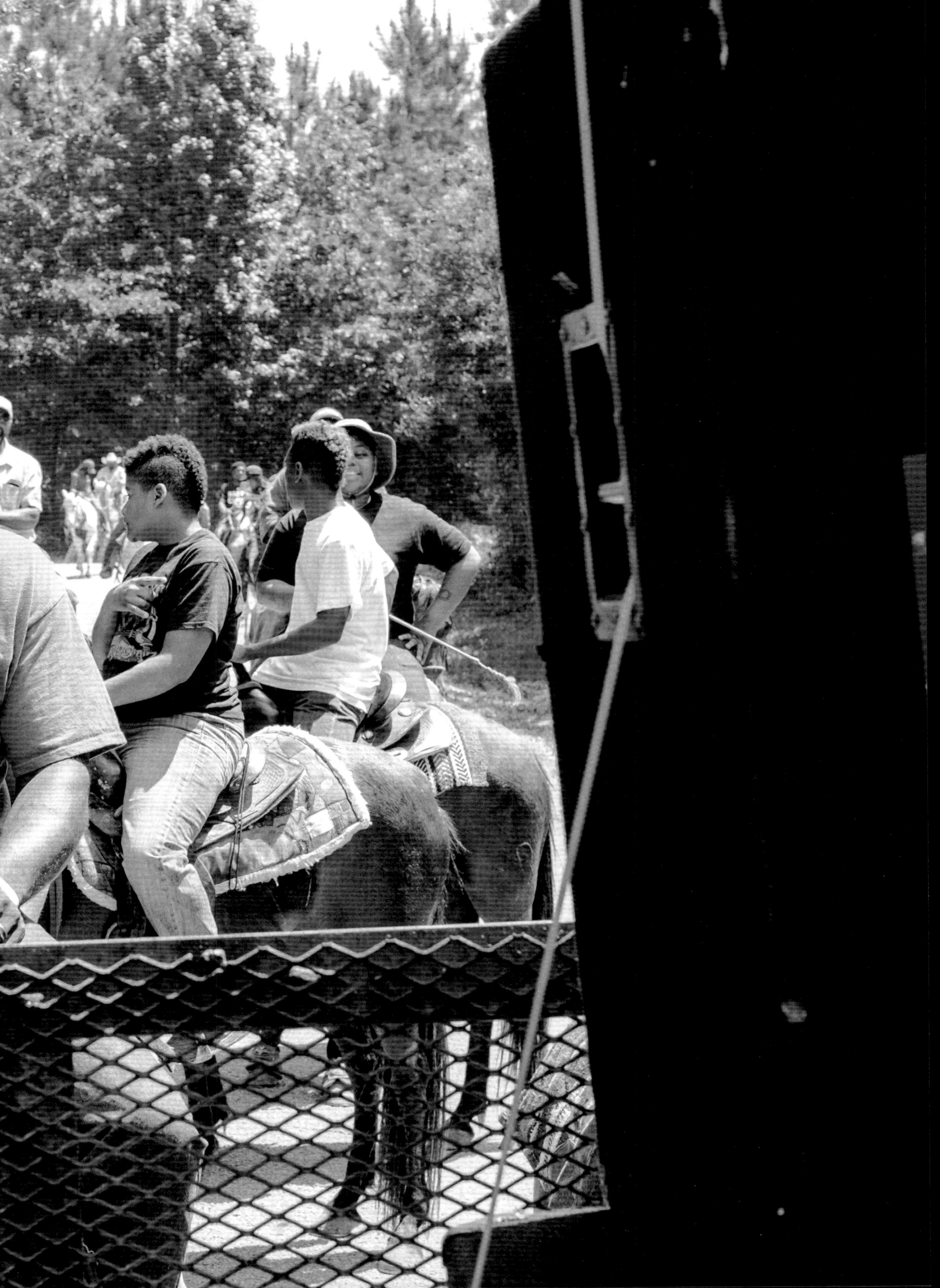

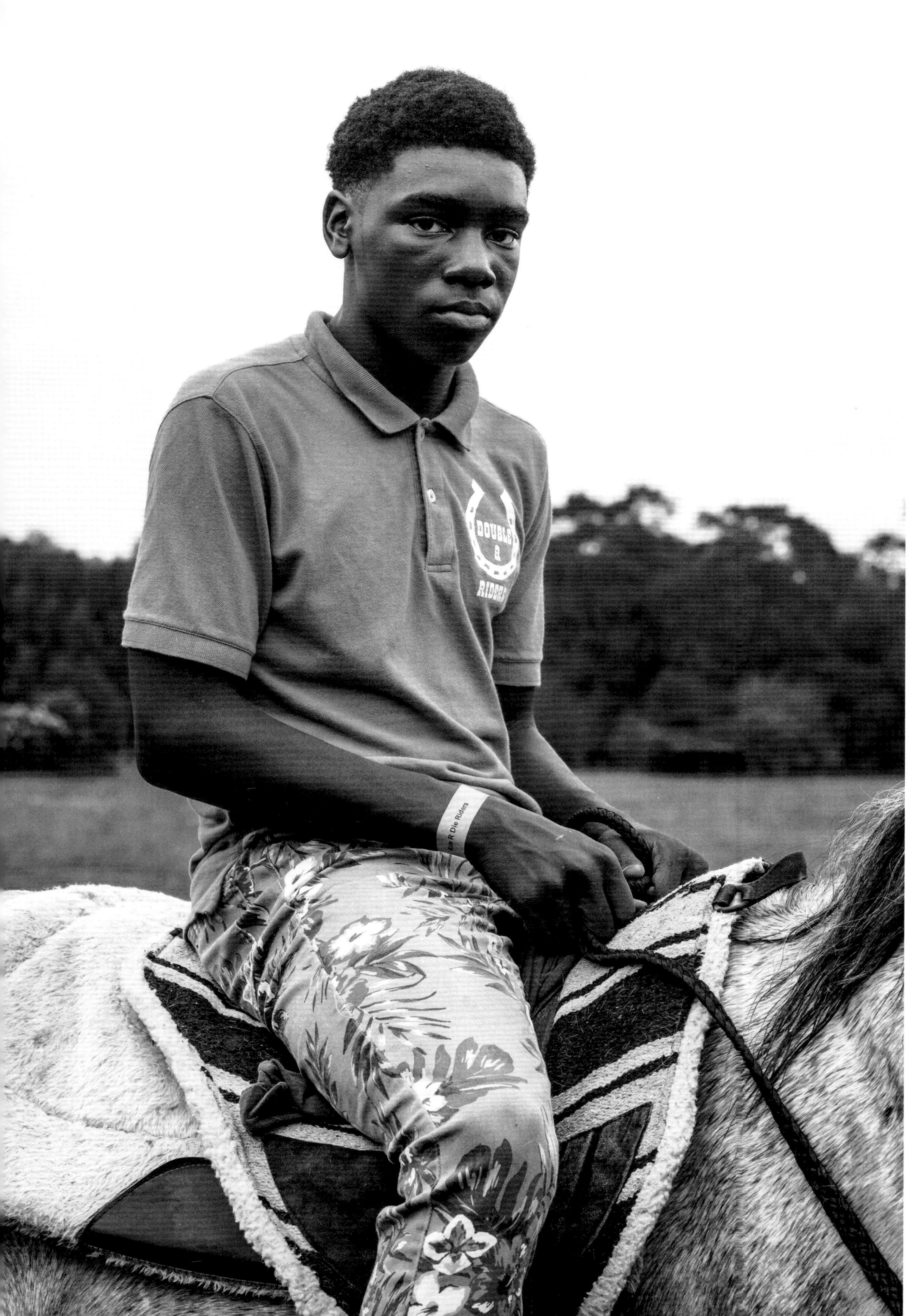
DOUBLE
R
RIDER
R Die Riders

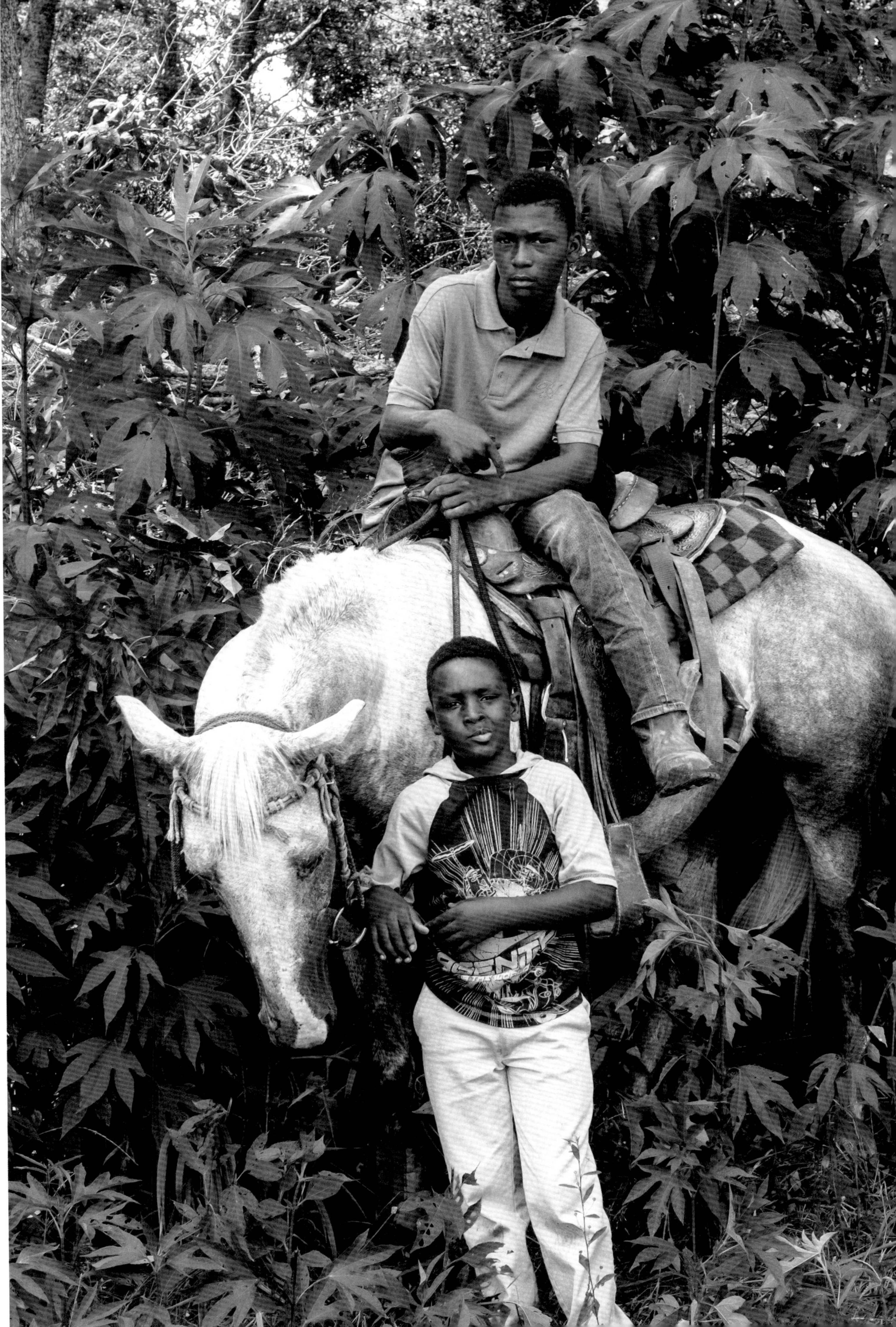

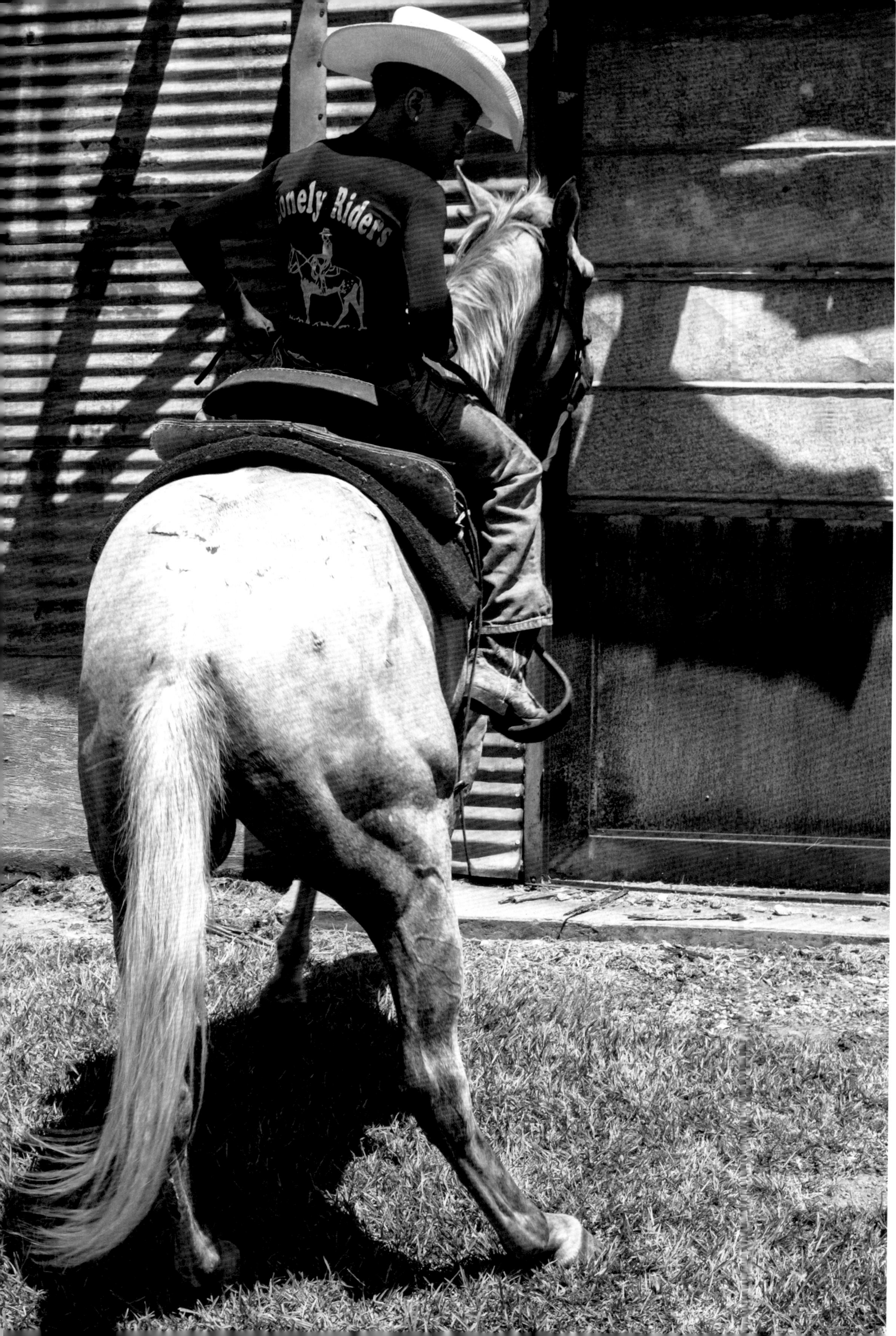
Lonely Riders

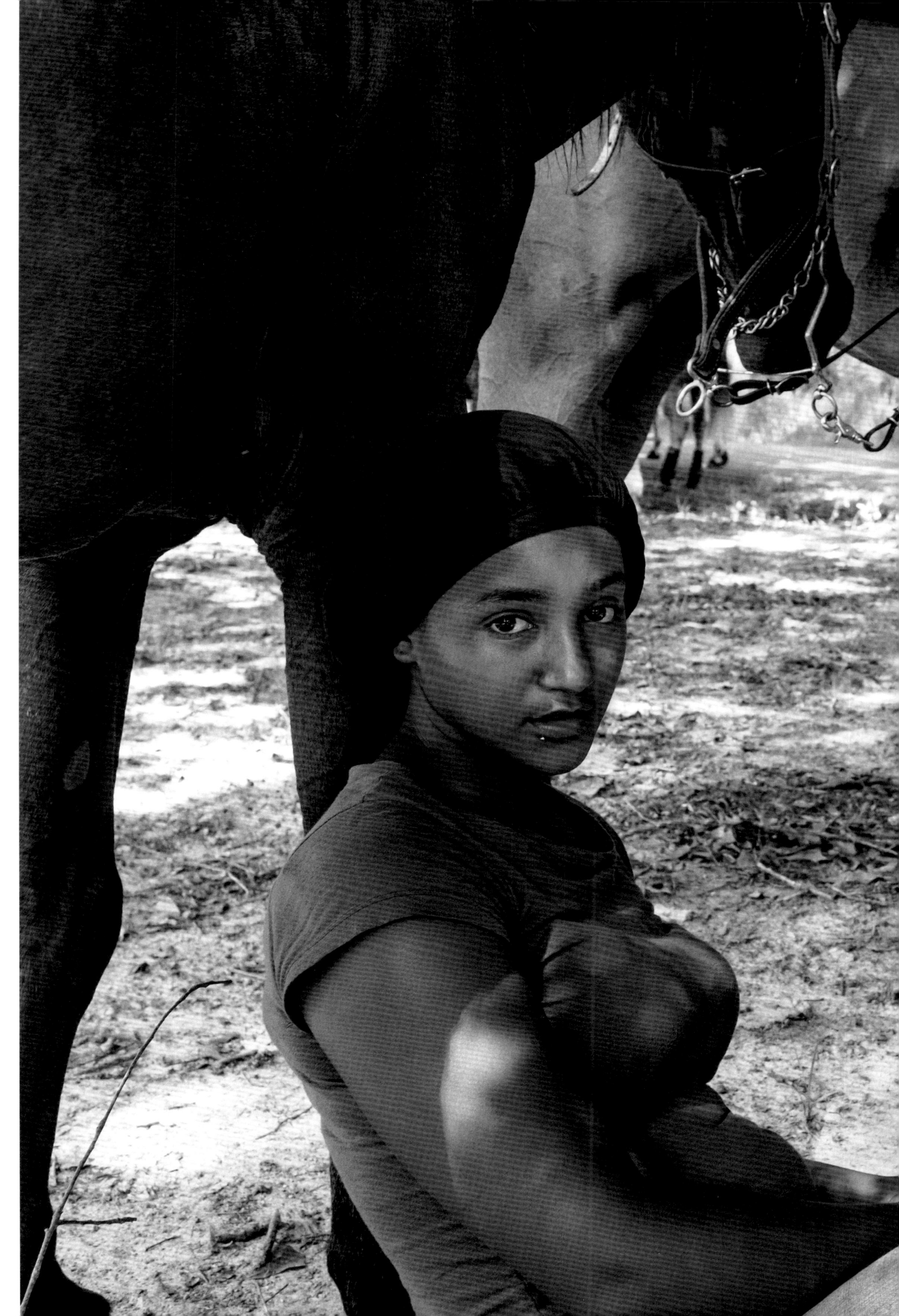

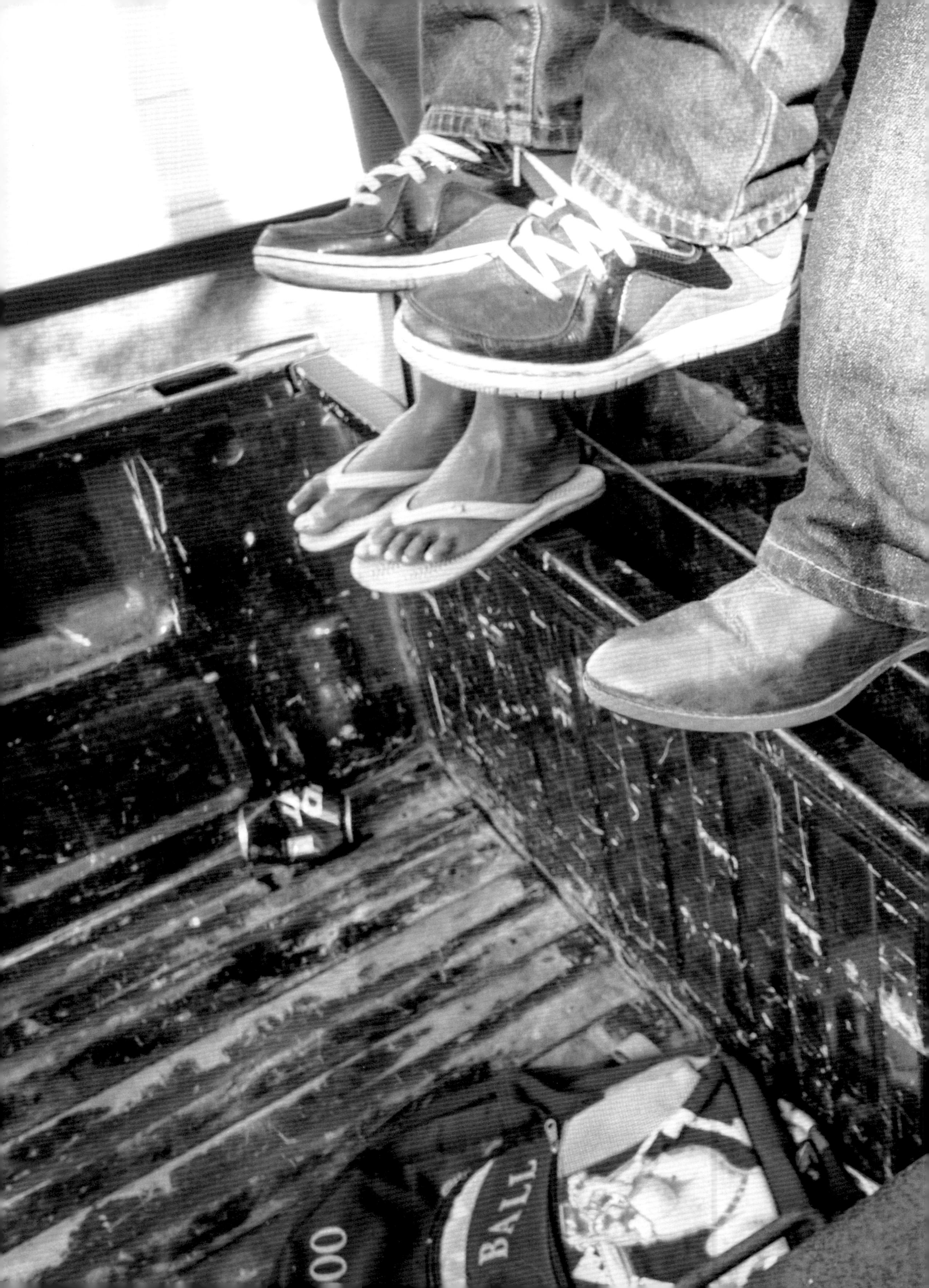
BALL

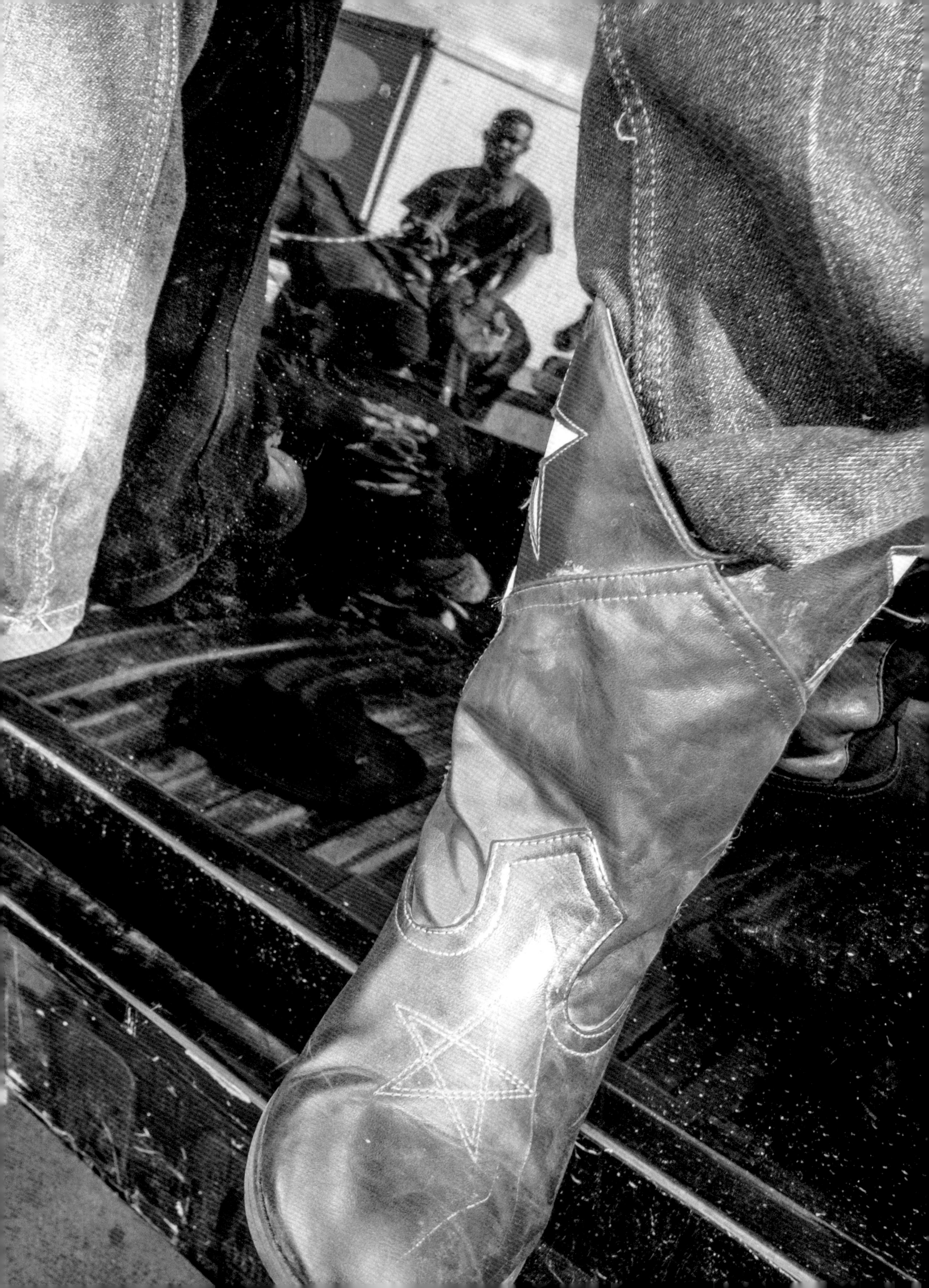

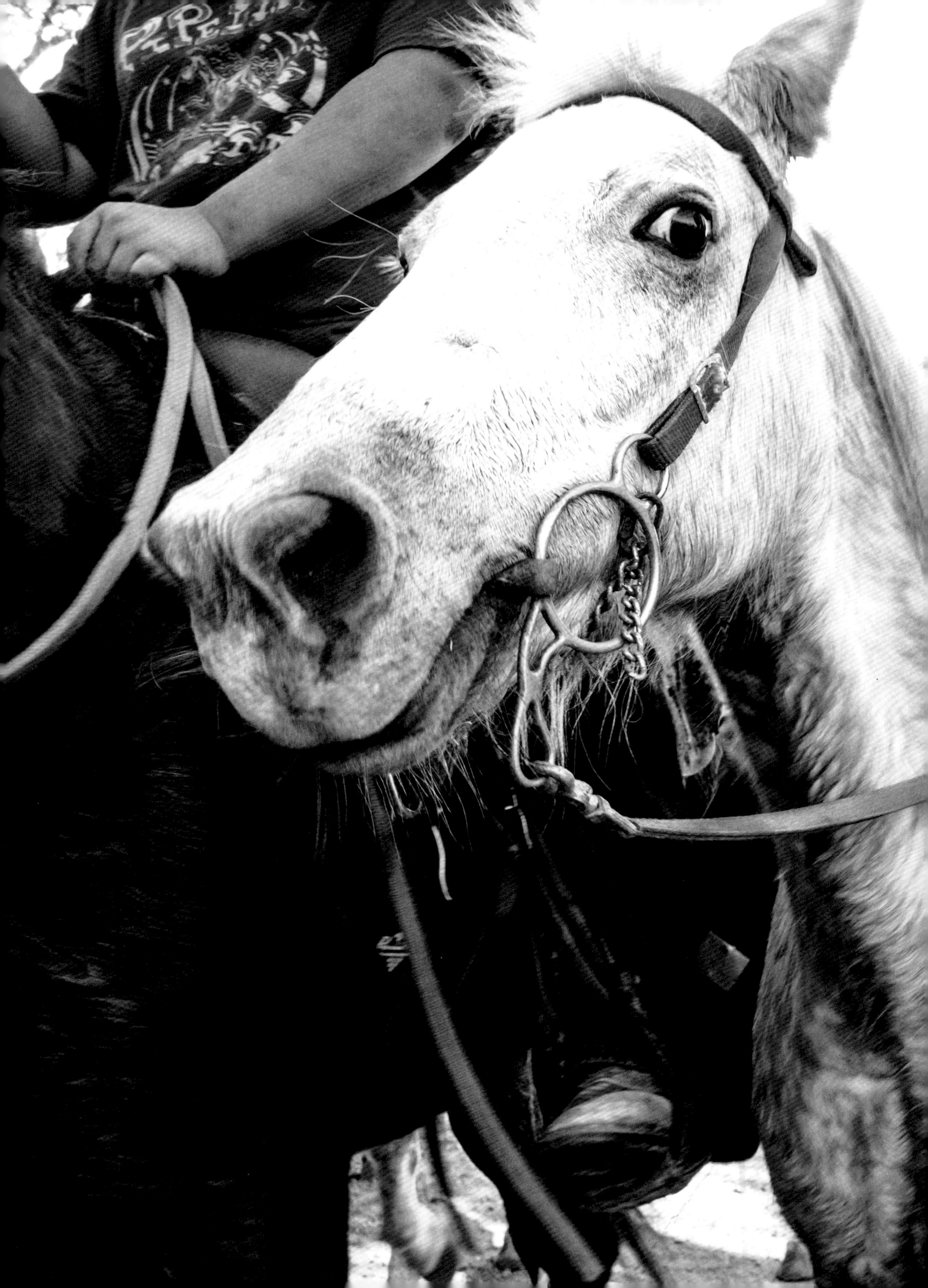

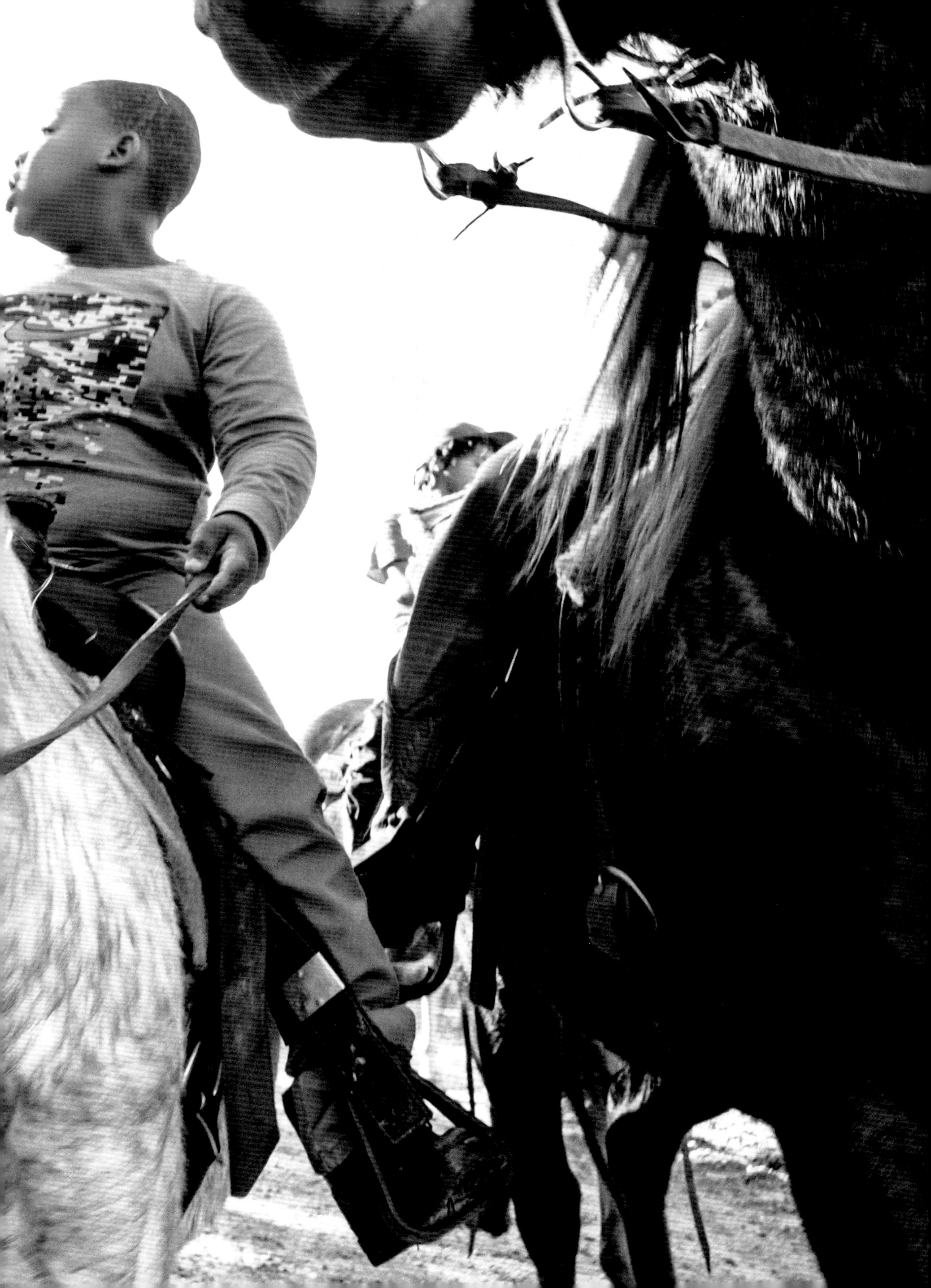

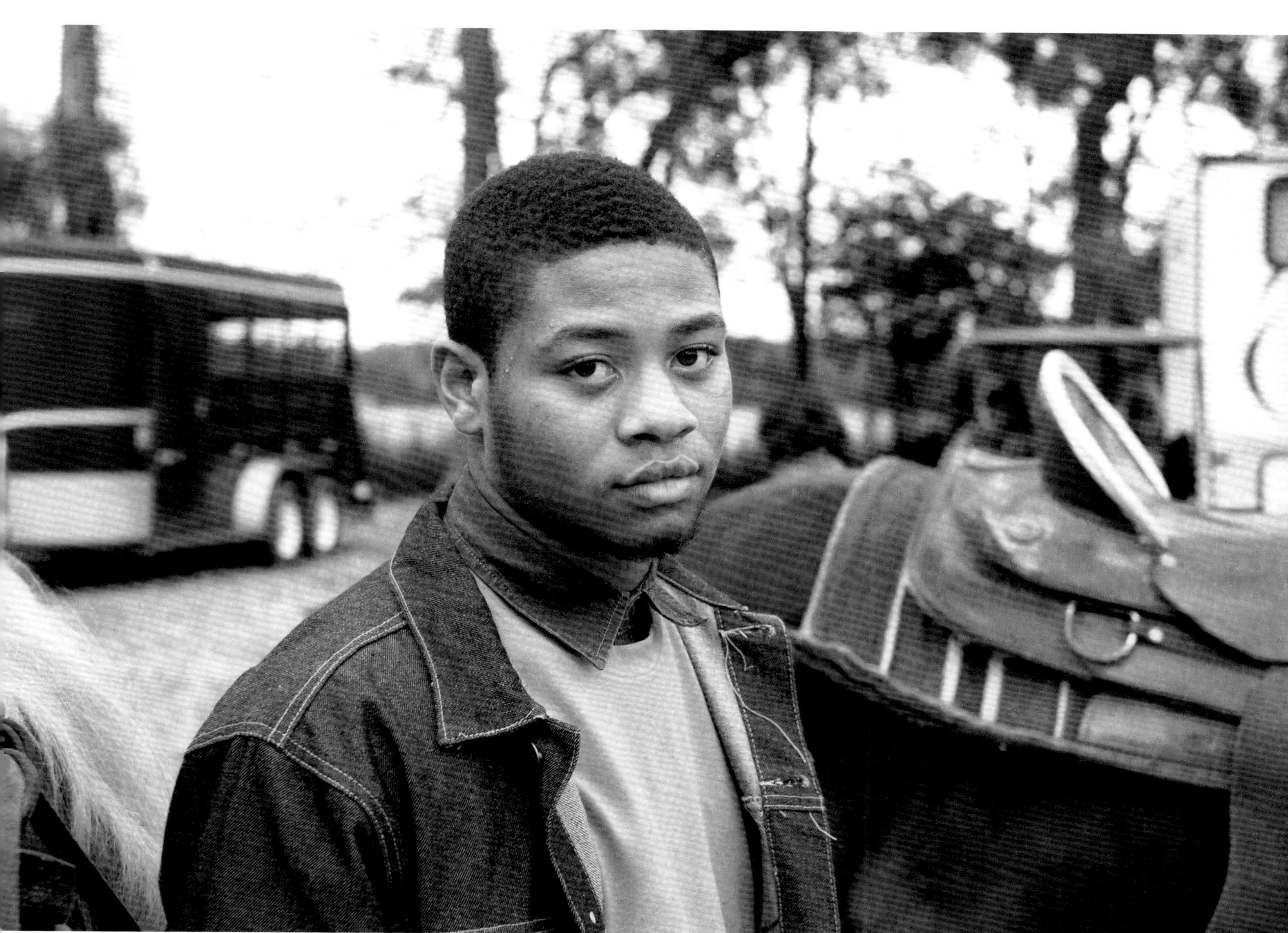

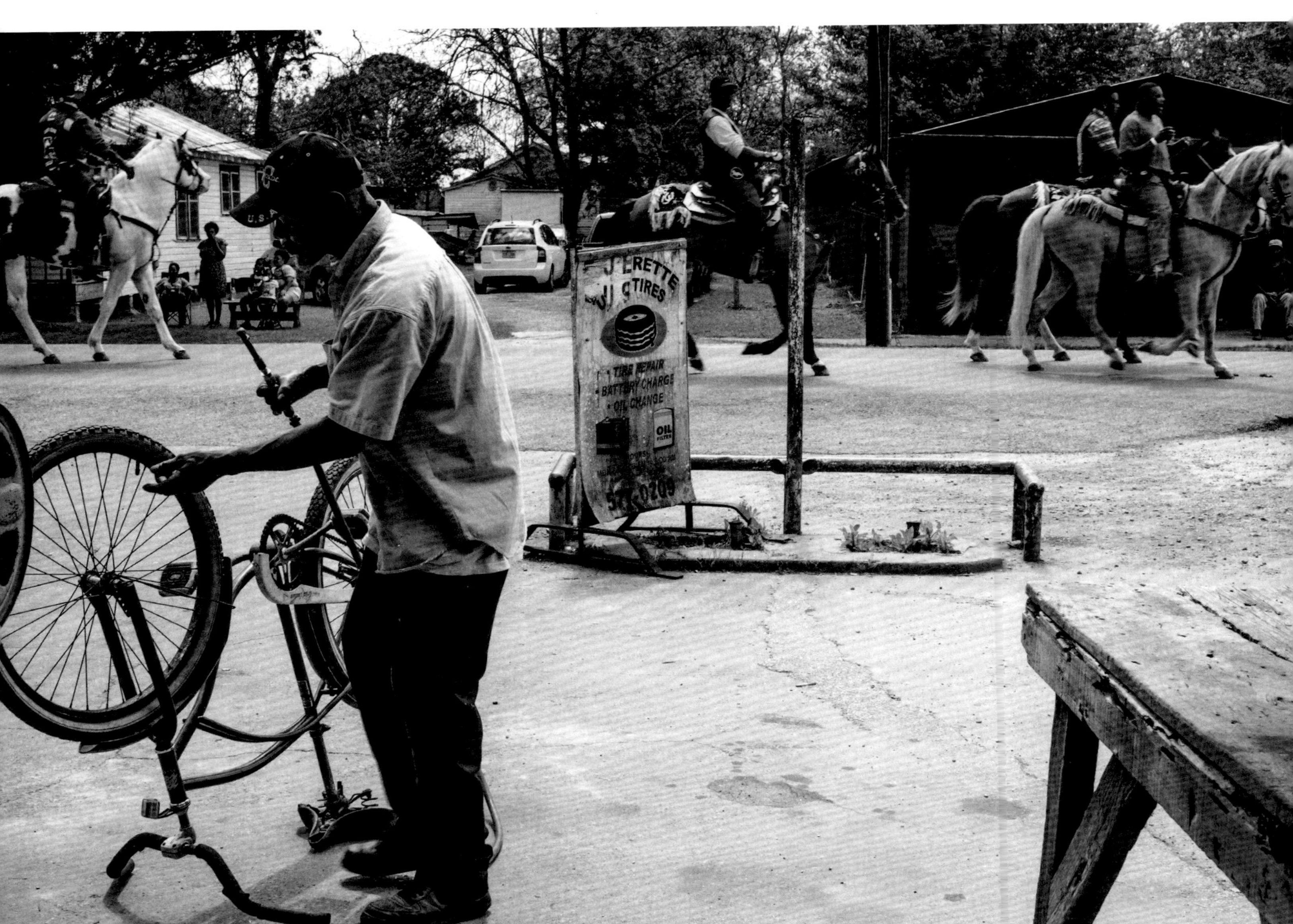
TIRES
TIRE REPAIR
BATTERY CHARGE
OIL CHANGE
OIL
FILTER

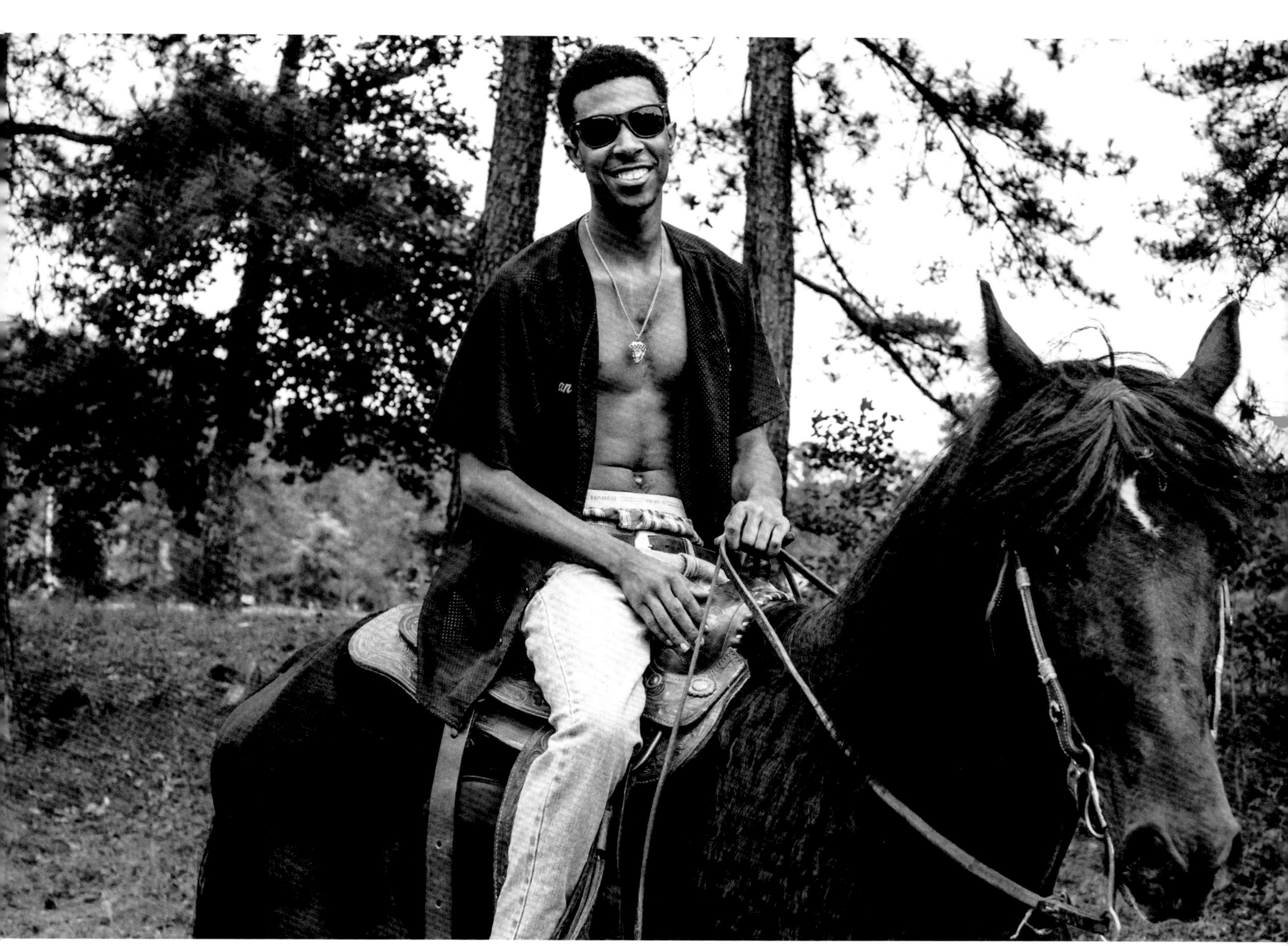

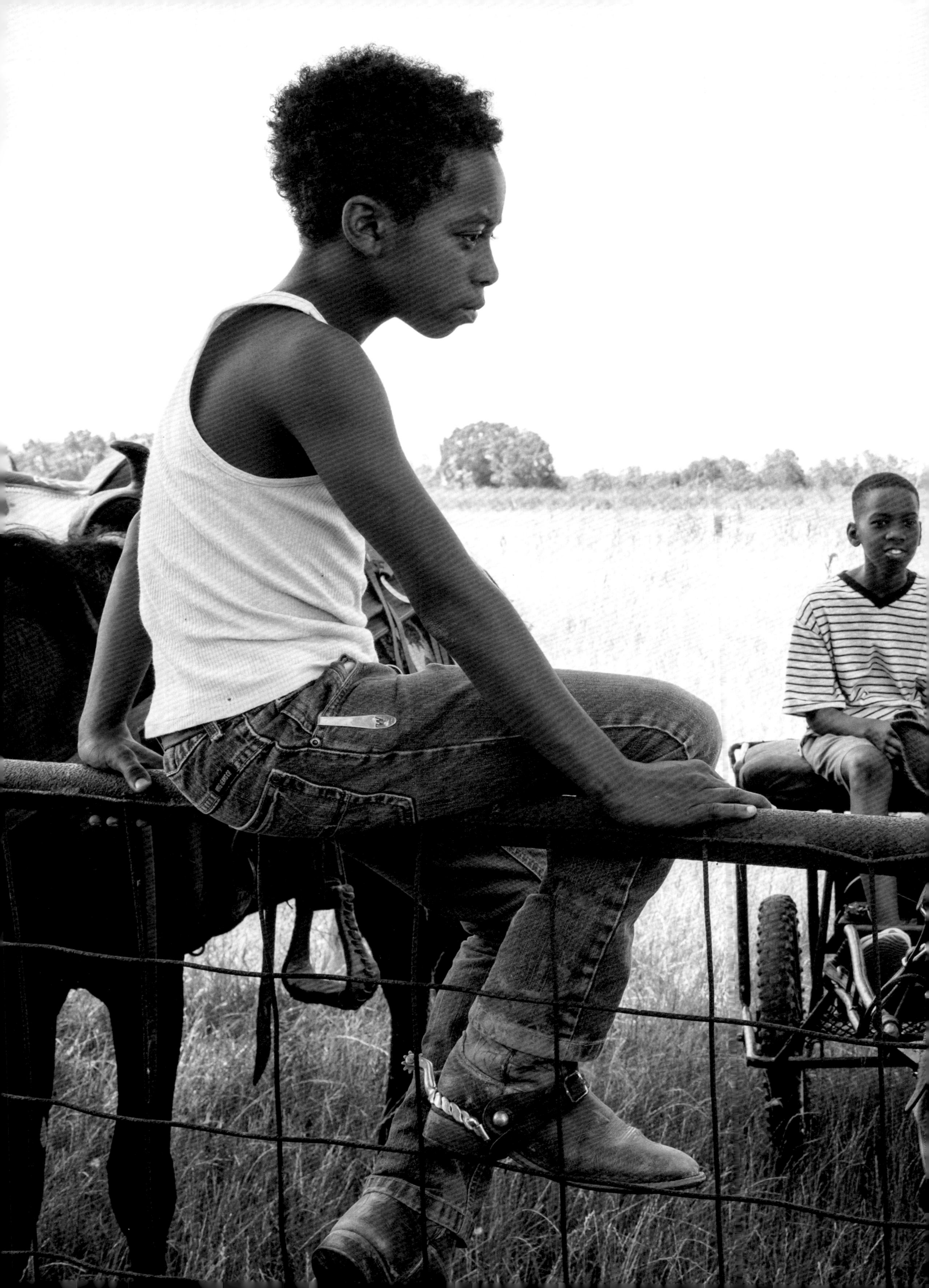

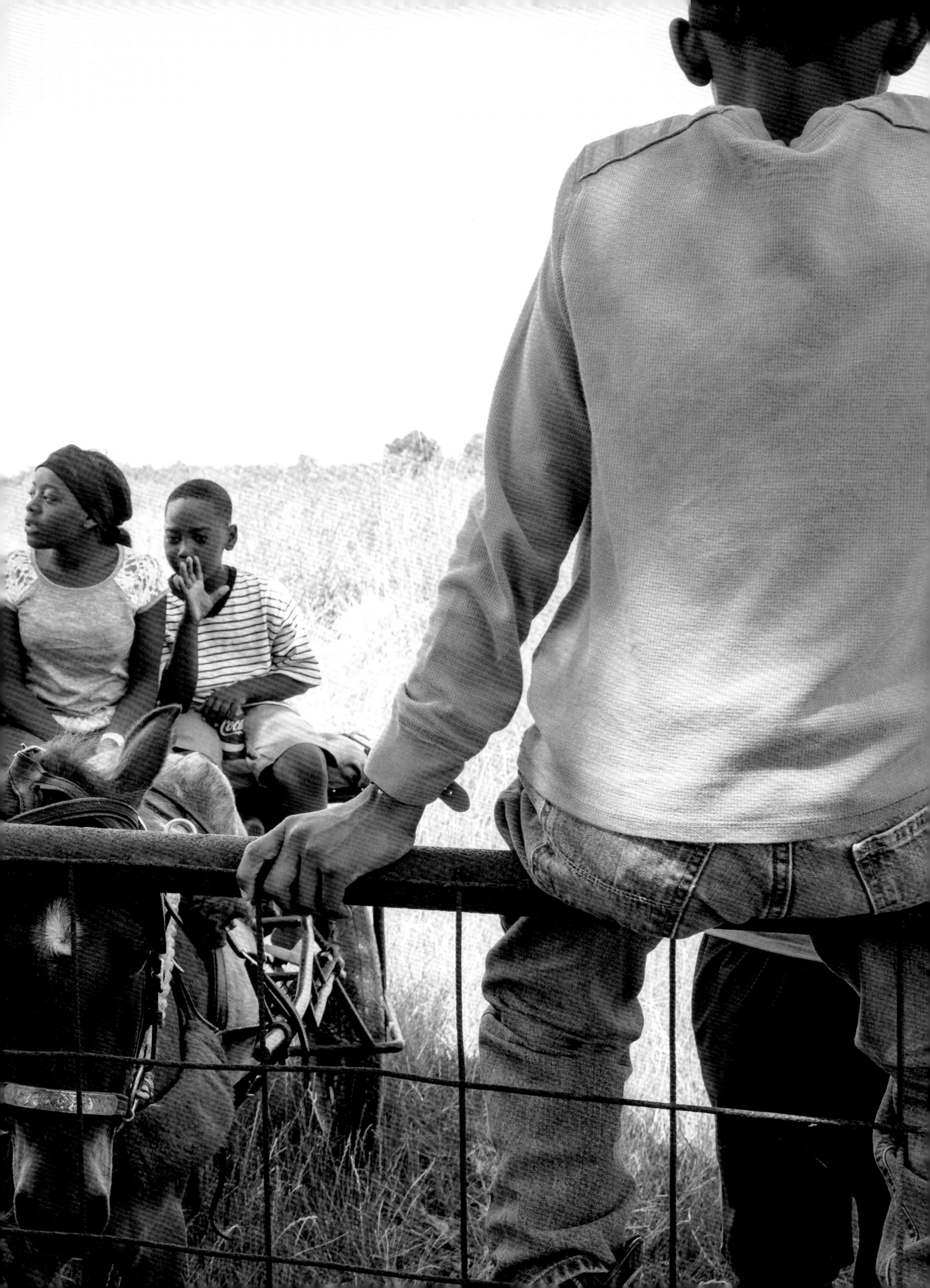

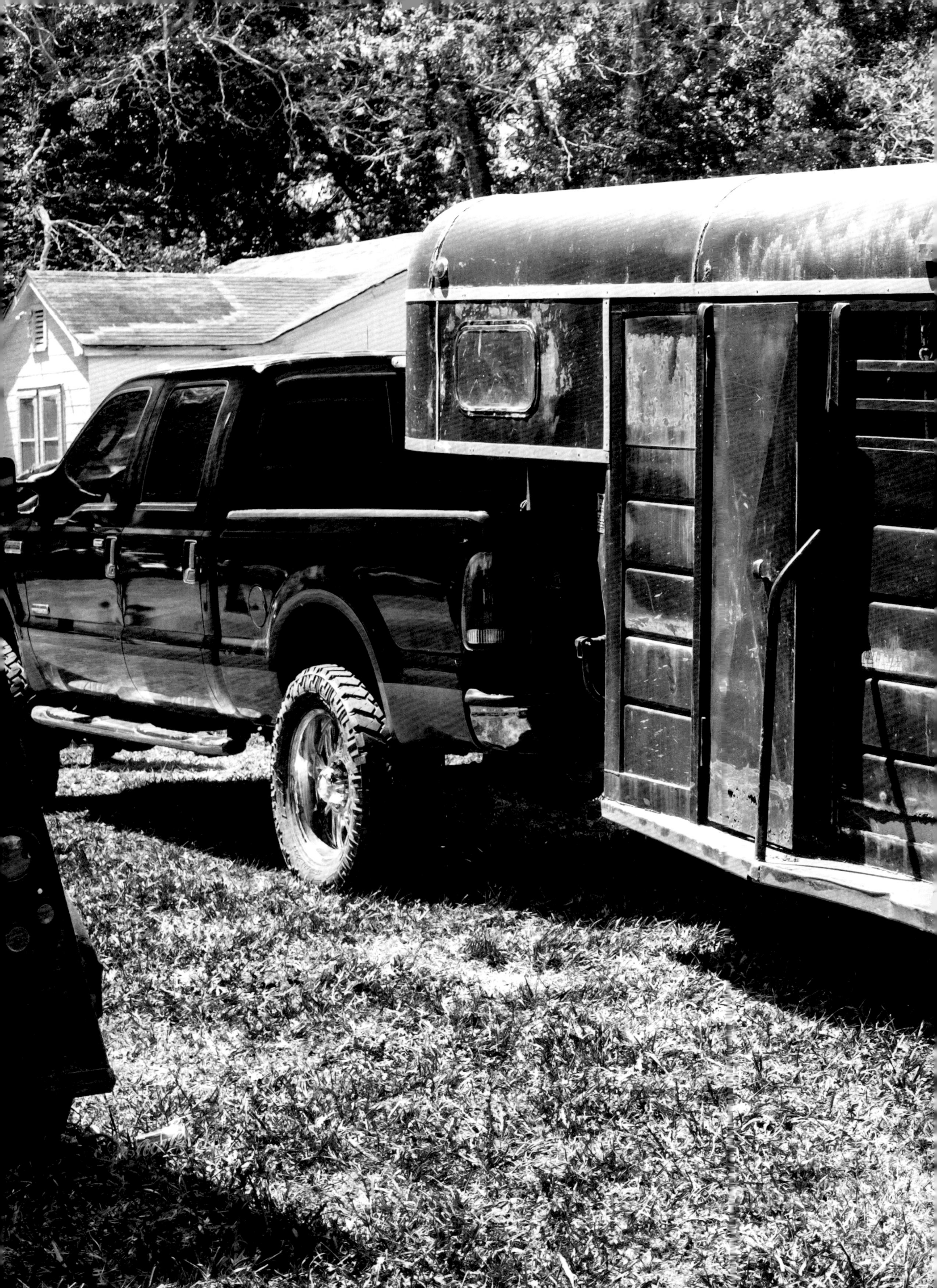

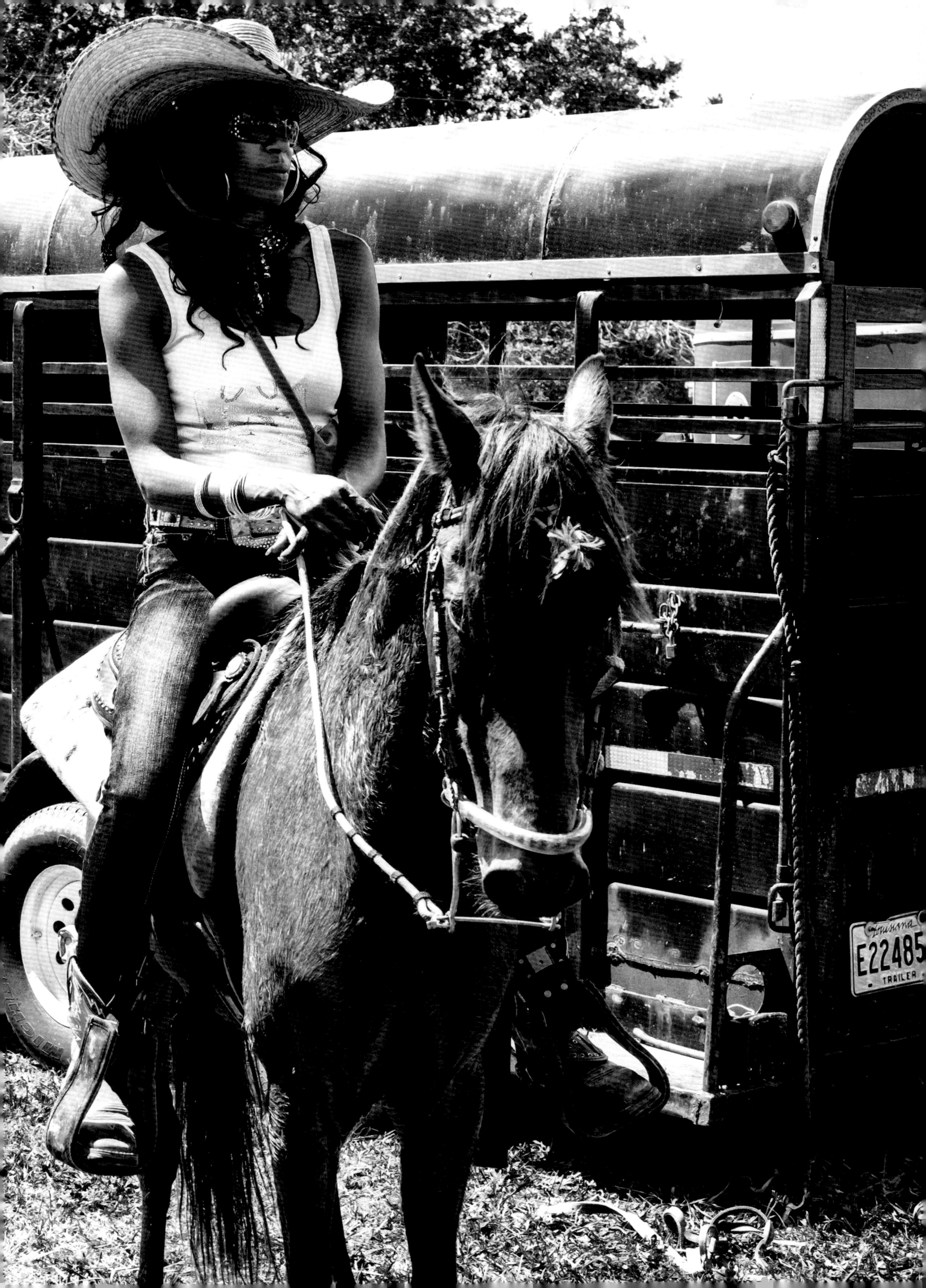
E22485
TRAILER

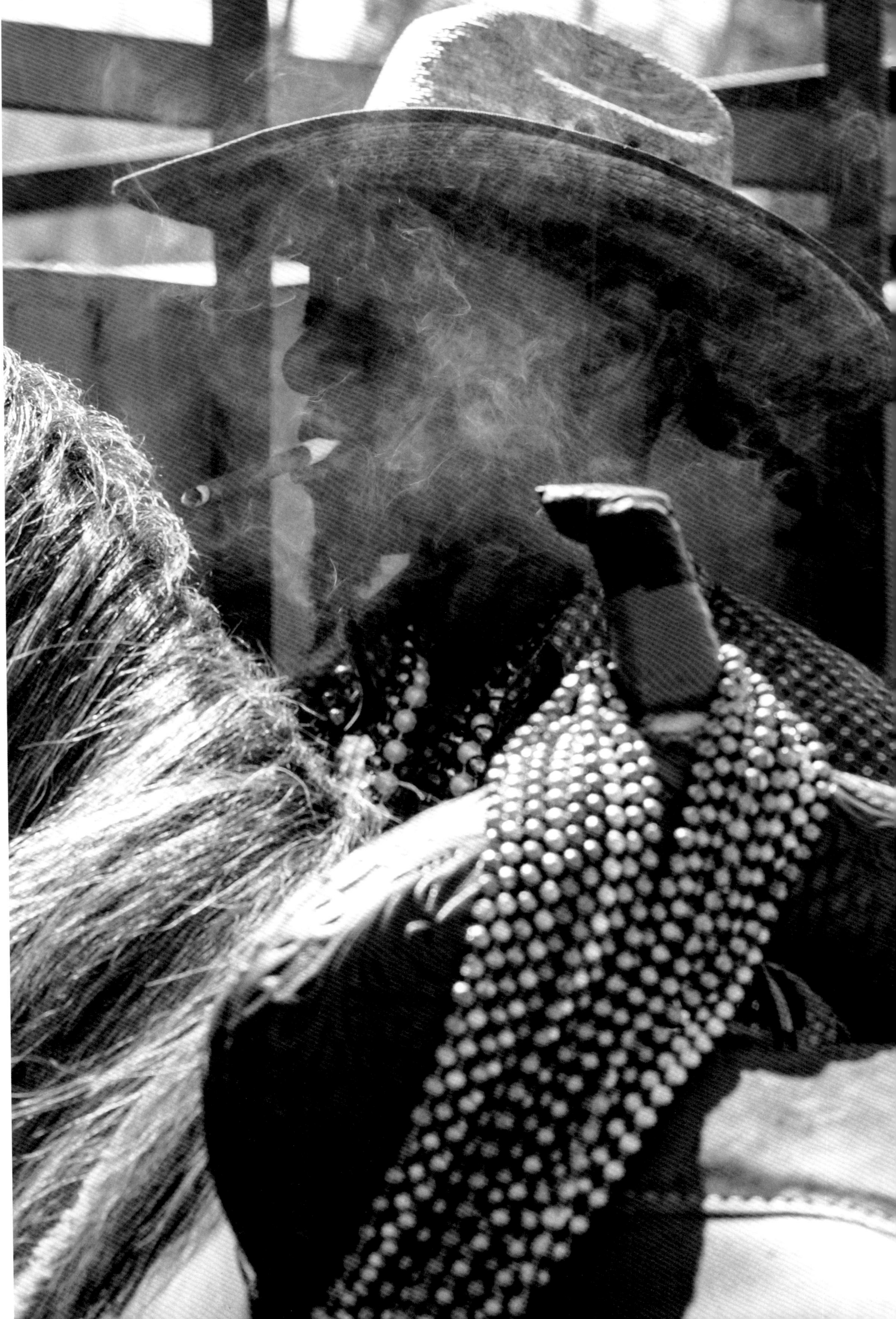

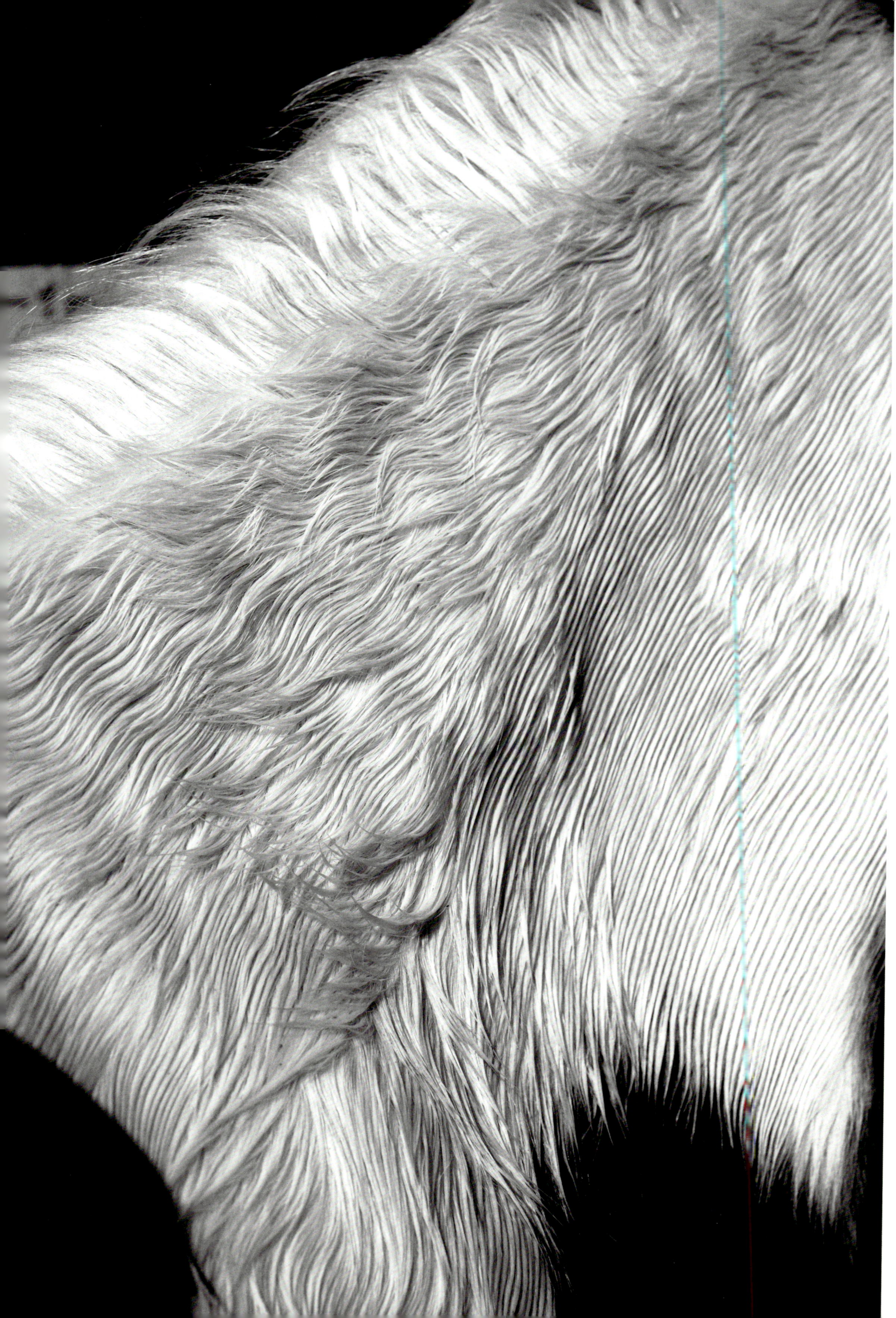

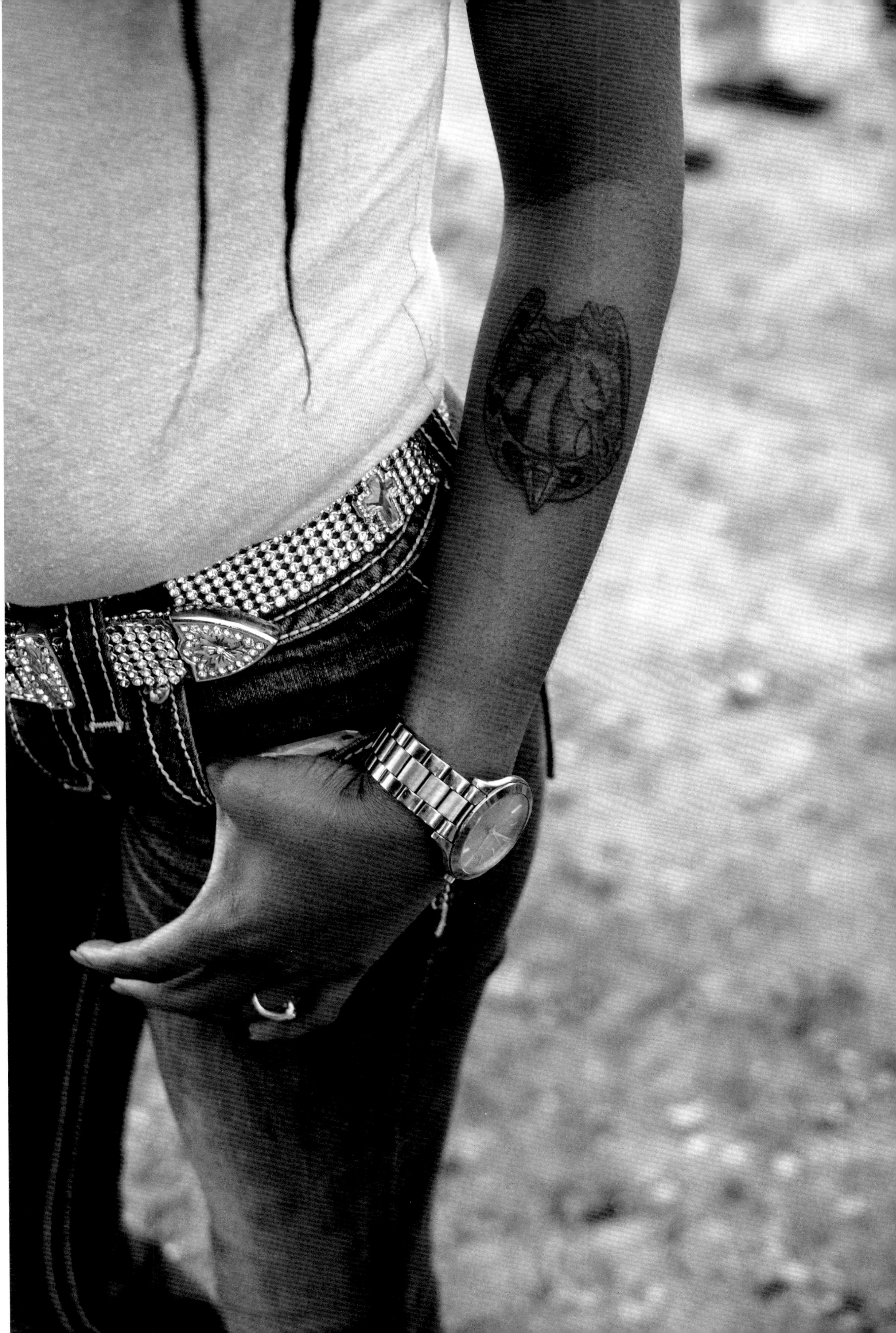

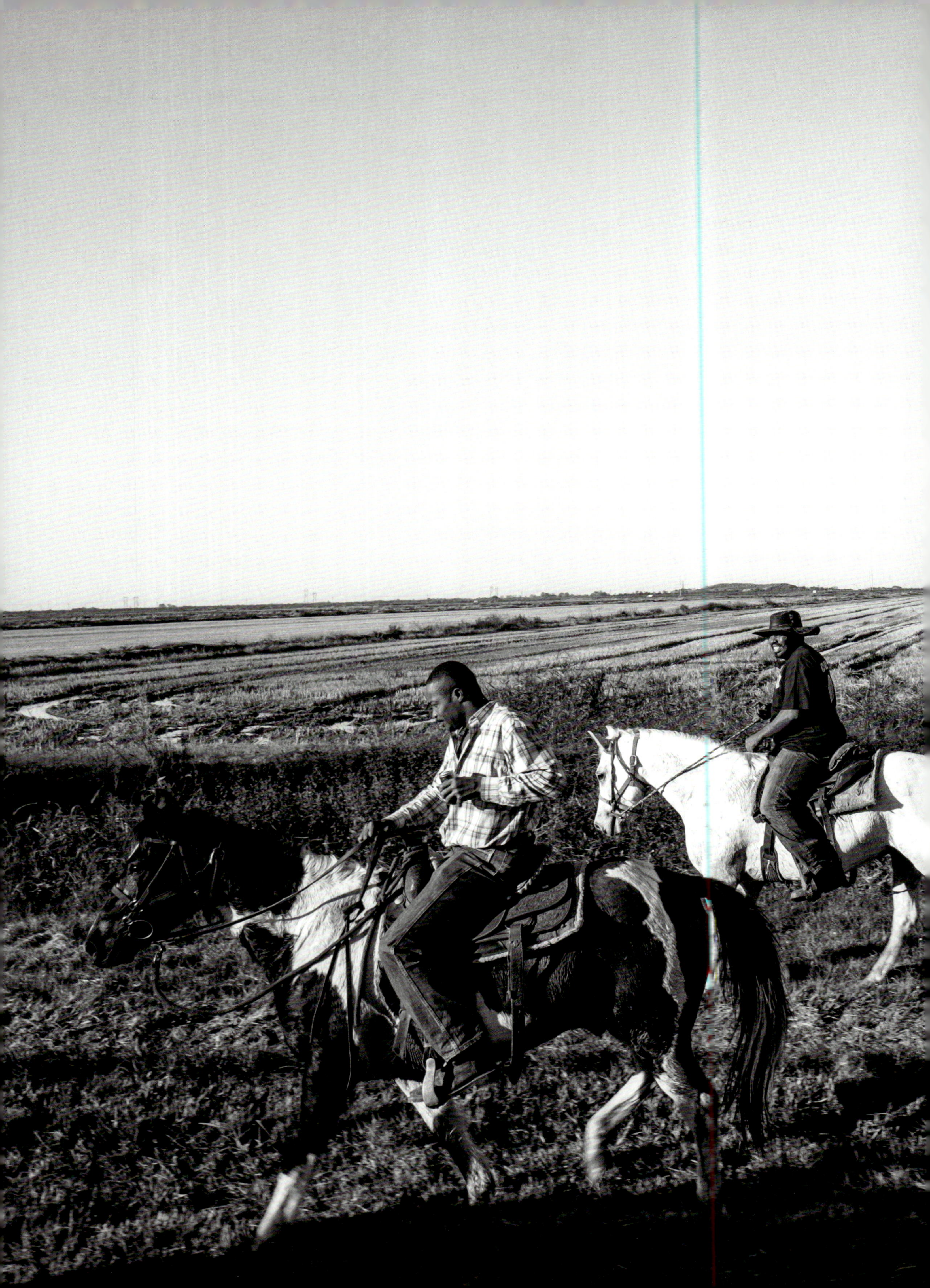

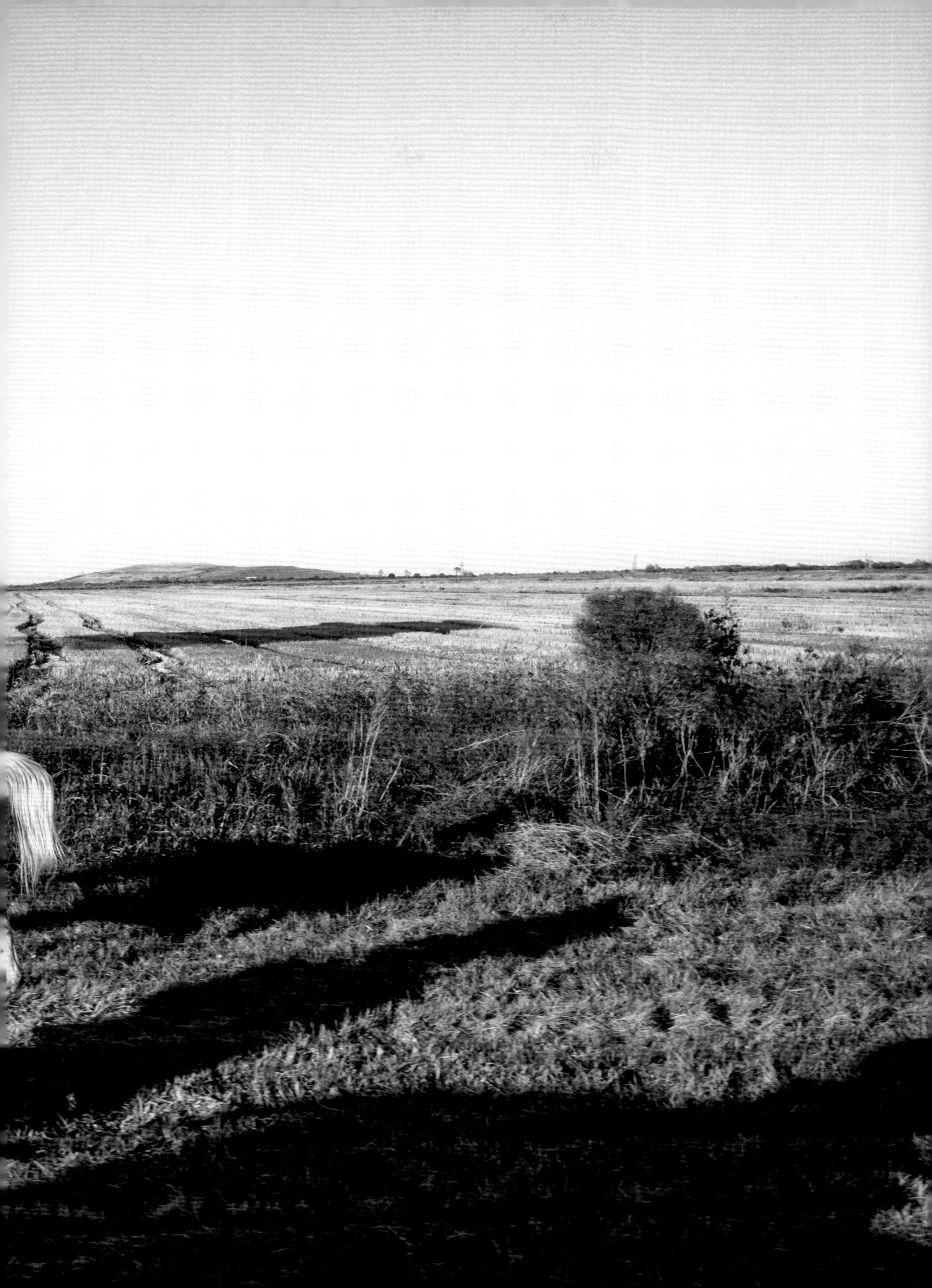

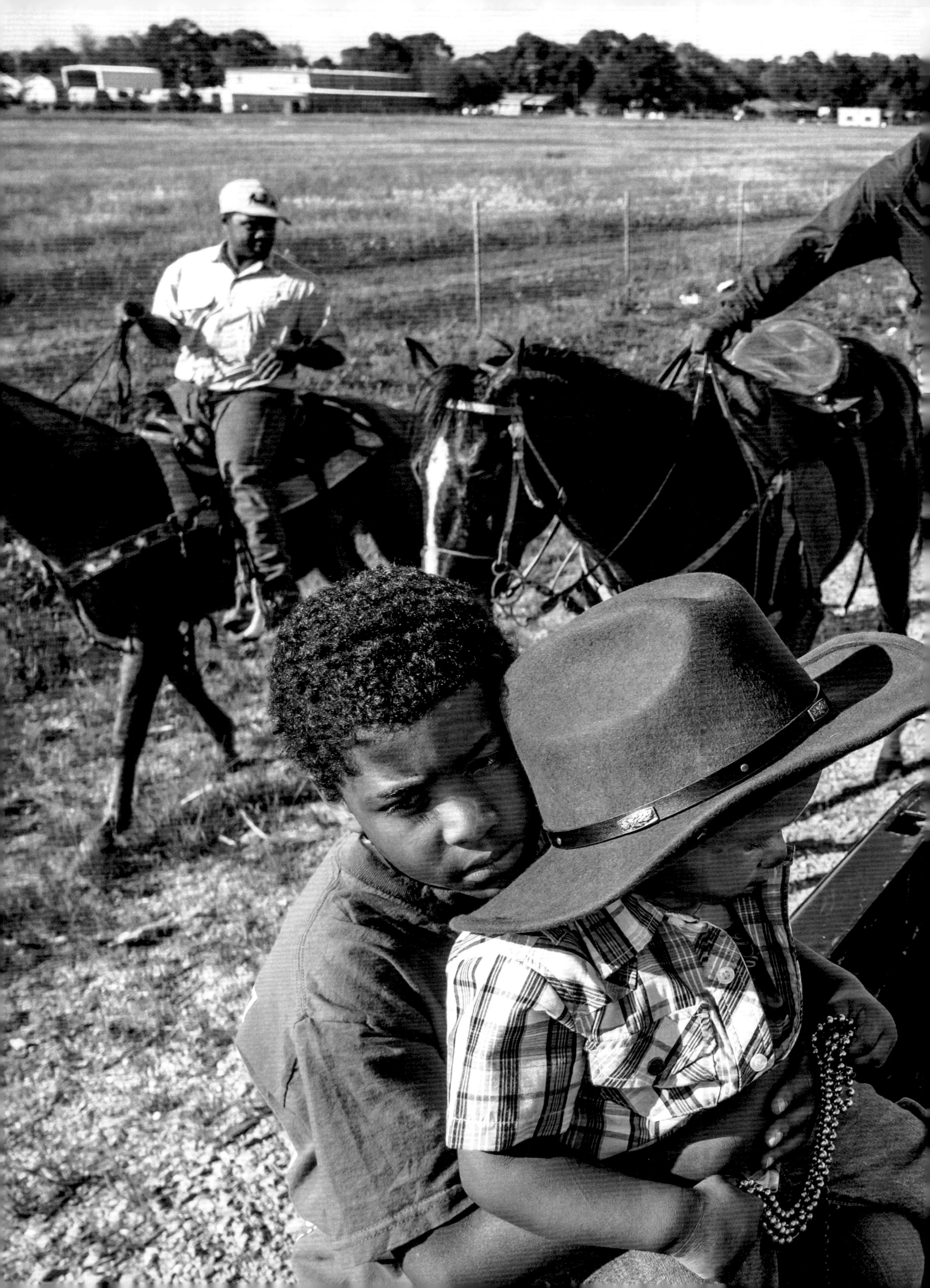

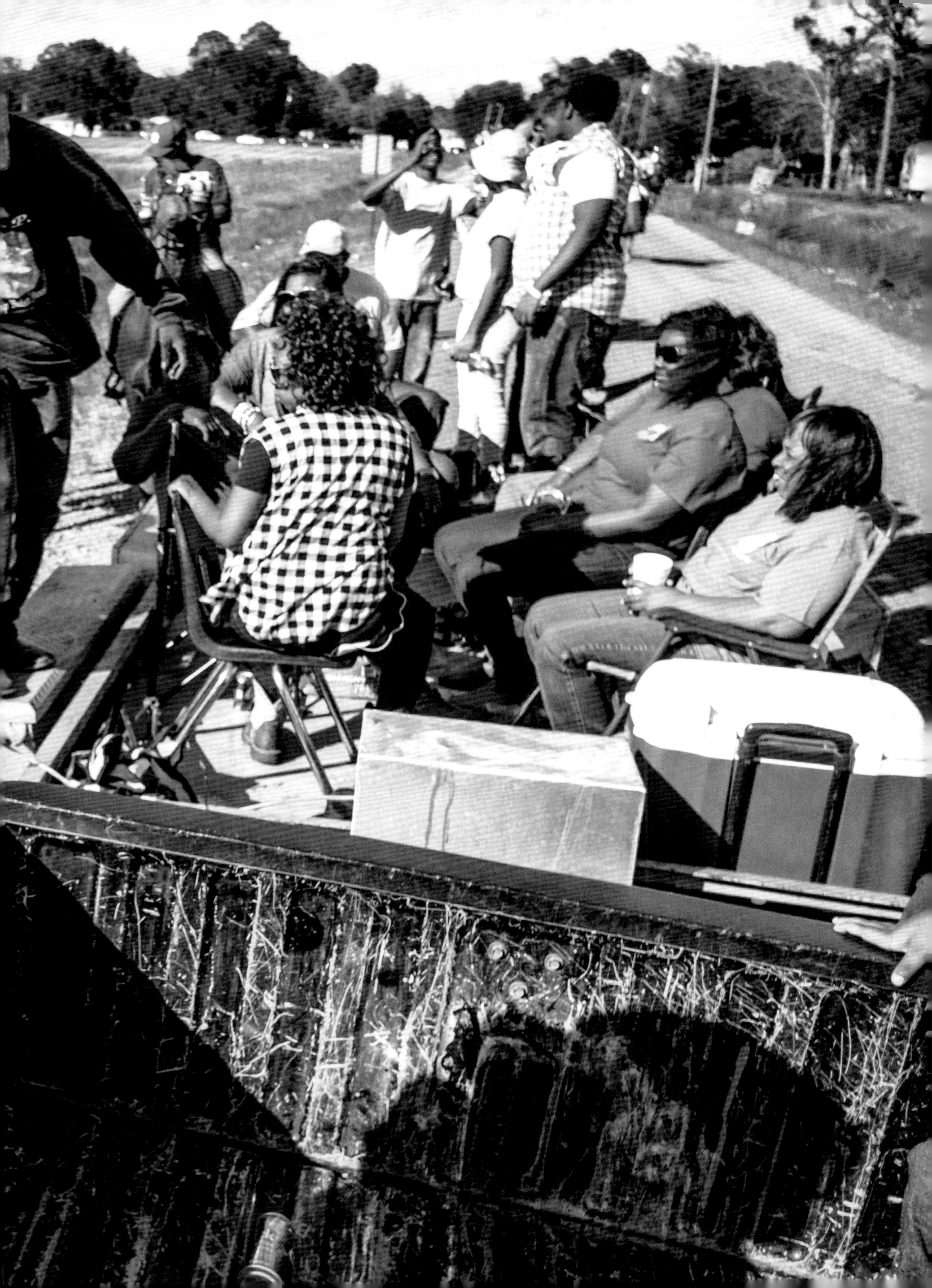

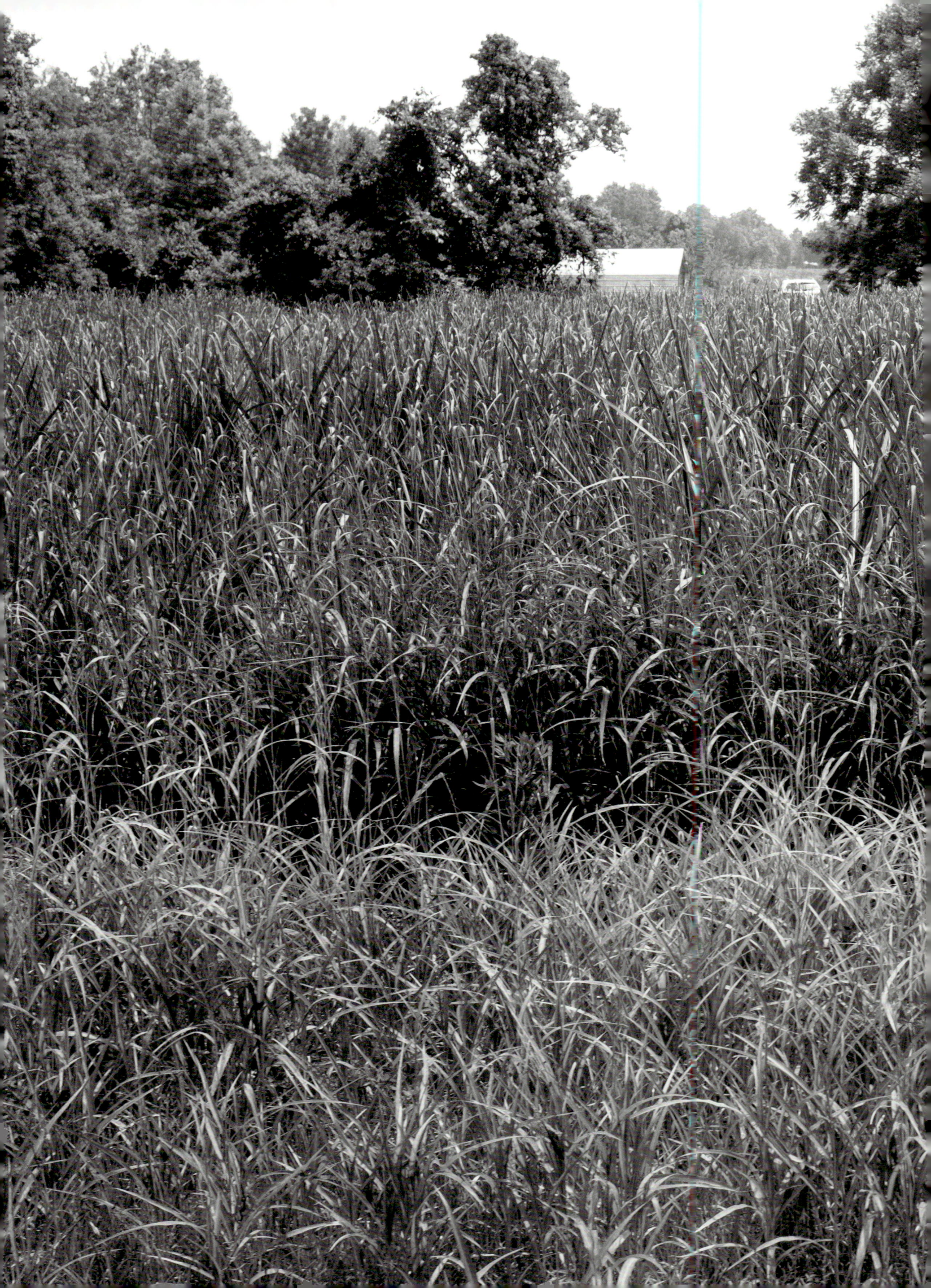

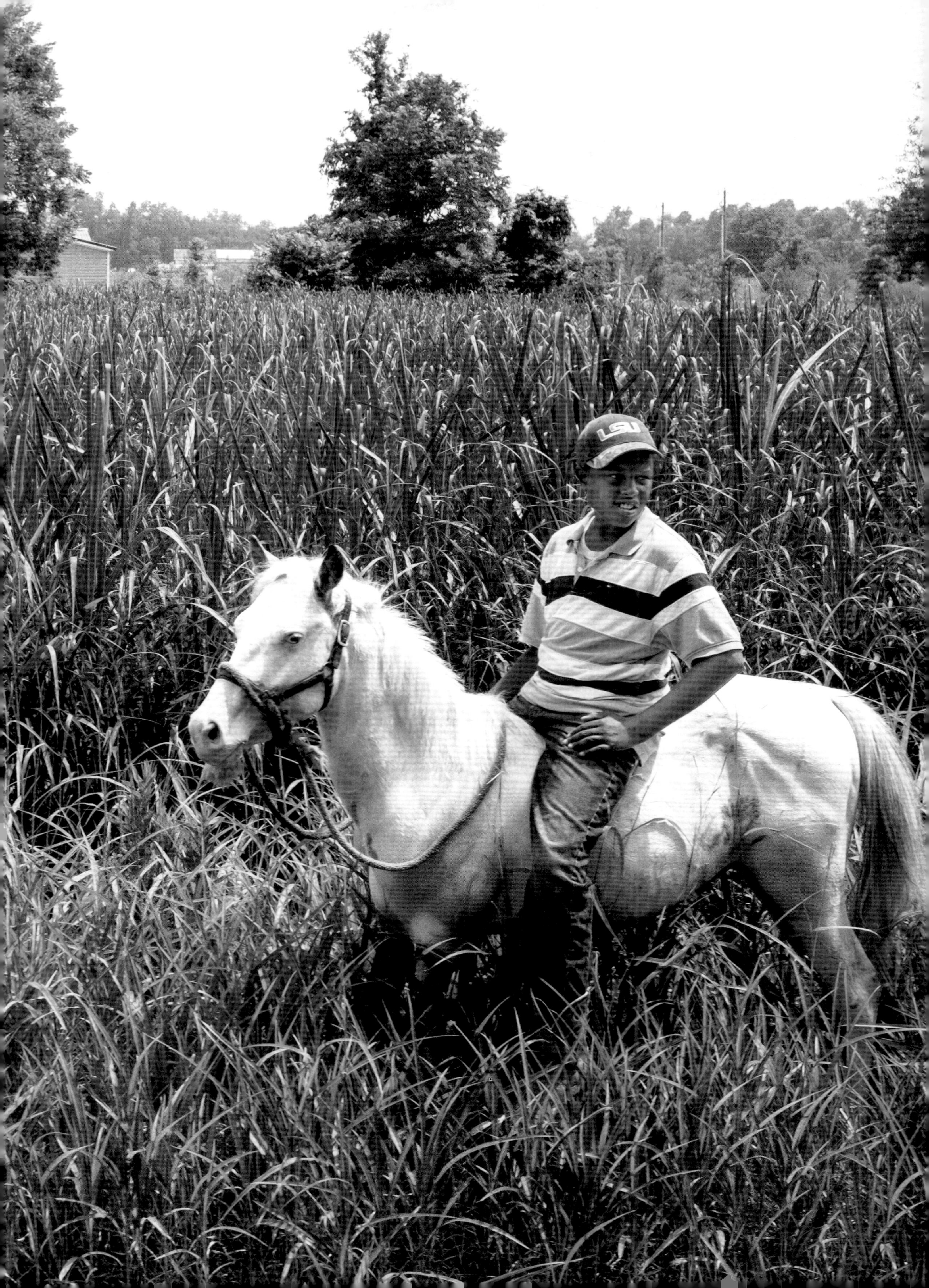
LSU

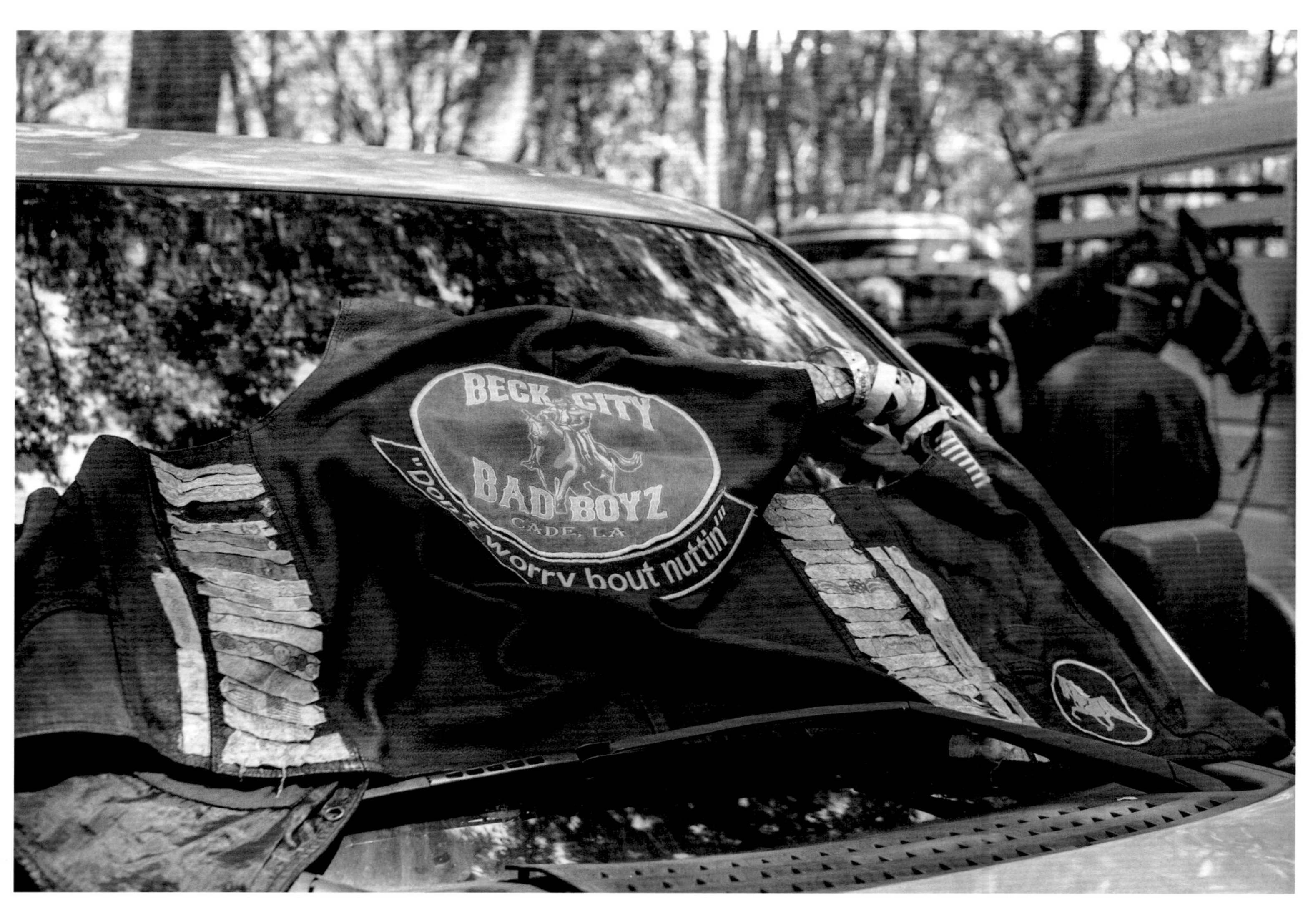
BECK CITY
BAD BOYZ
CADE, LA
"Don't worry bout nuttin'"

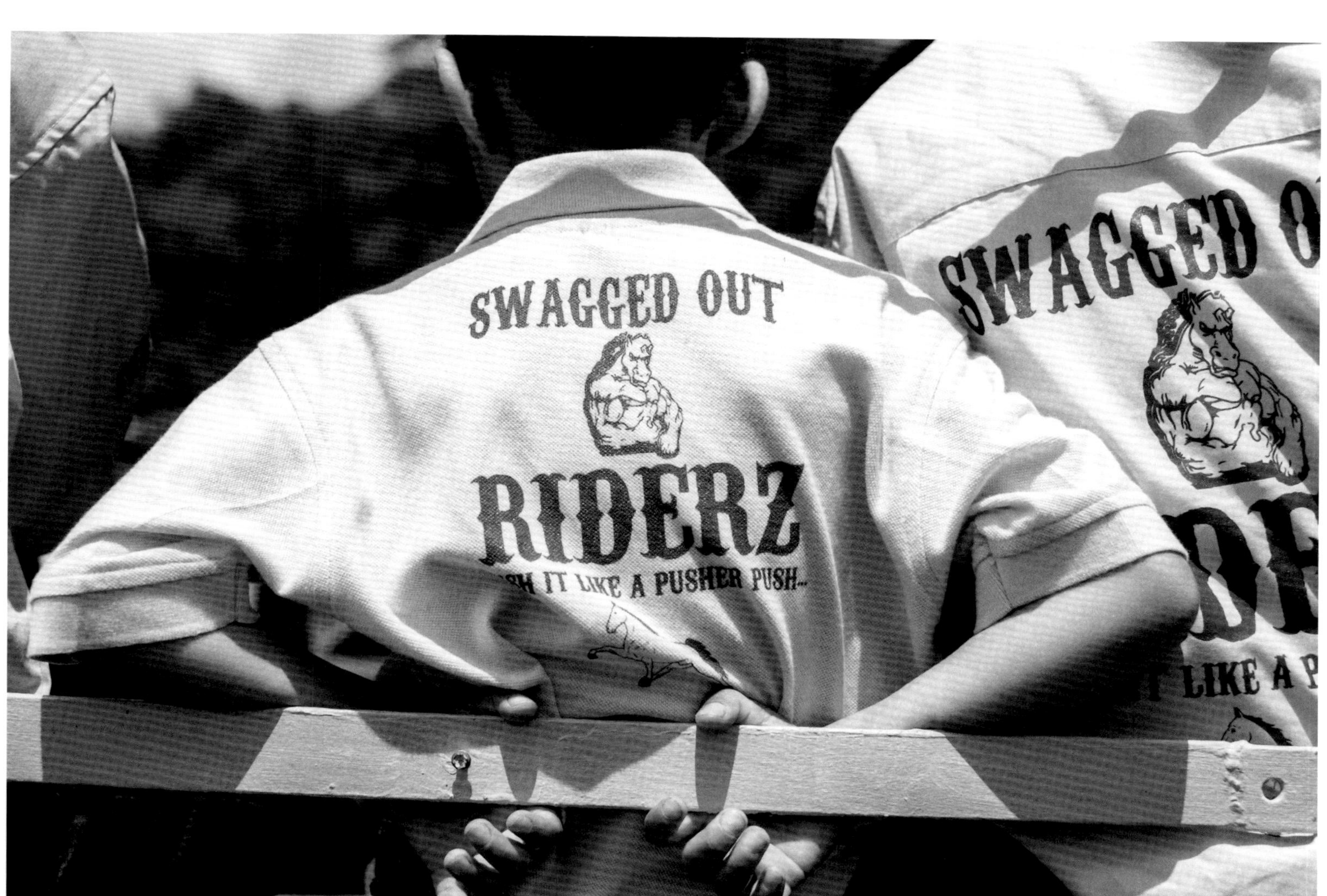
SWAGGED OUT
RIDERZ
IT LIKE A PUSHER PUSH...

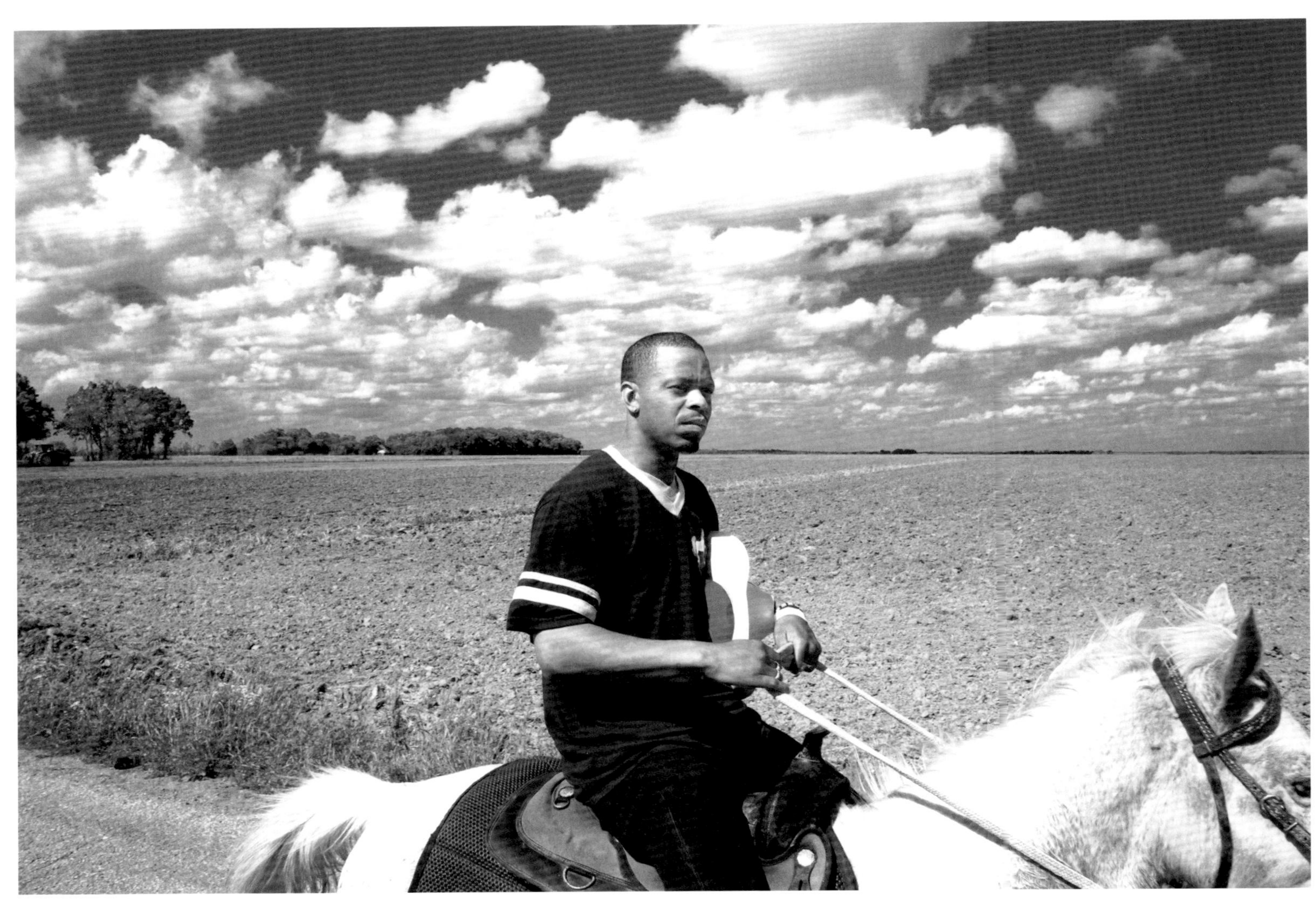

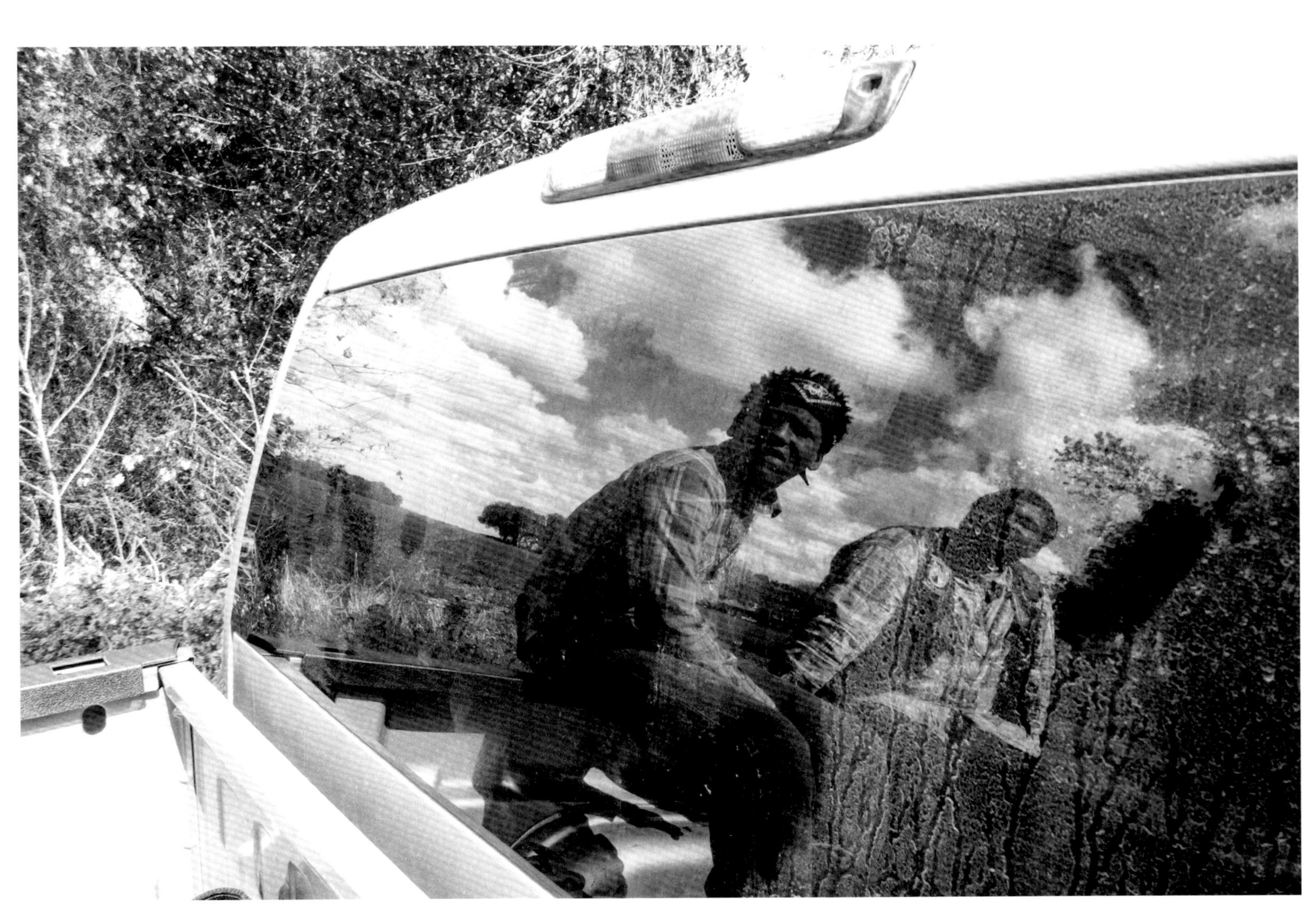

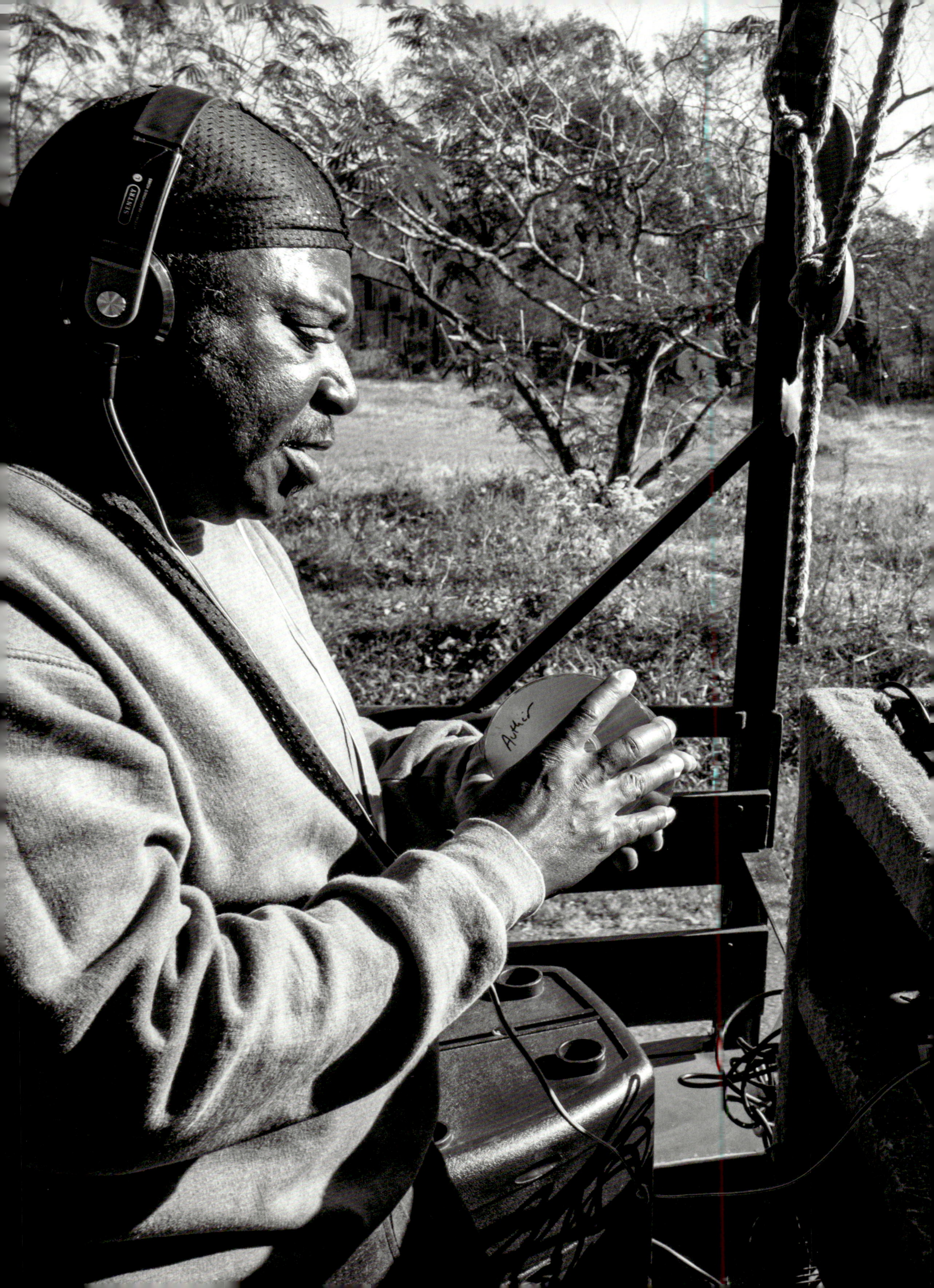
SENTRY
Arthur

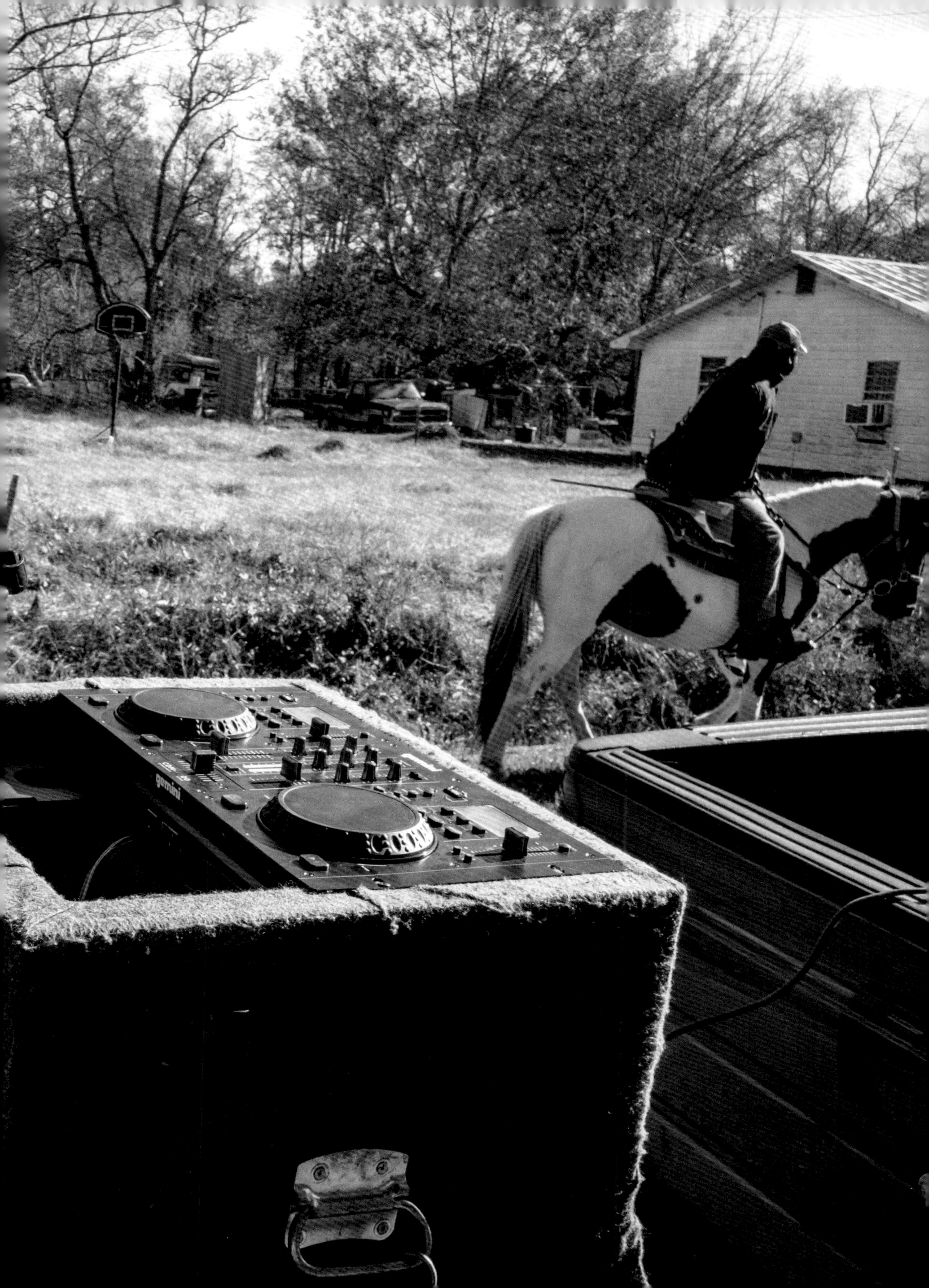
gemini

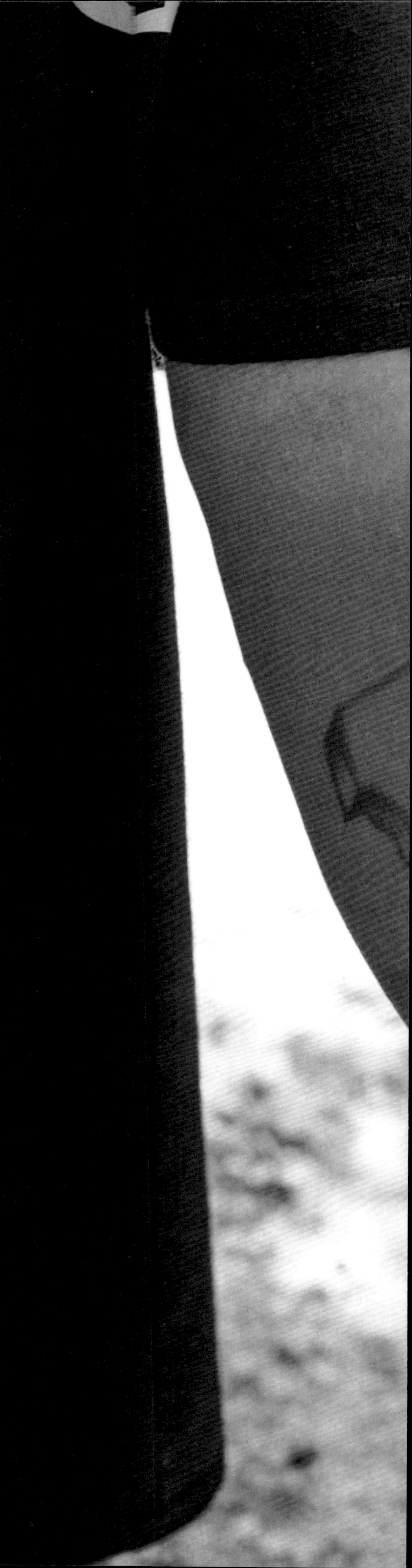

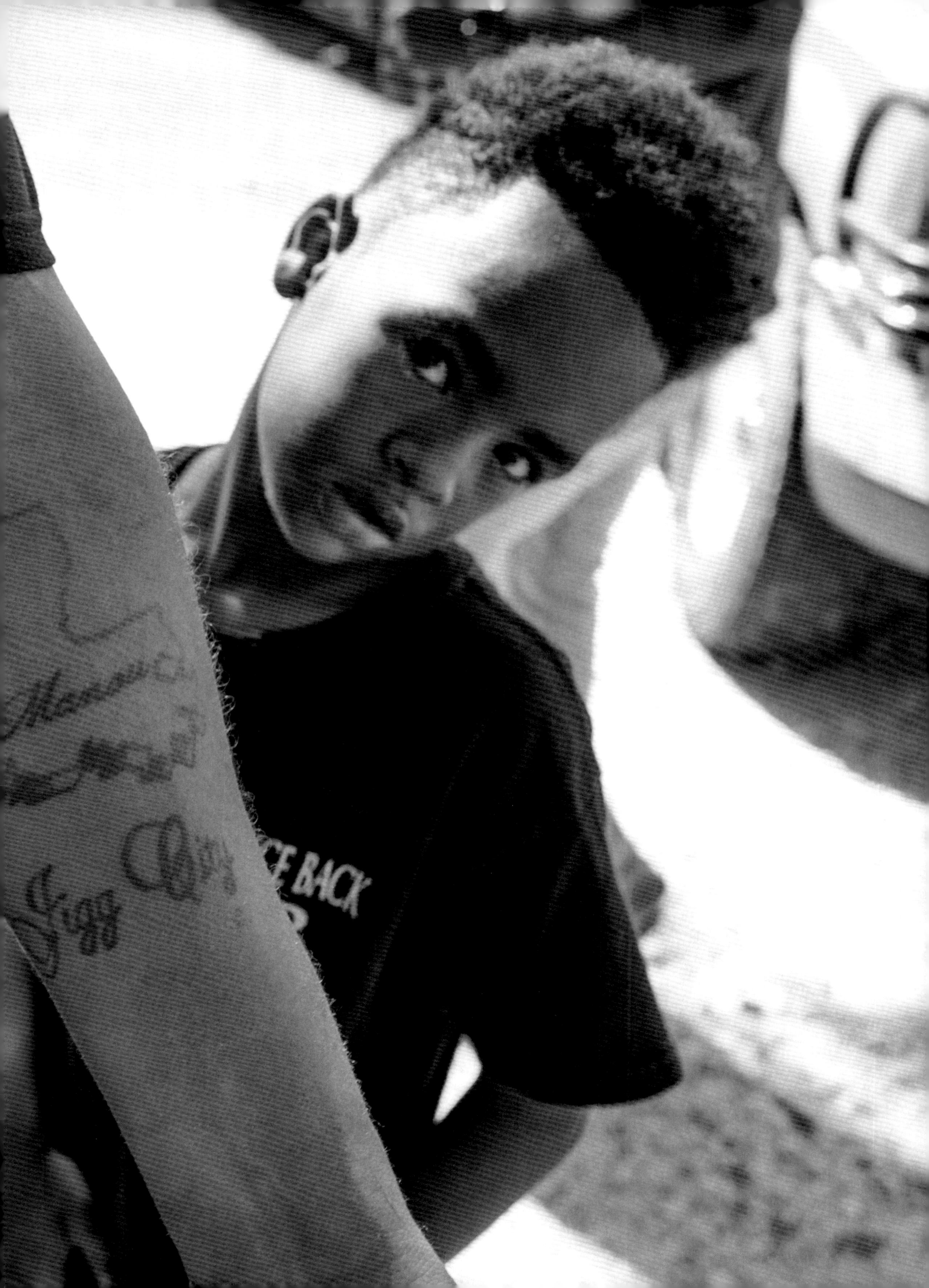

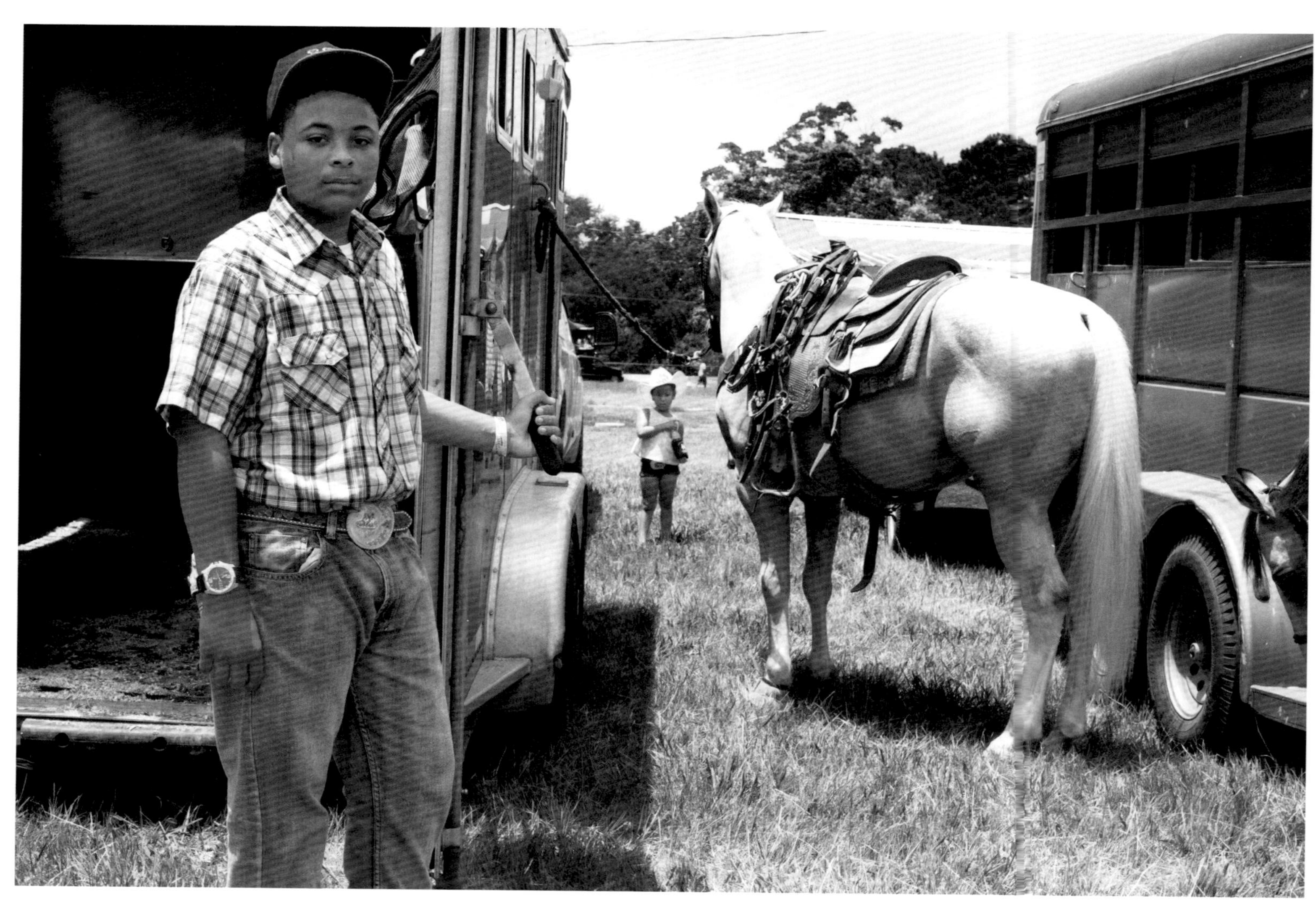

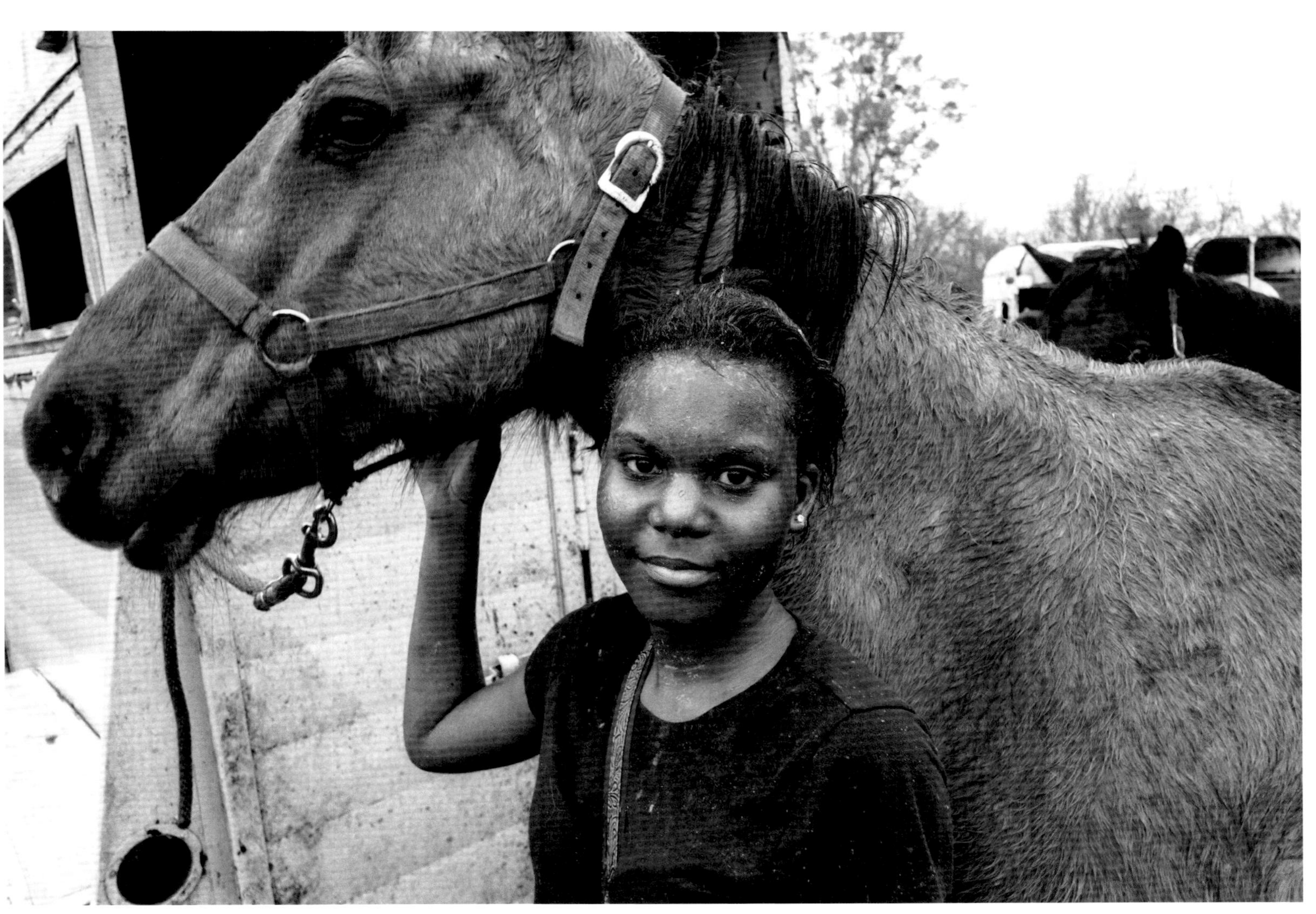

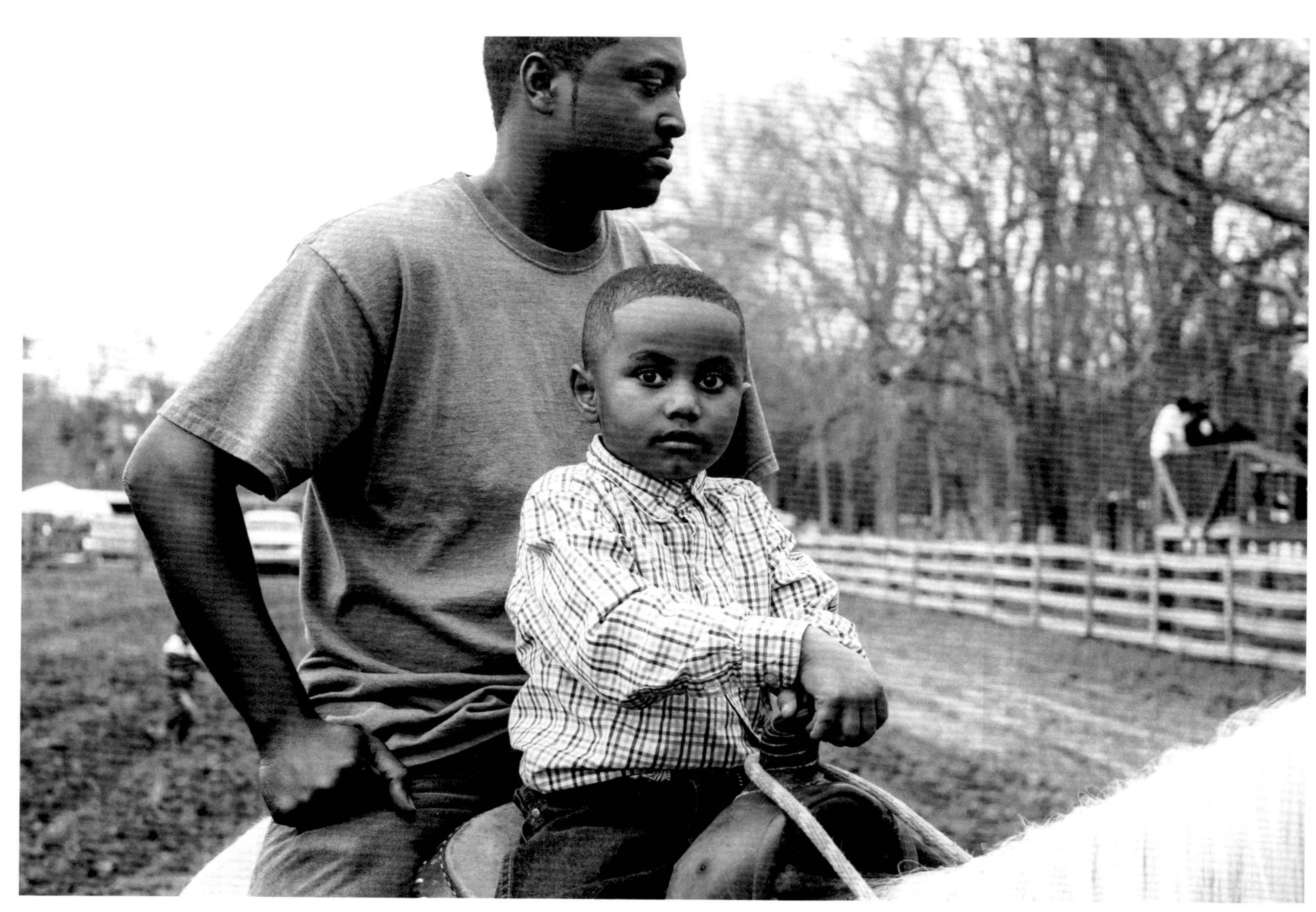

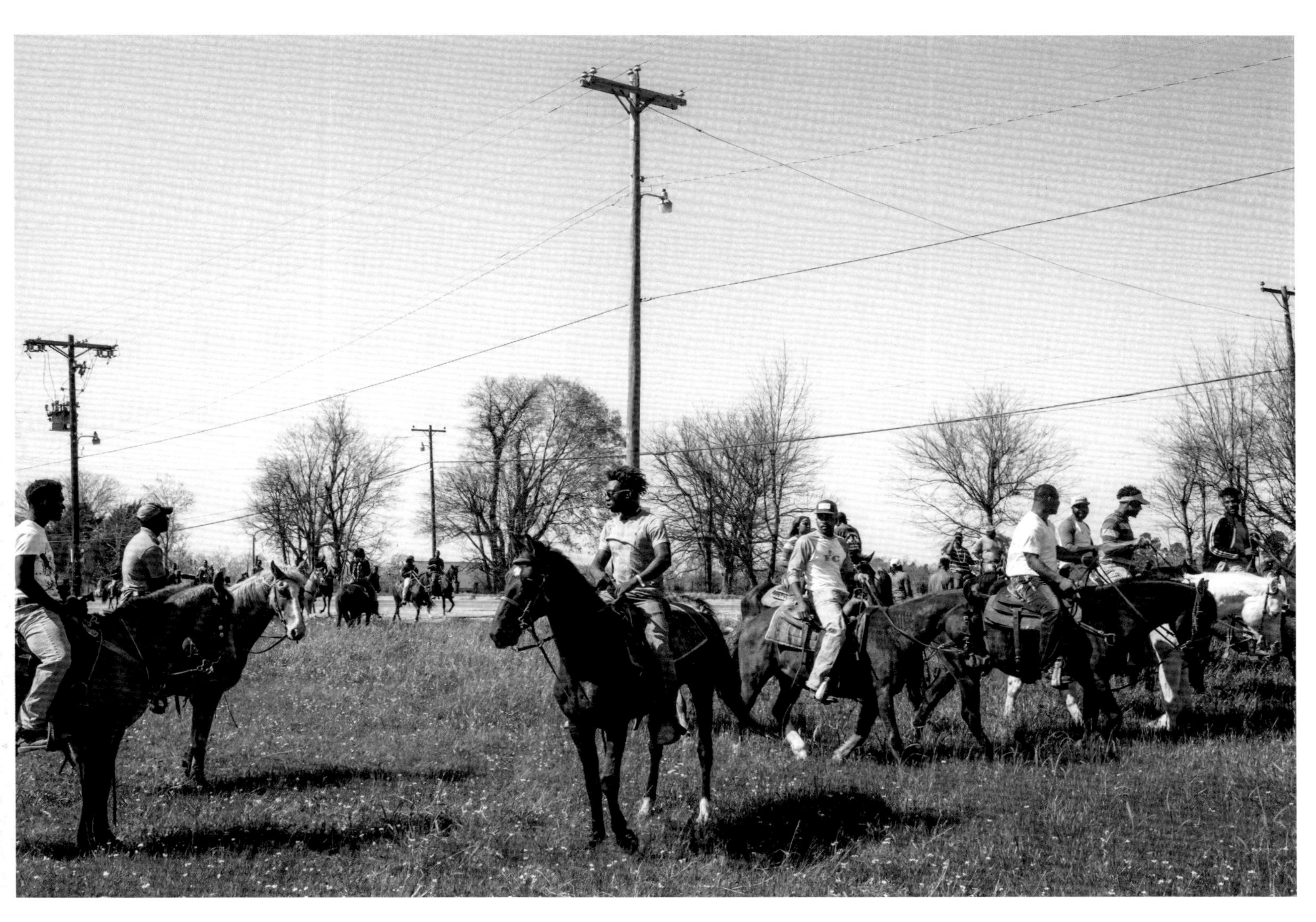

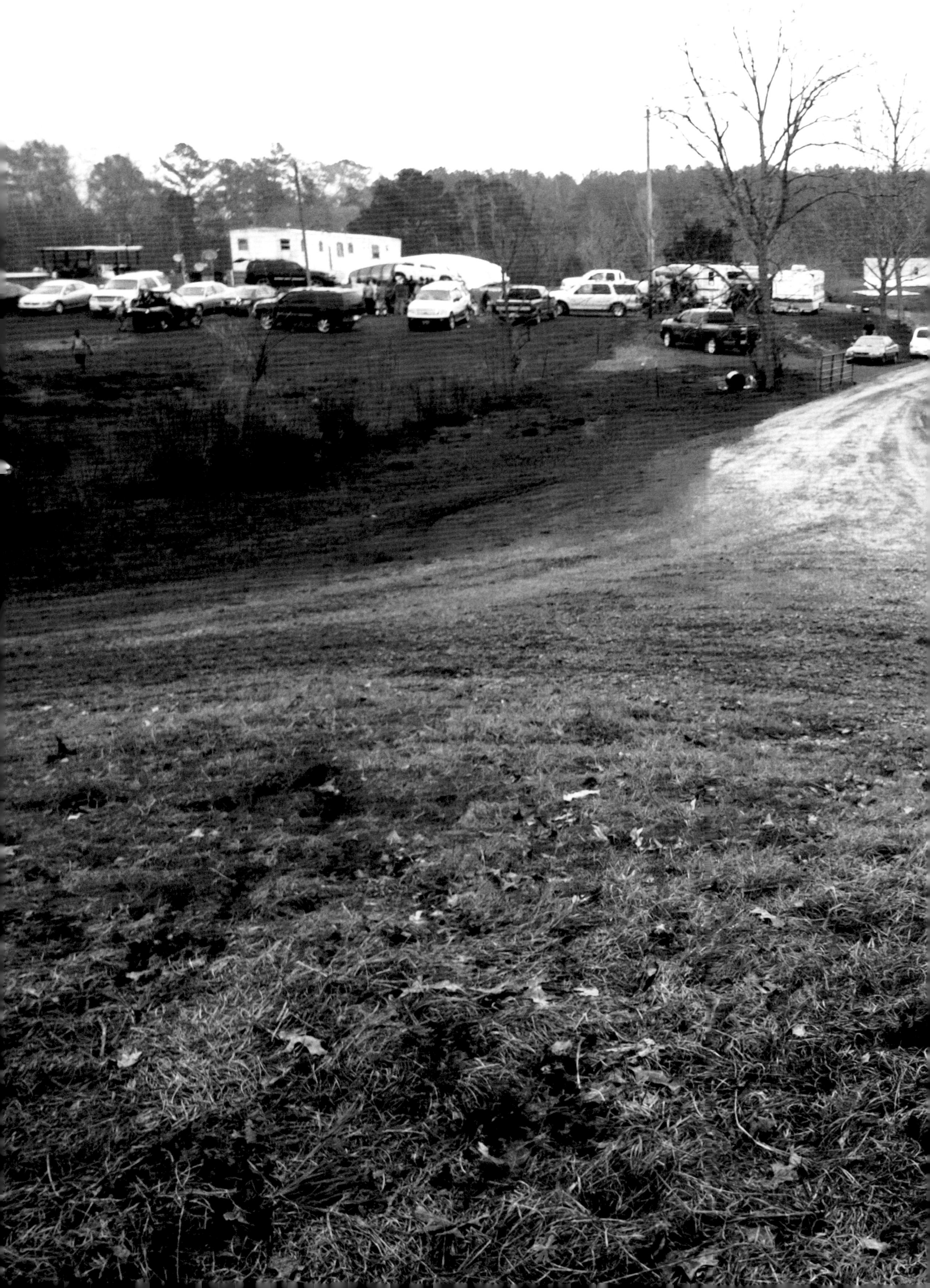

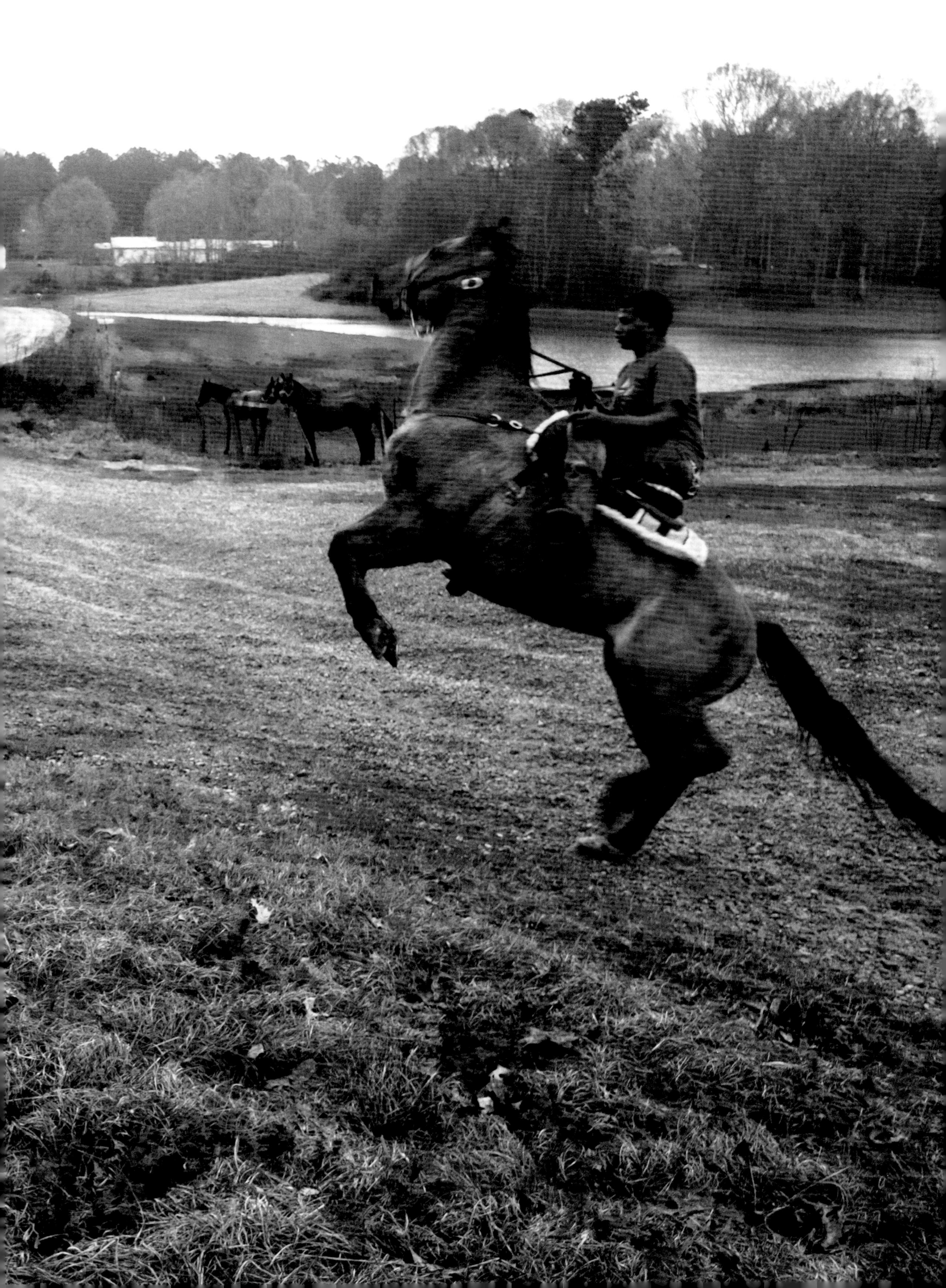

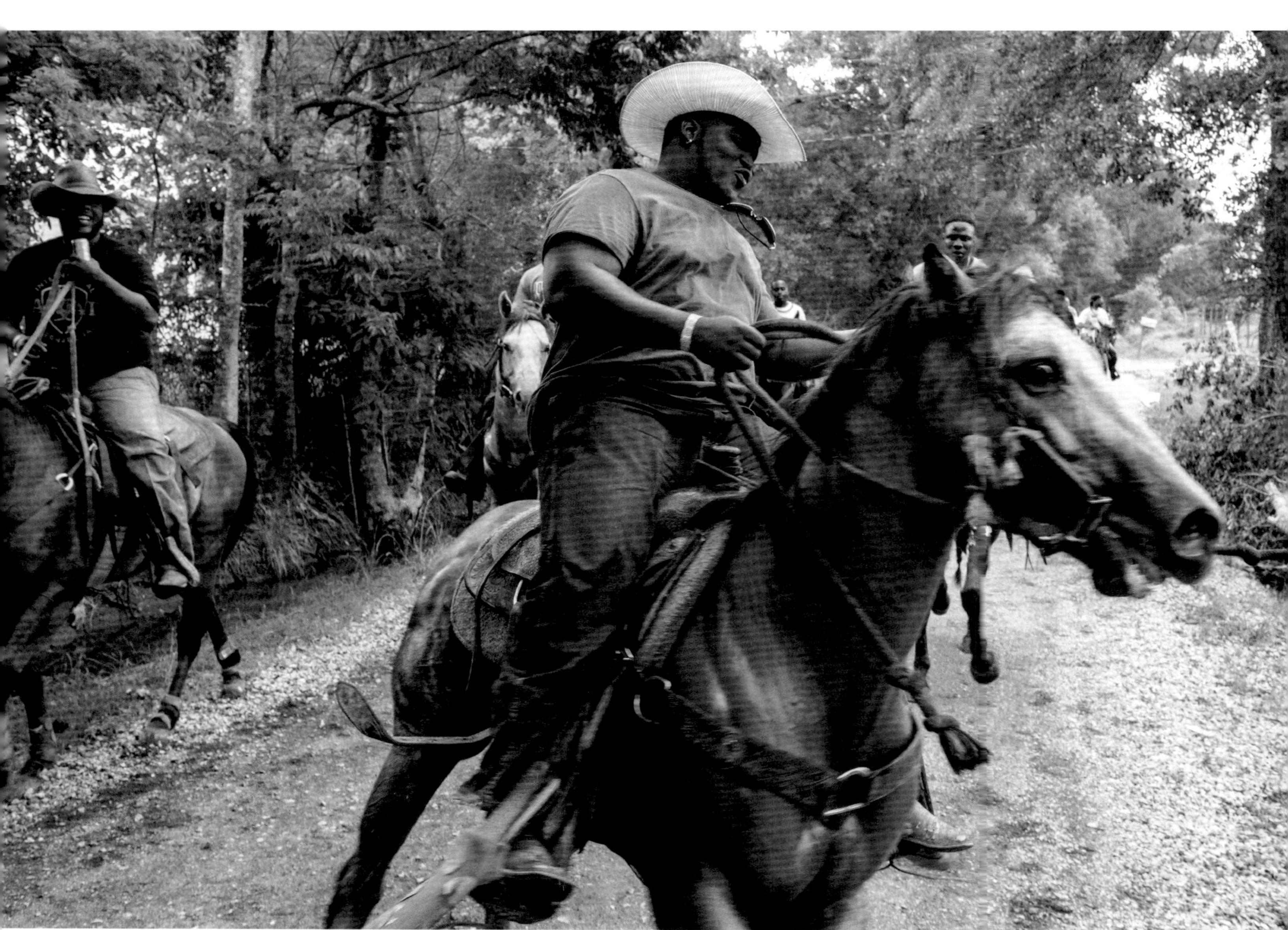

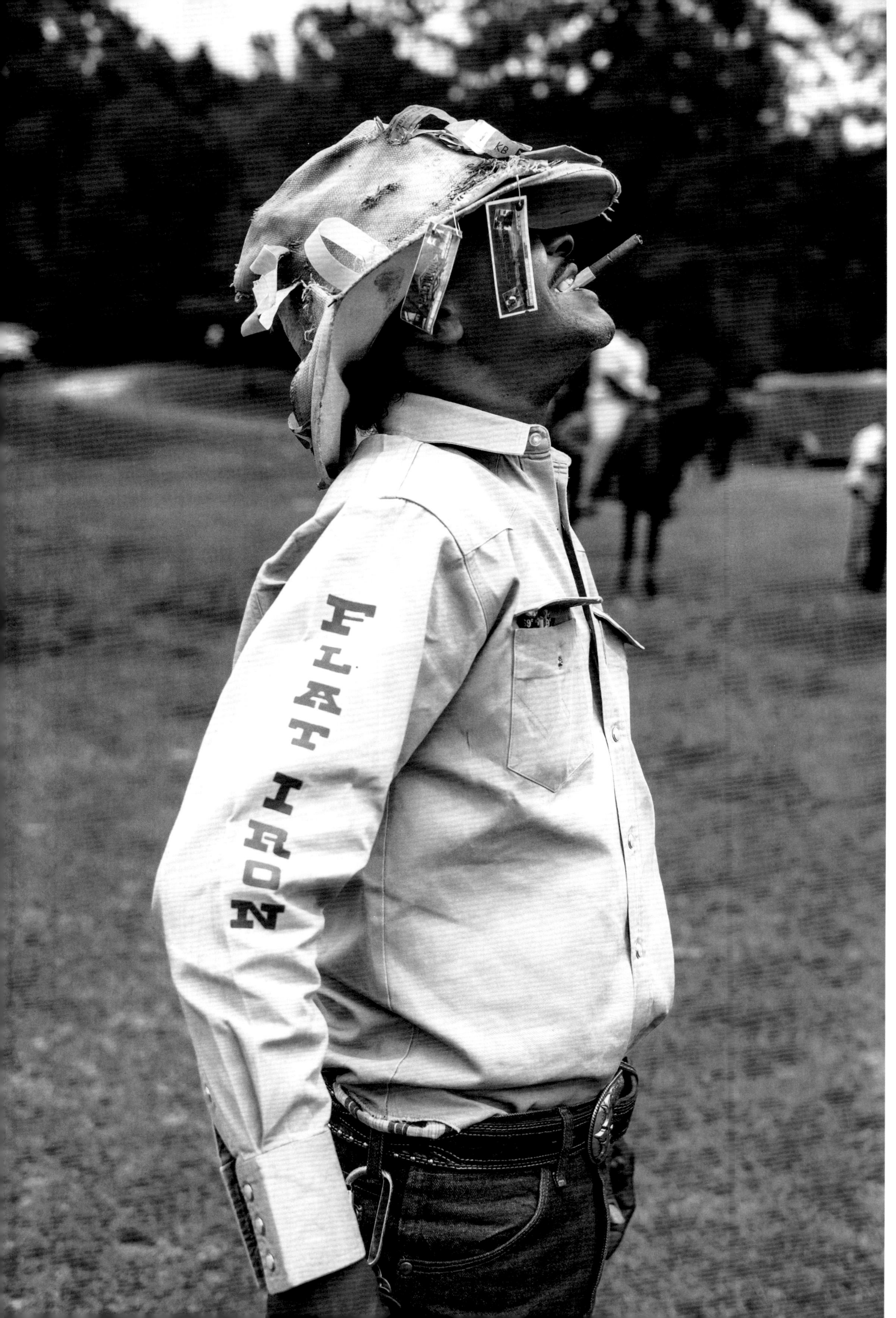
FLAT IRON

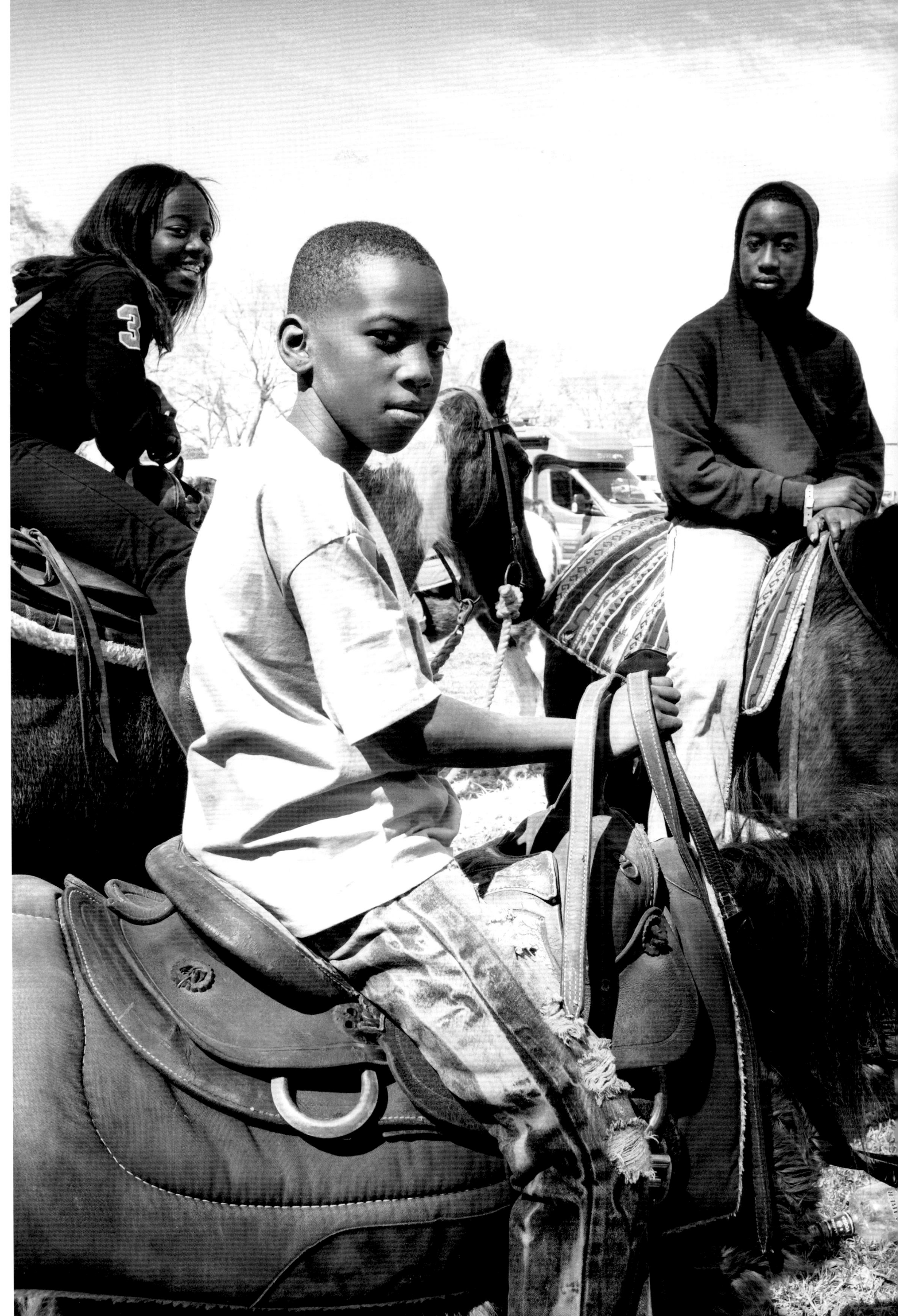

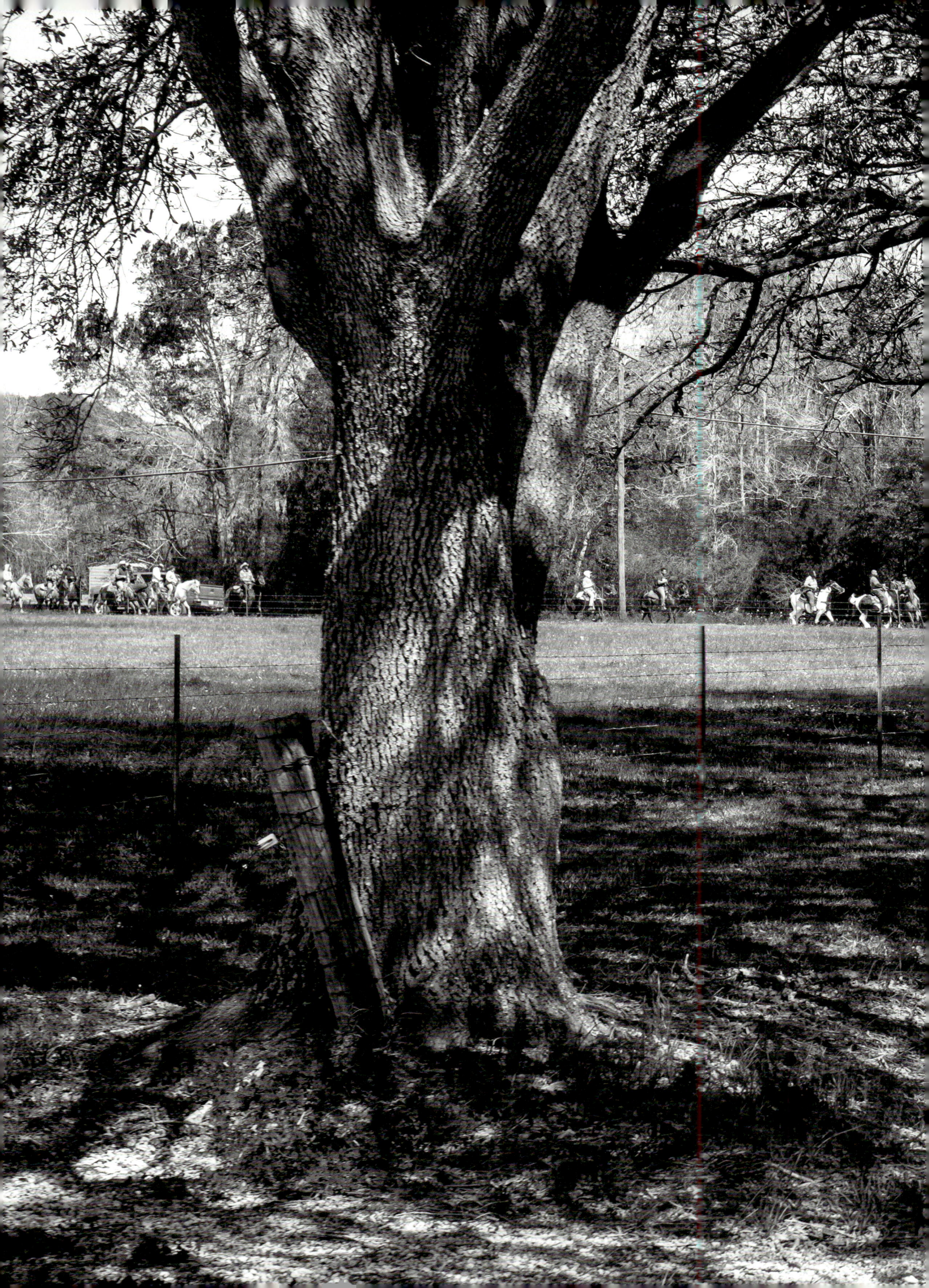

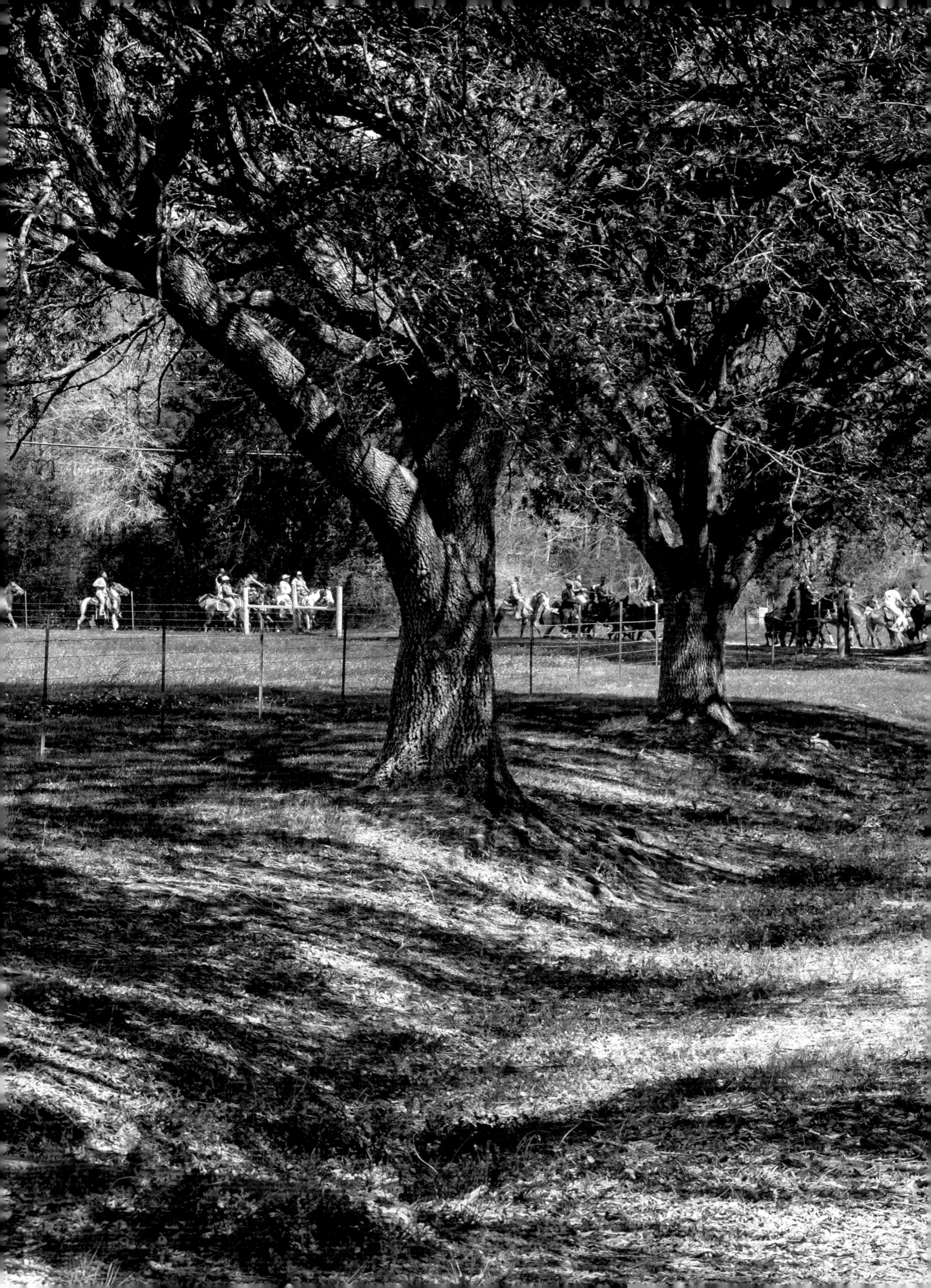

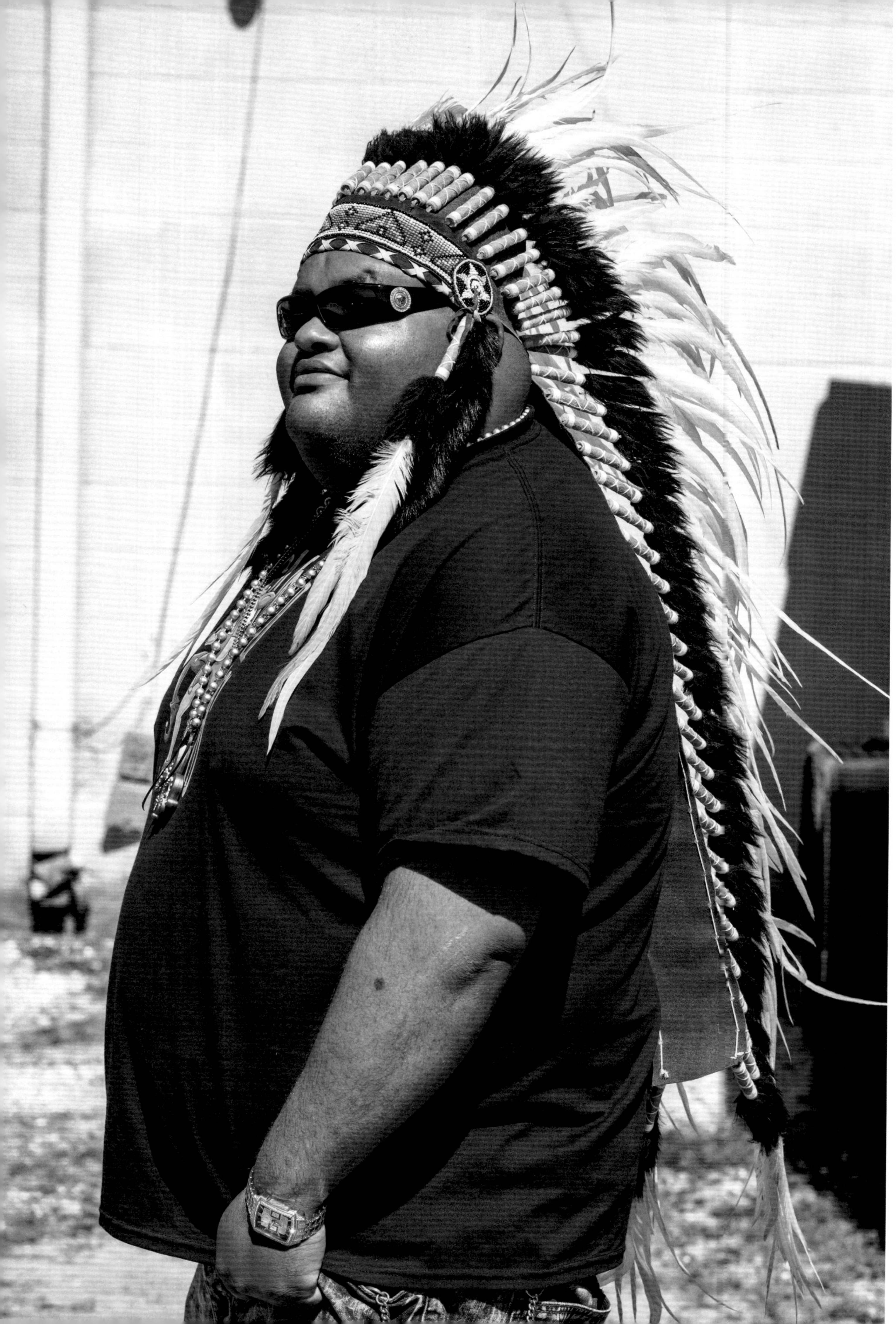

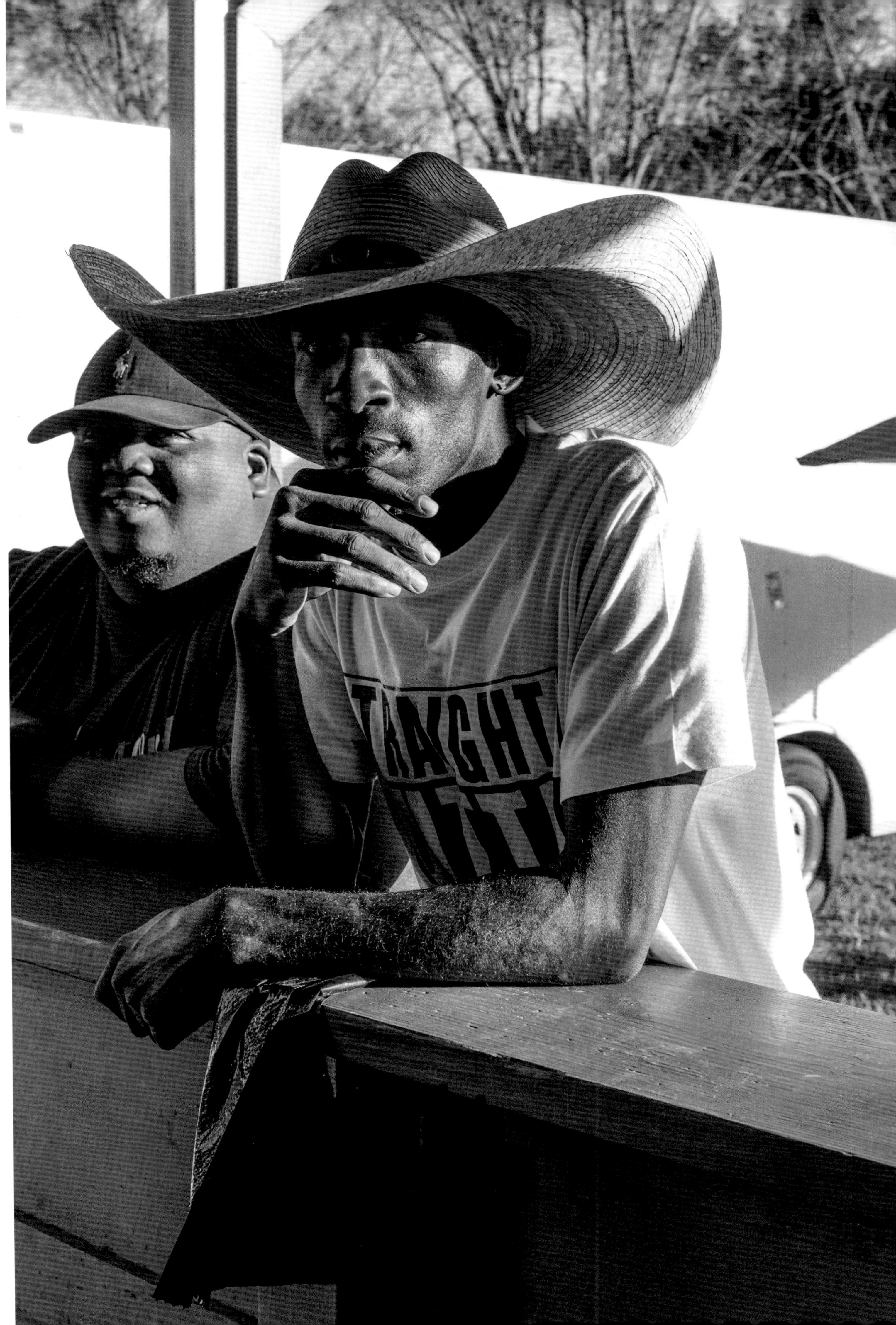

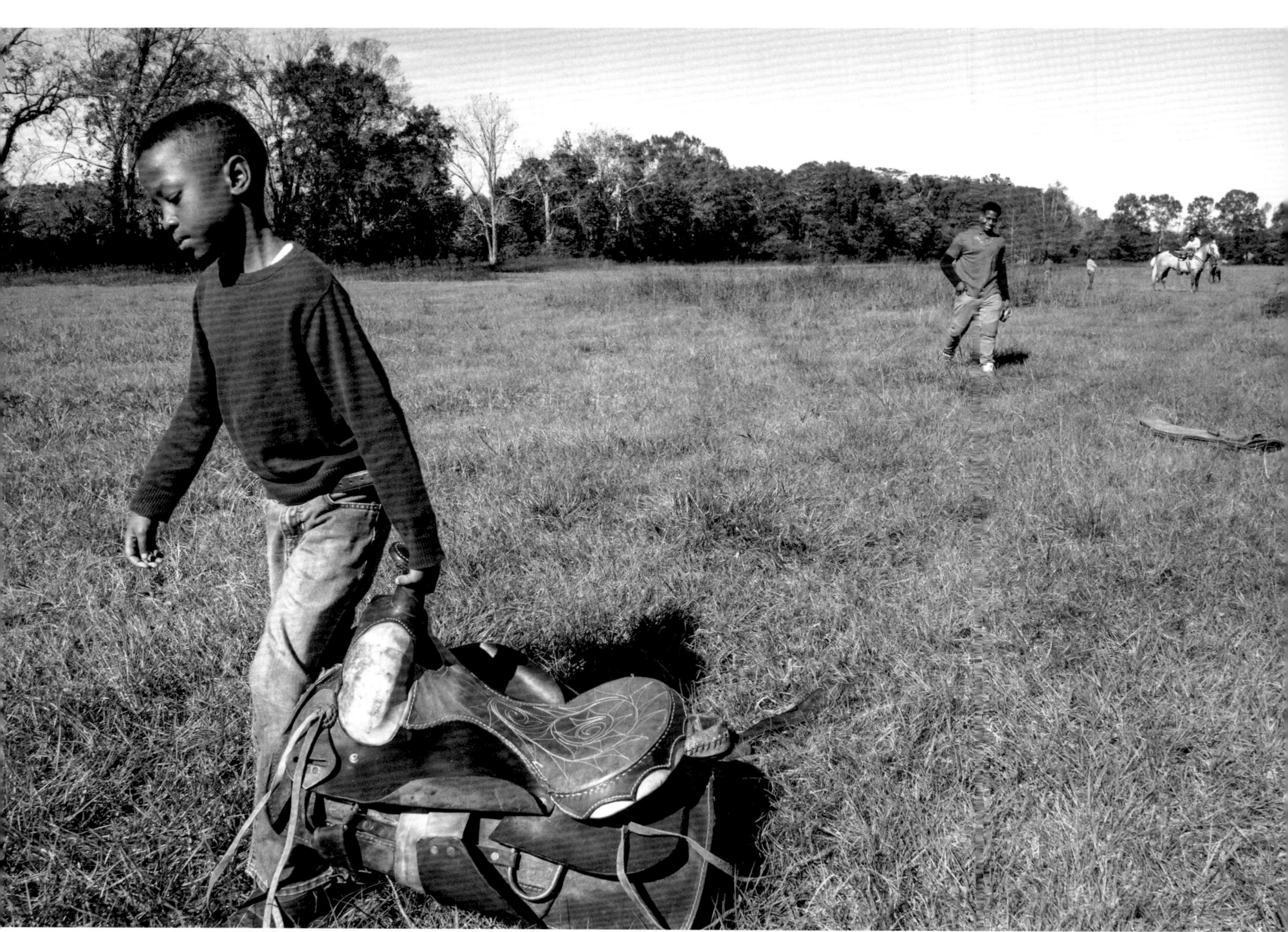

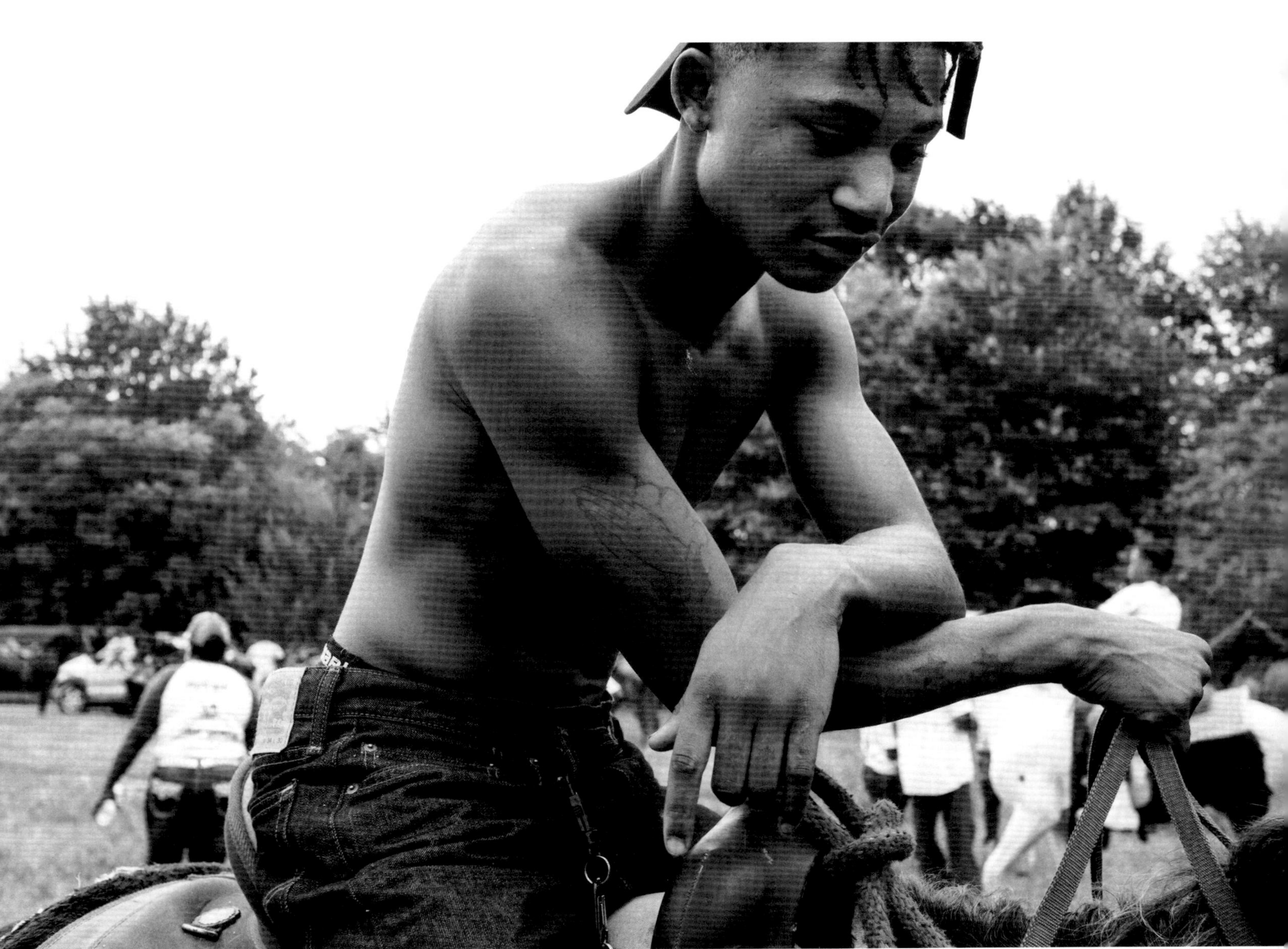

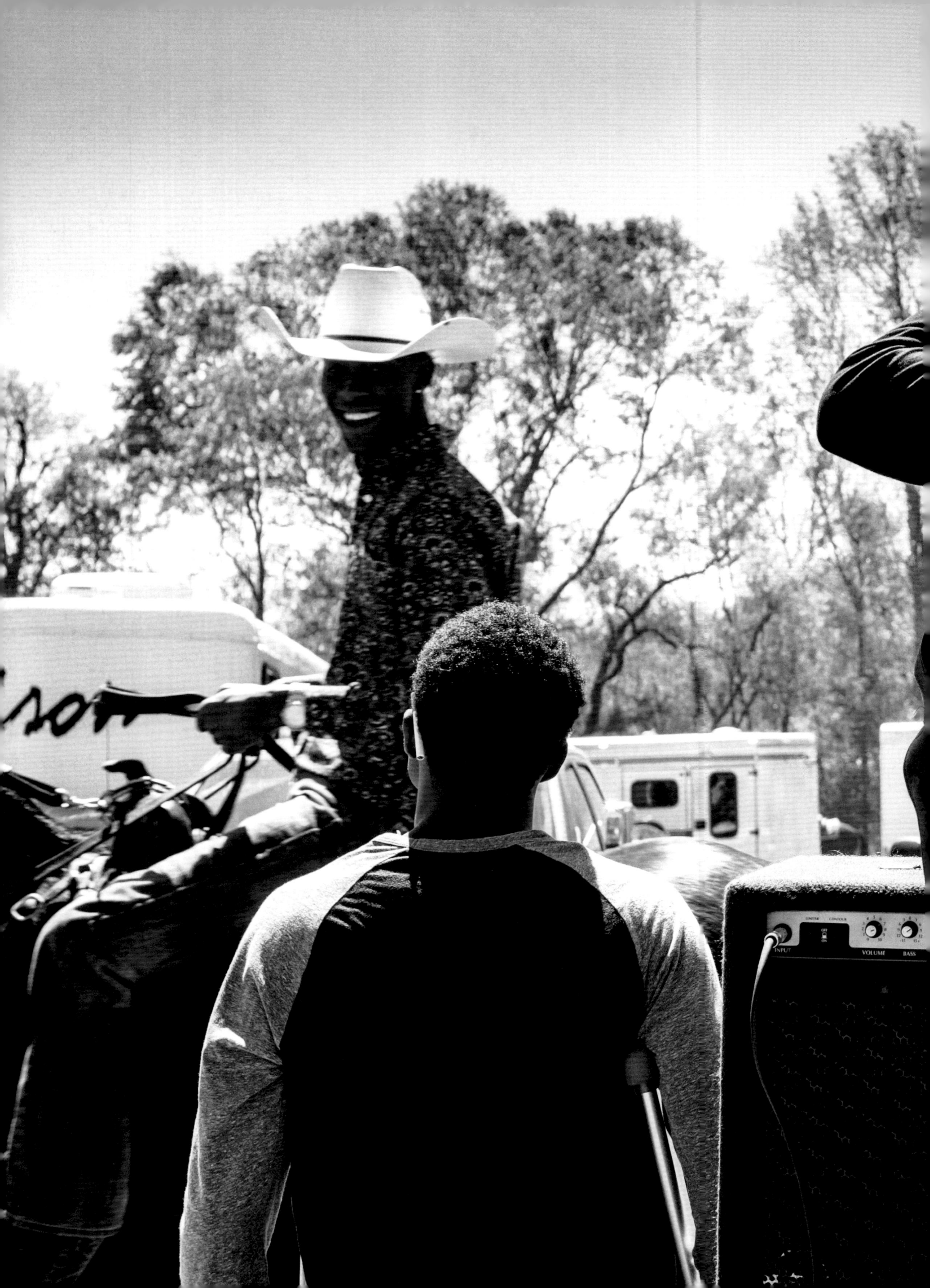
INPUT
VOLUME
BASS

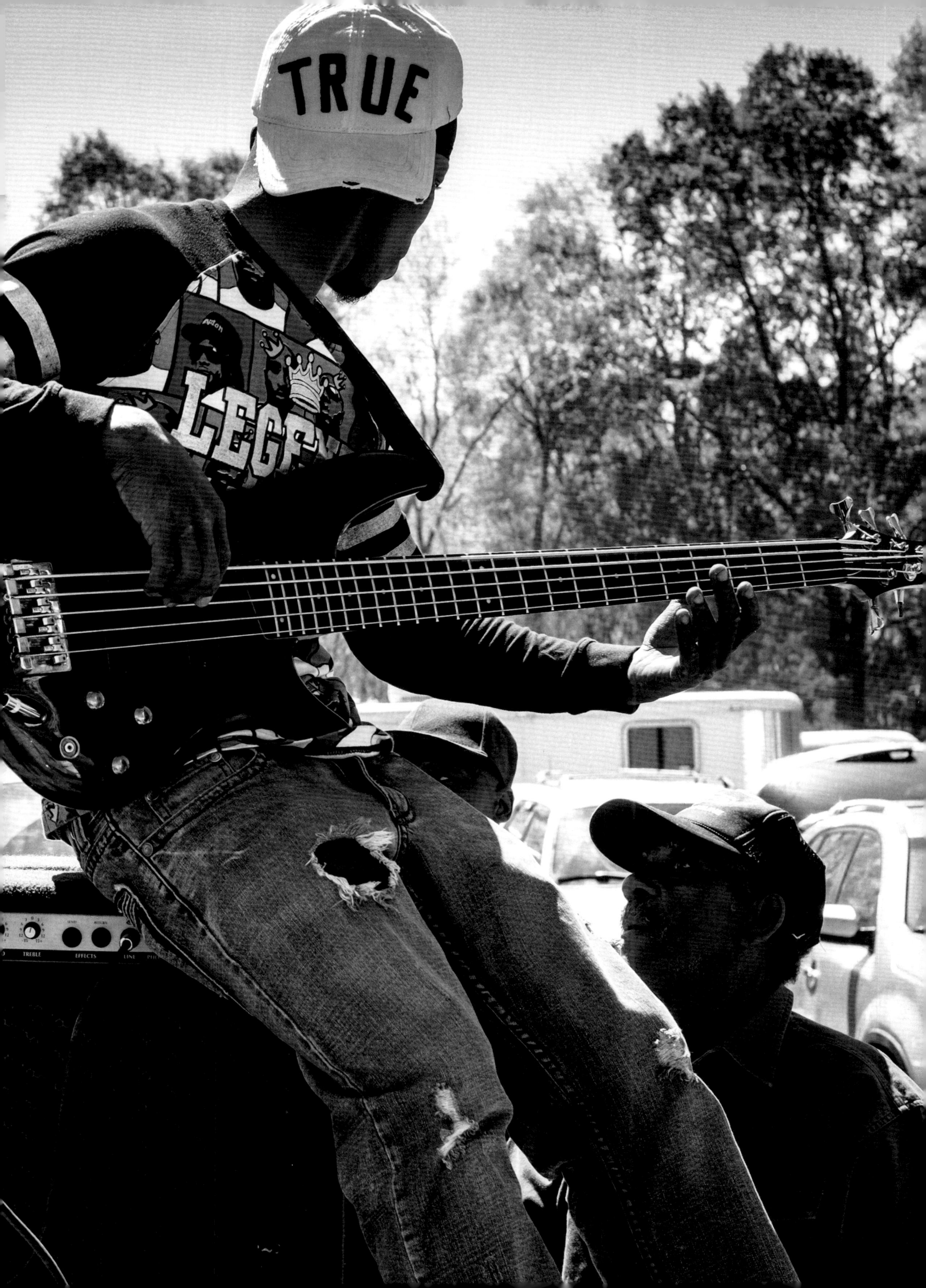
TRUE
TREBLE
EFFECTS
LINE

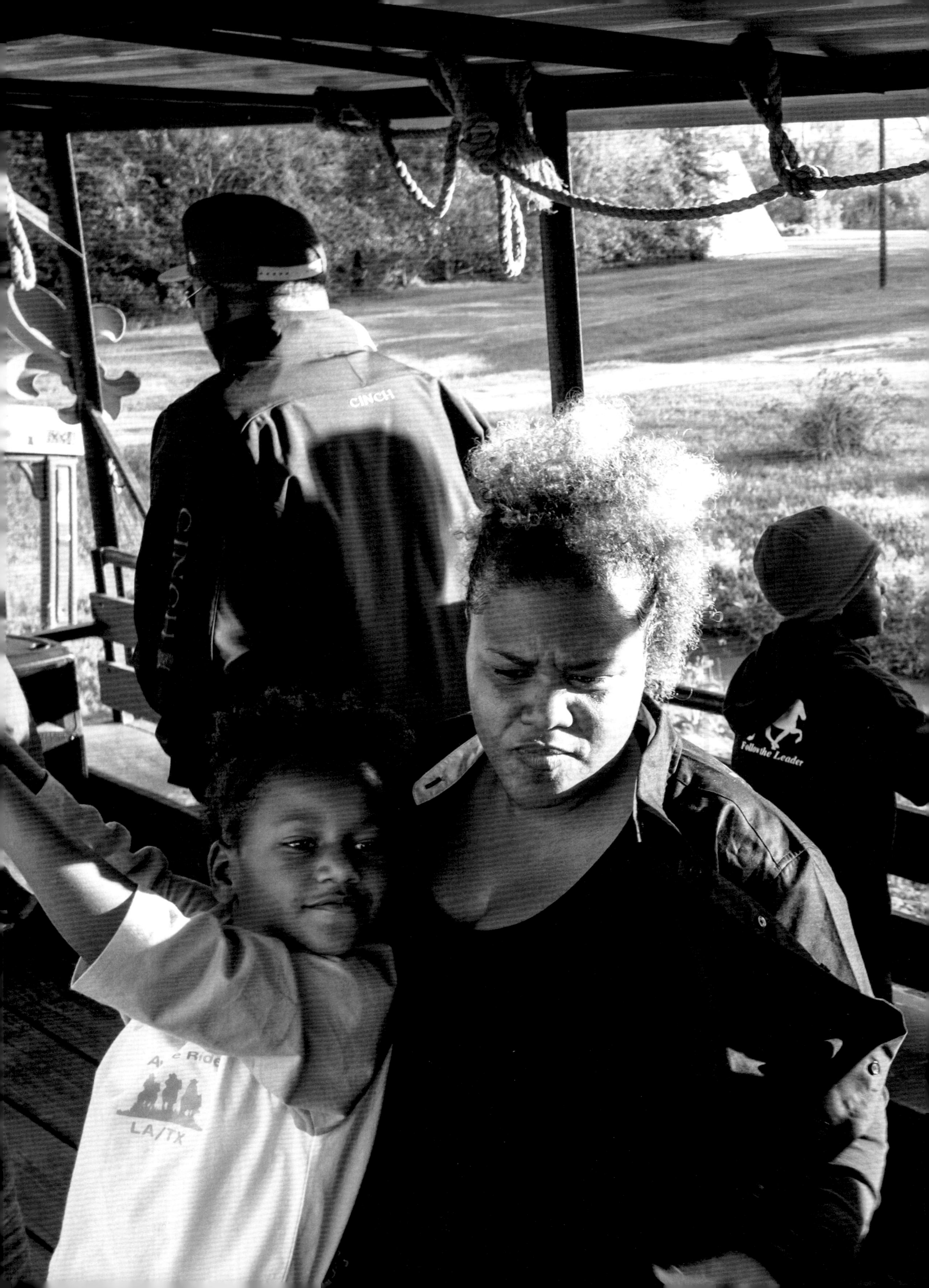
CINCH
CINCH
Follow the Leader
LA/TX

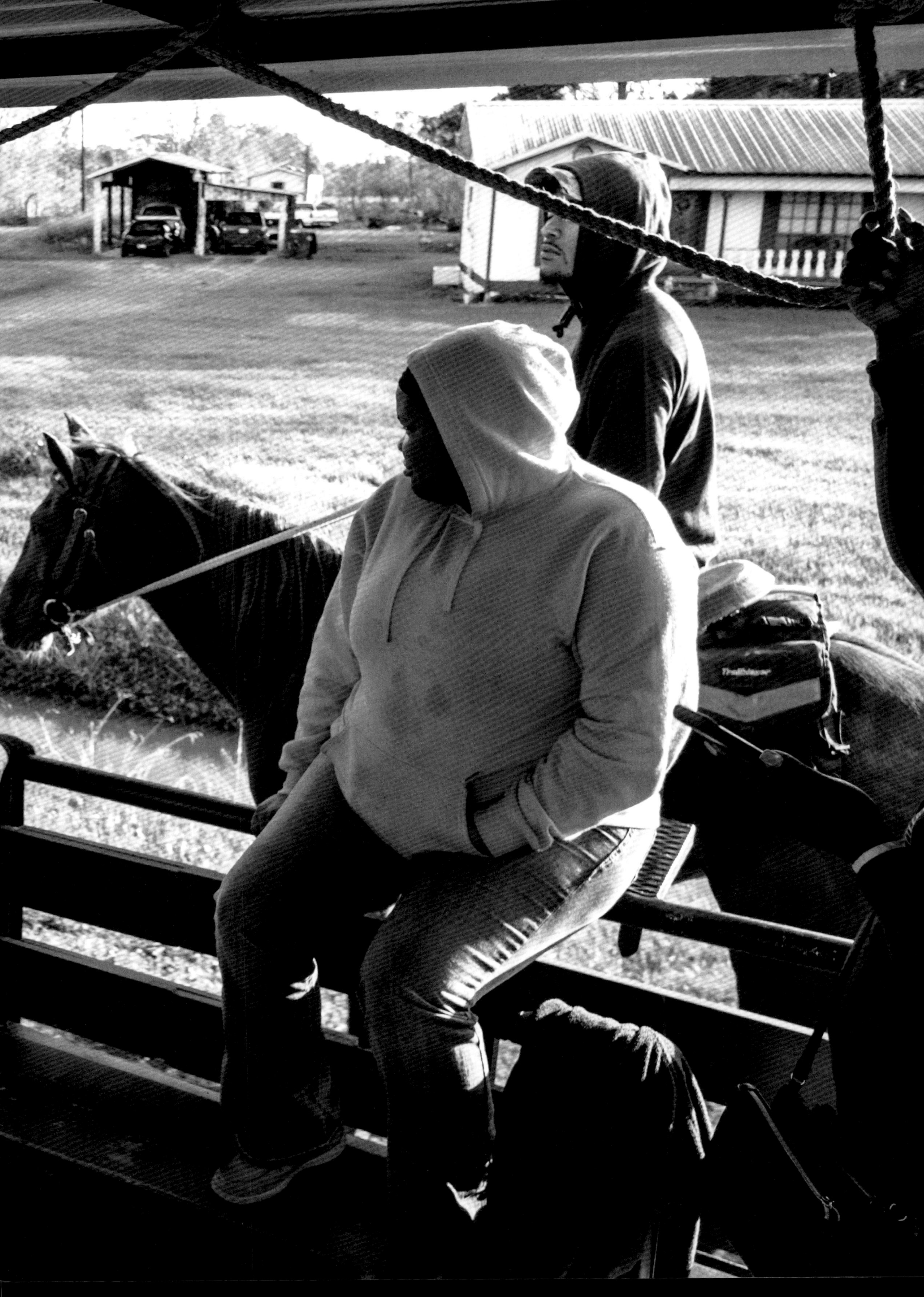

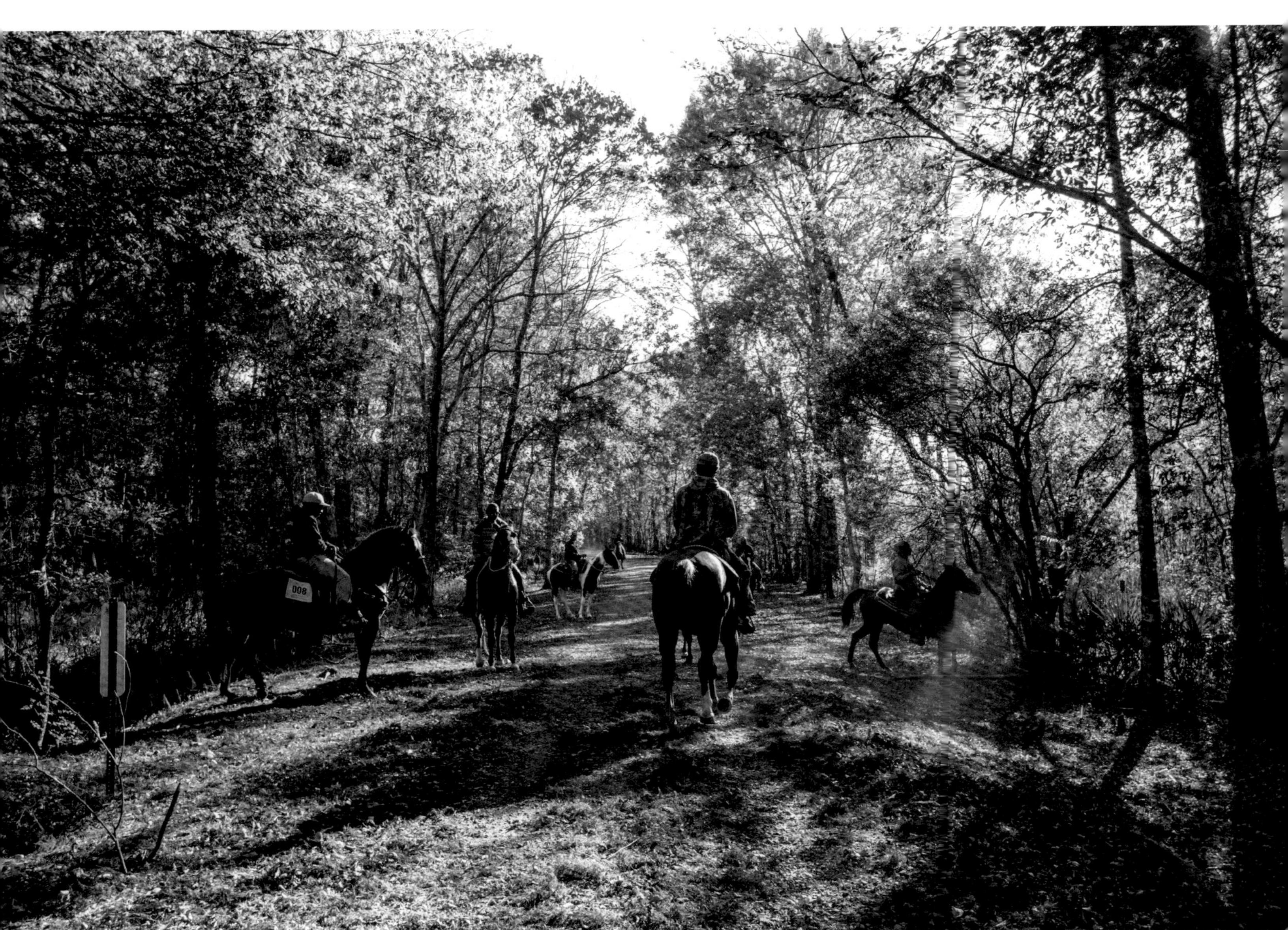
008

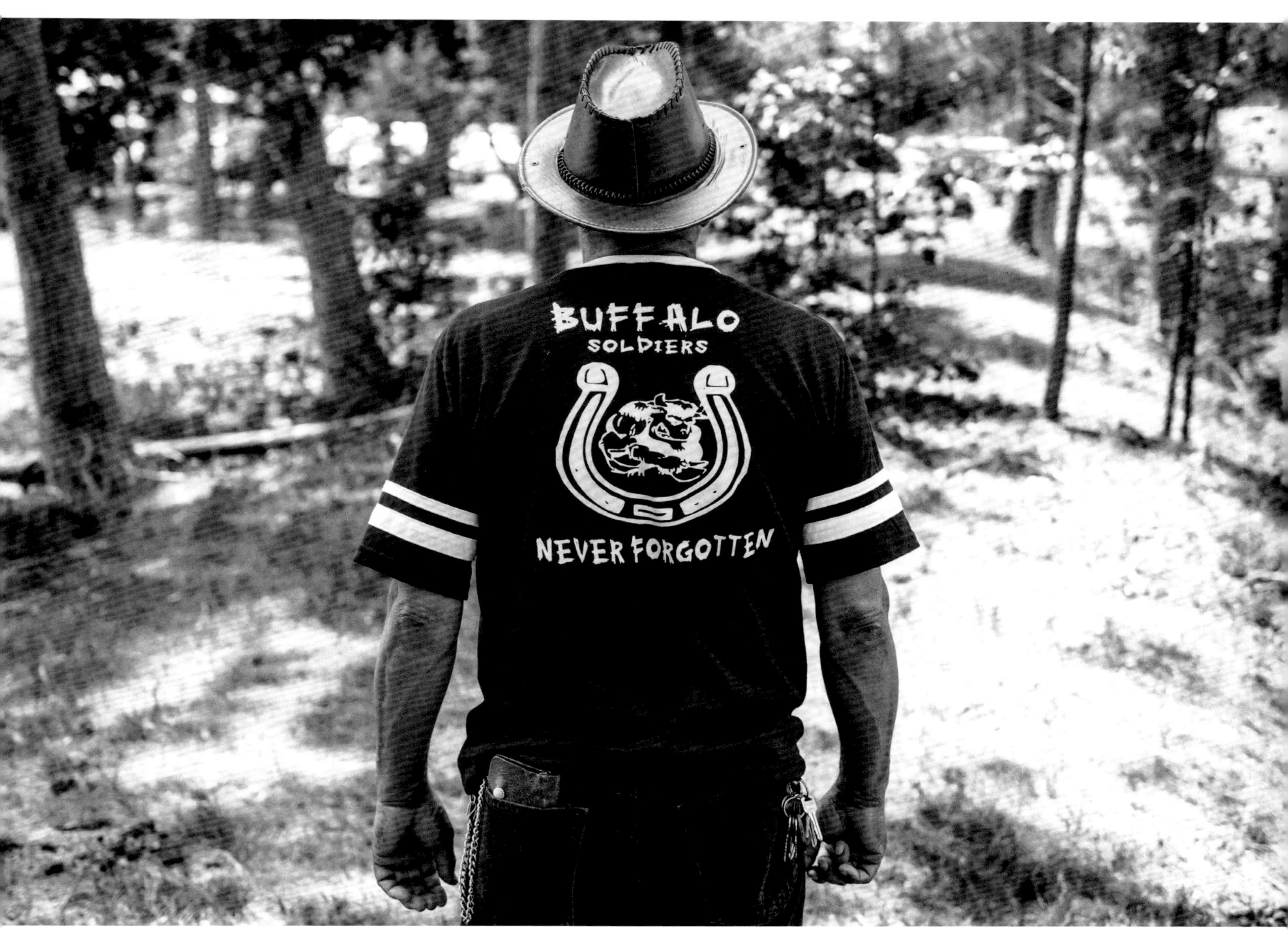
BUFFALO
SOLDIERS
NEVER FORGOTTEN

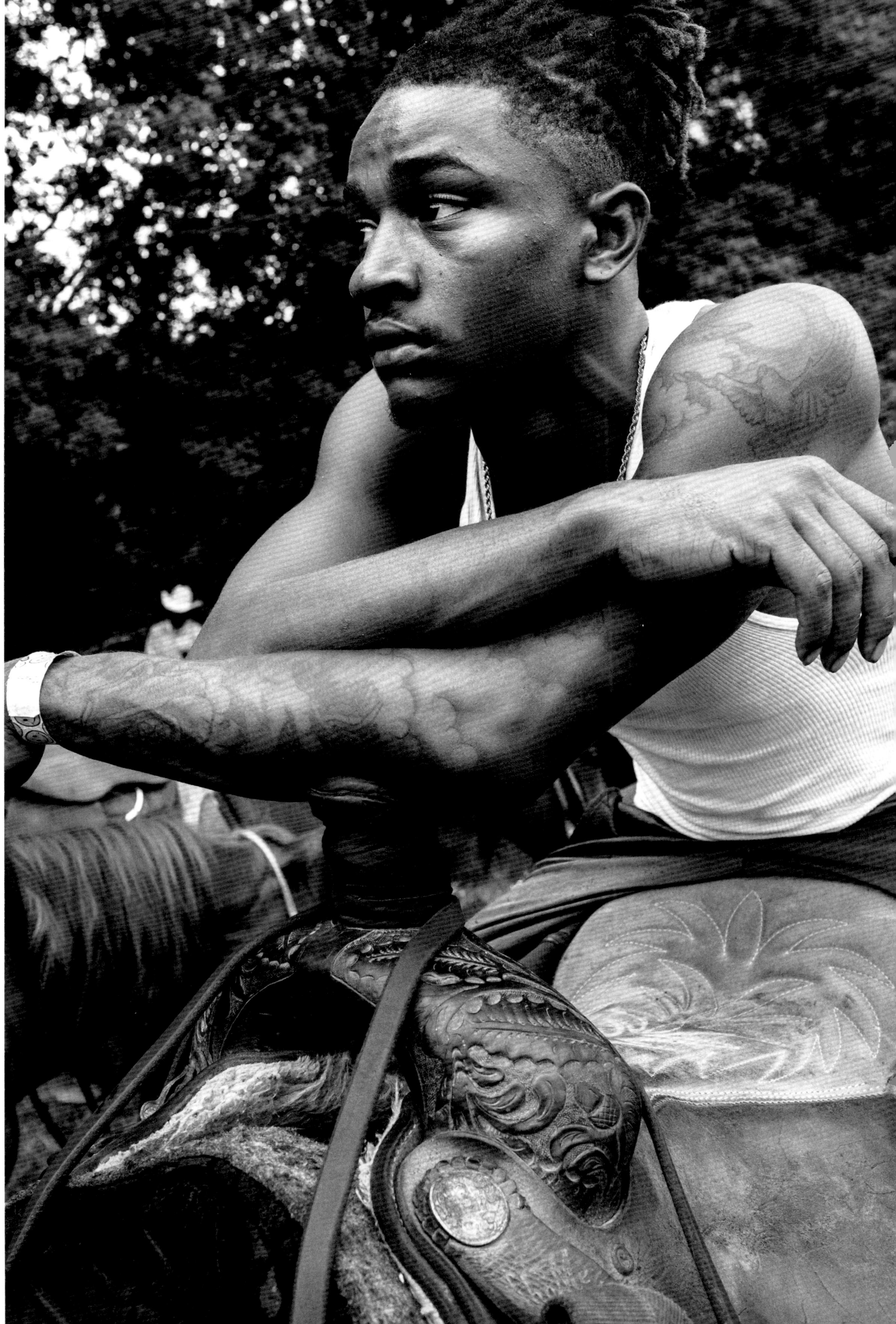

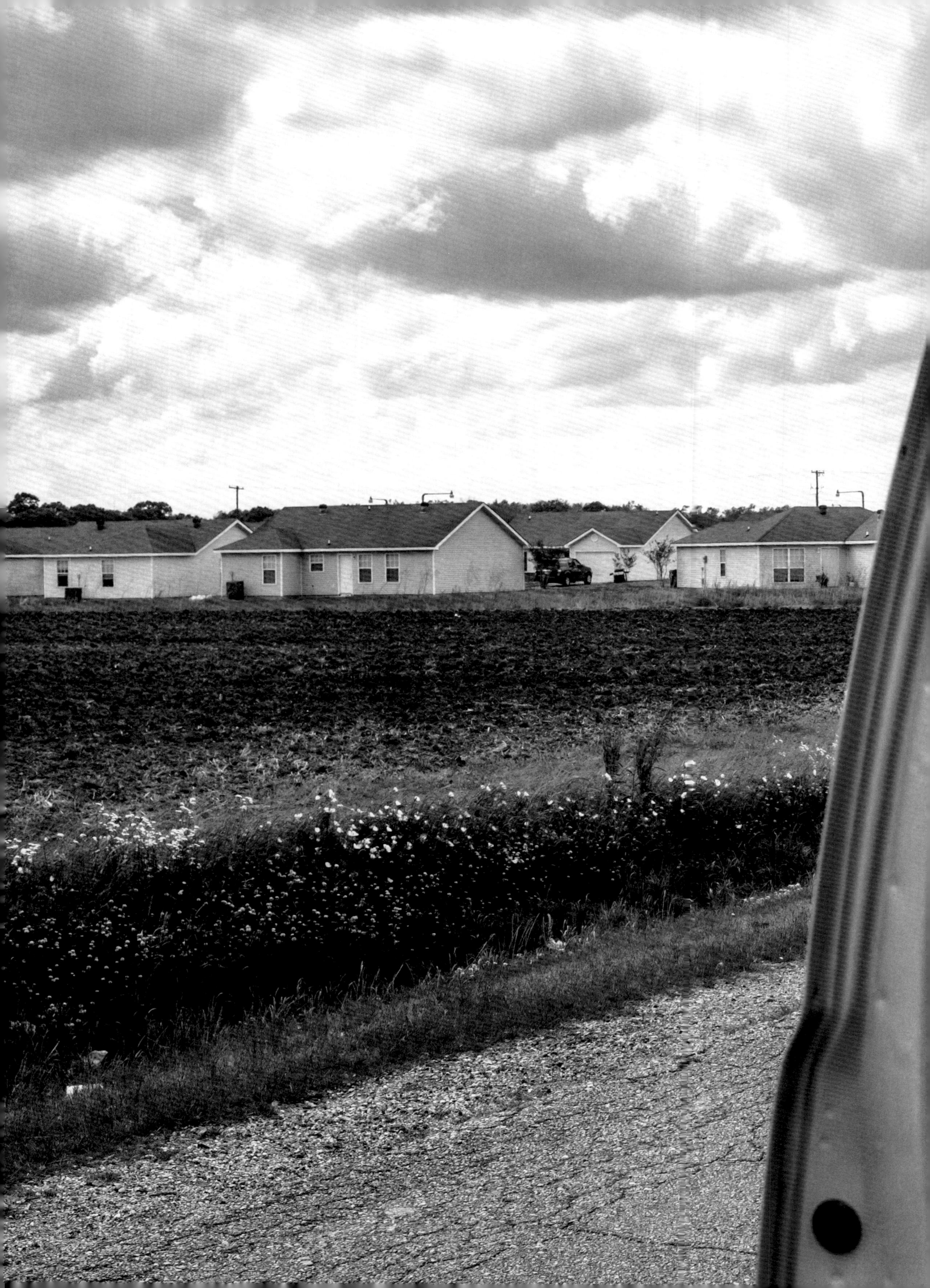

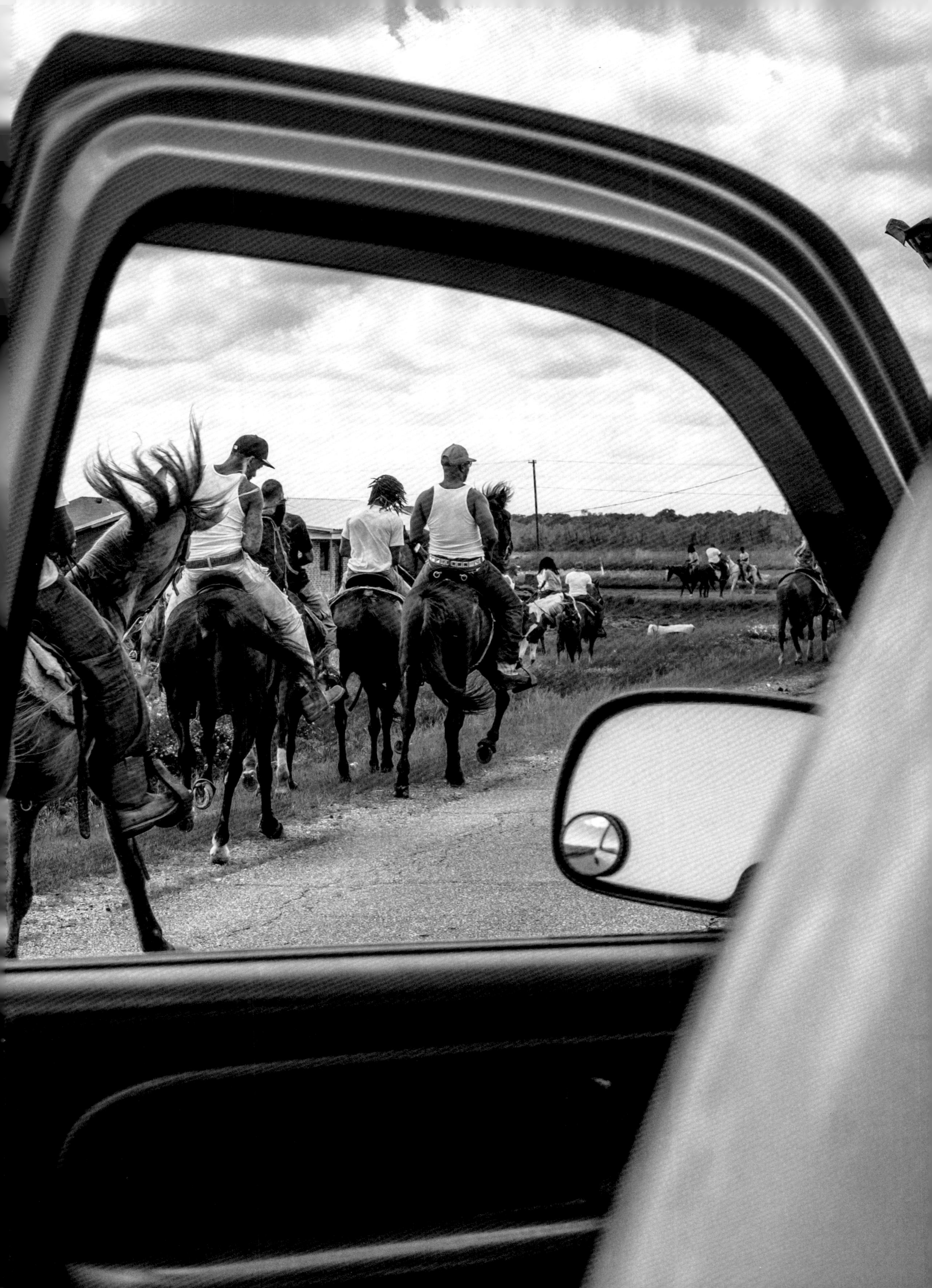

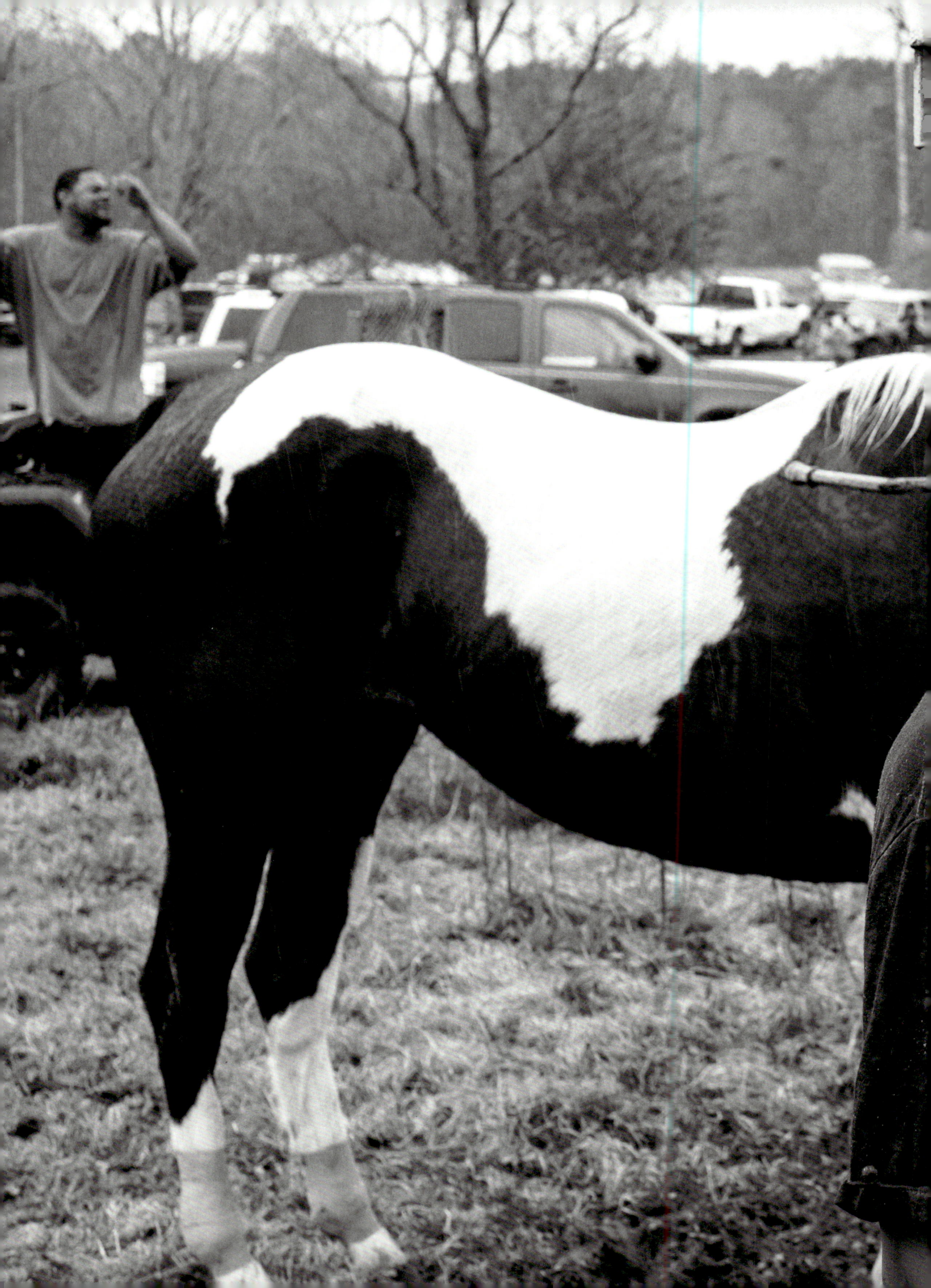

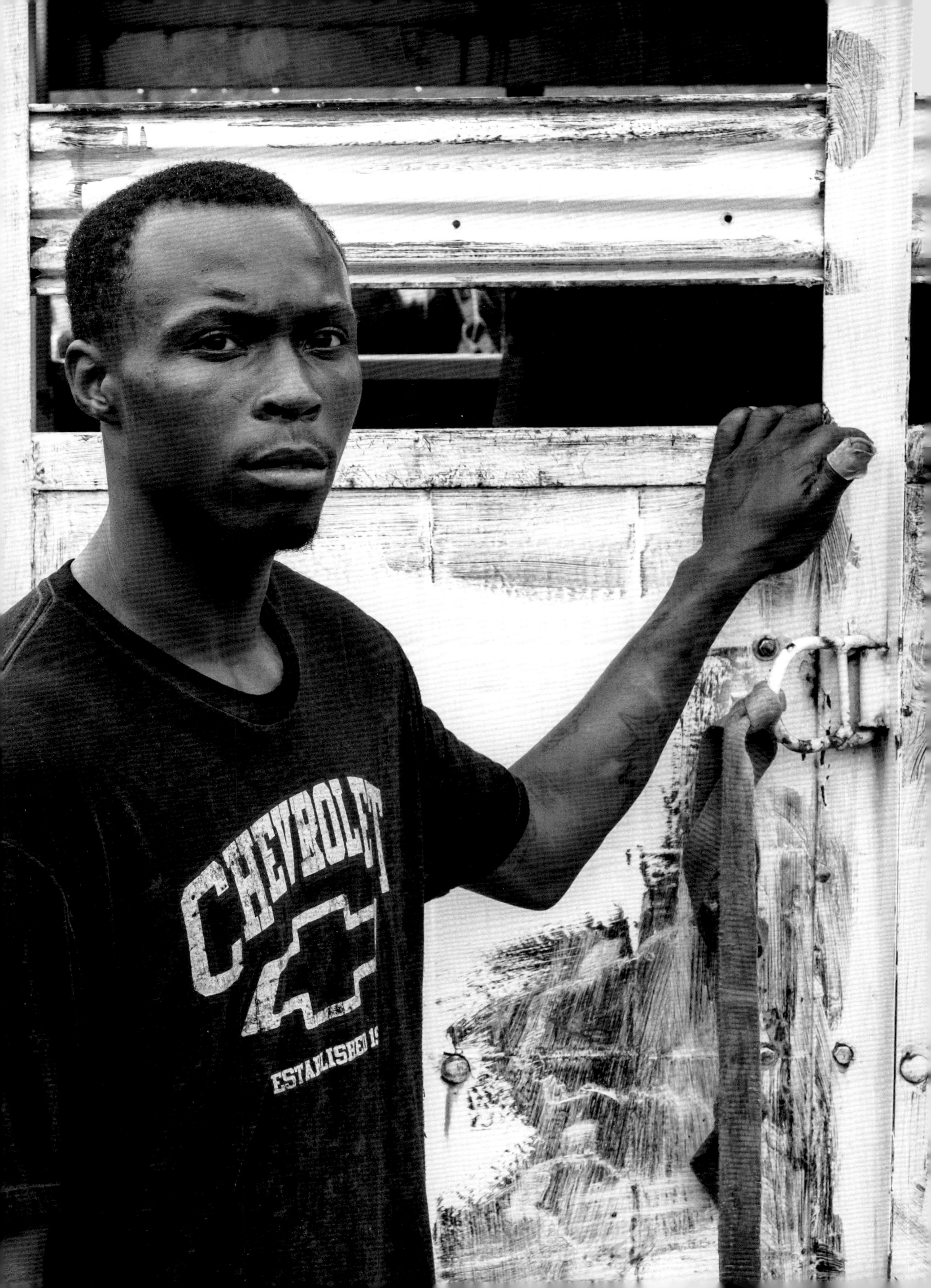
CHEVROLET
ESTABLISHED 19

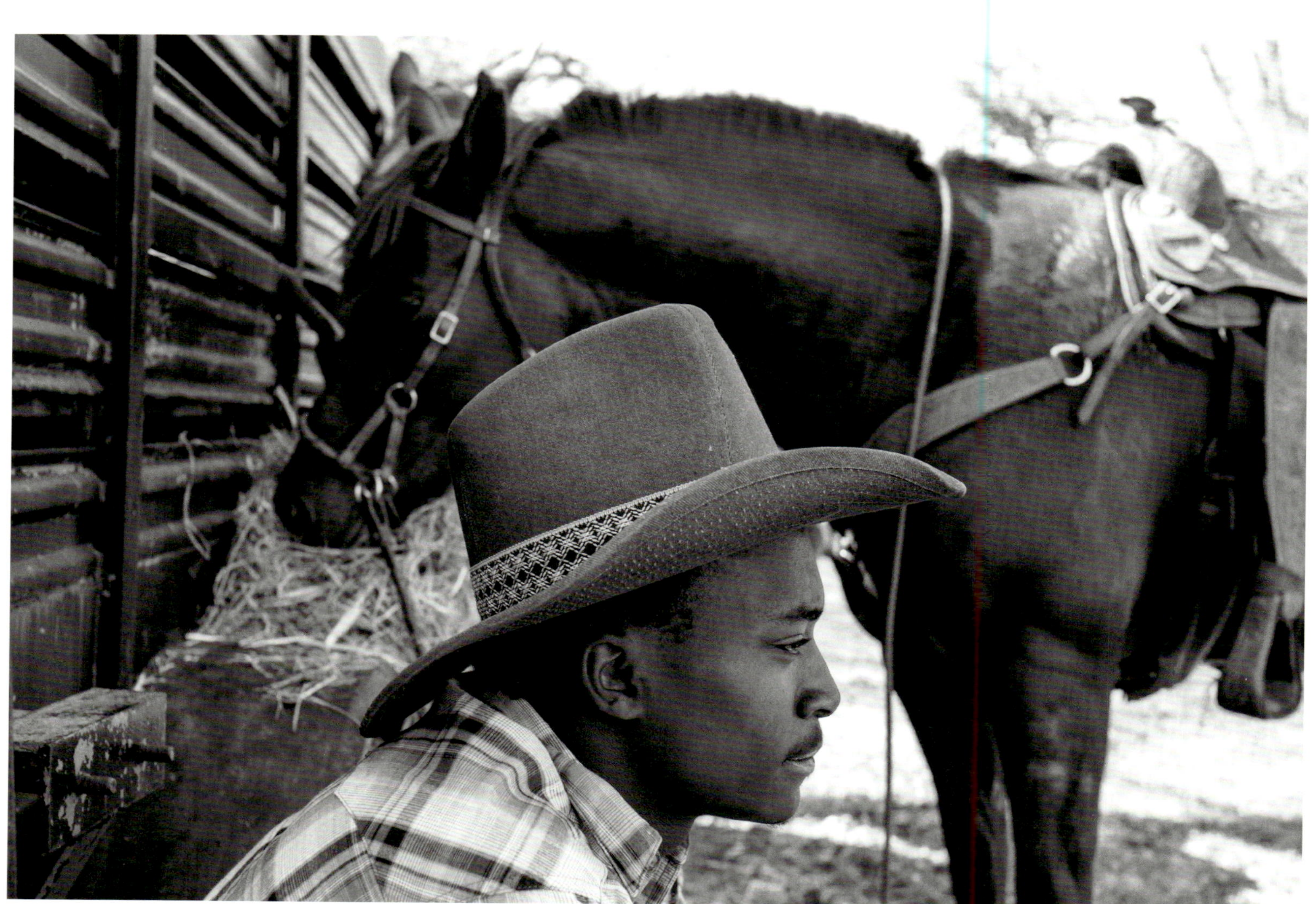

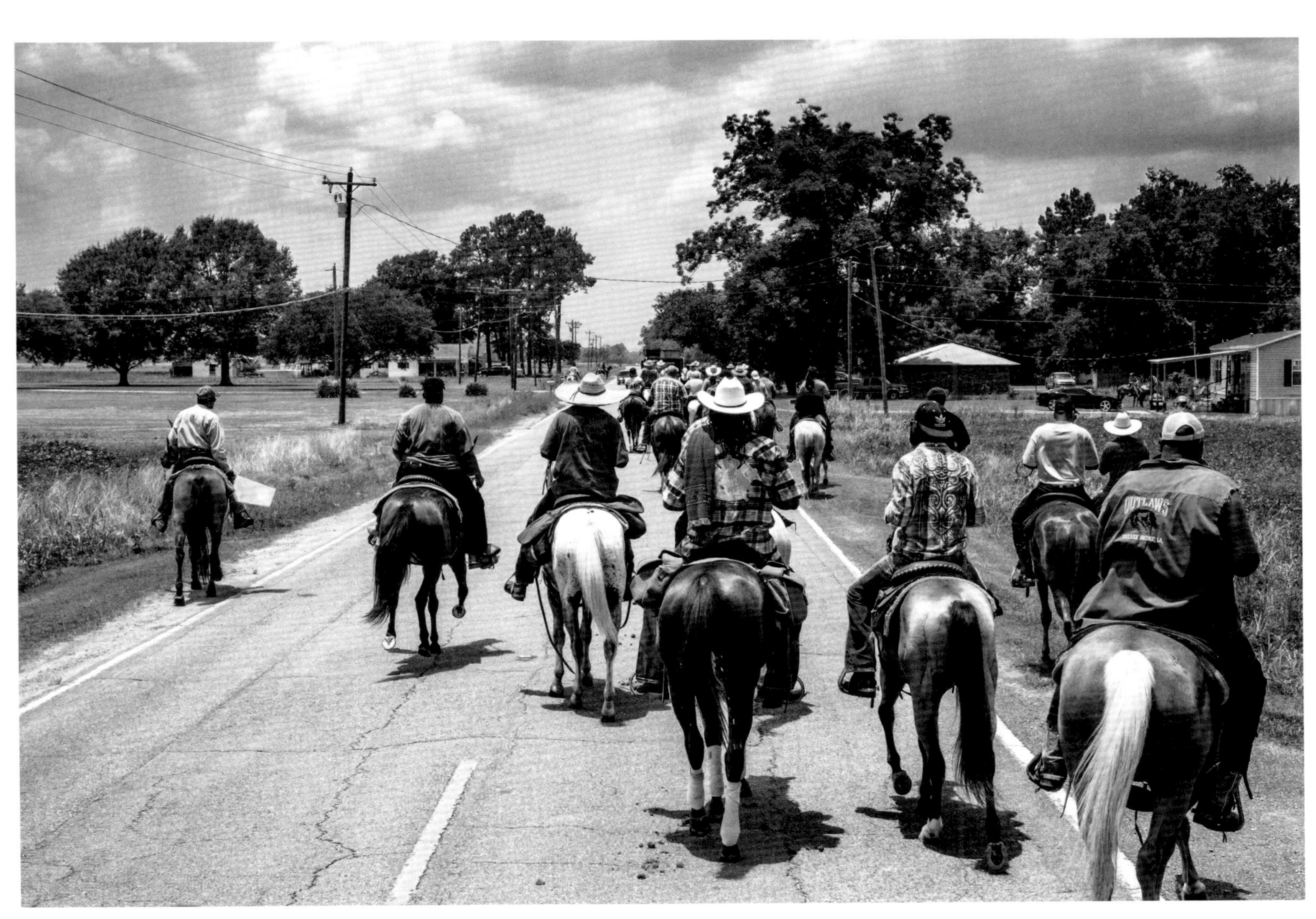
OUTLAWS

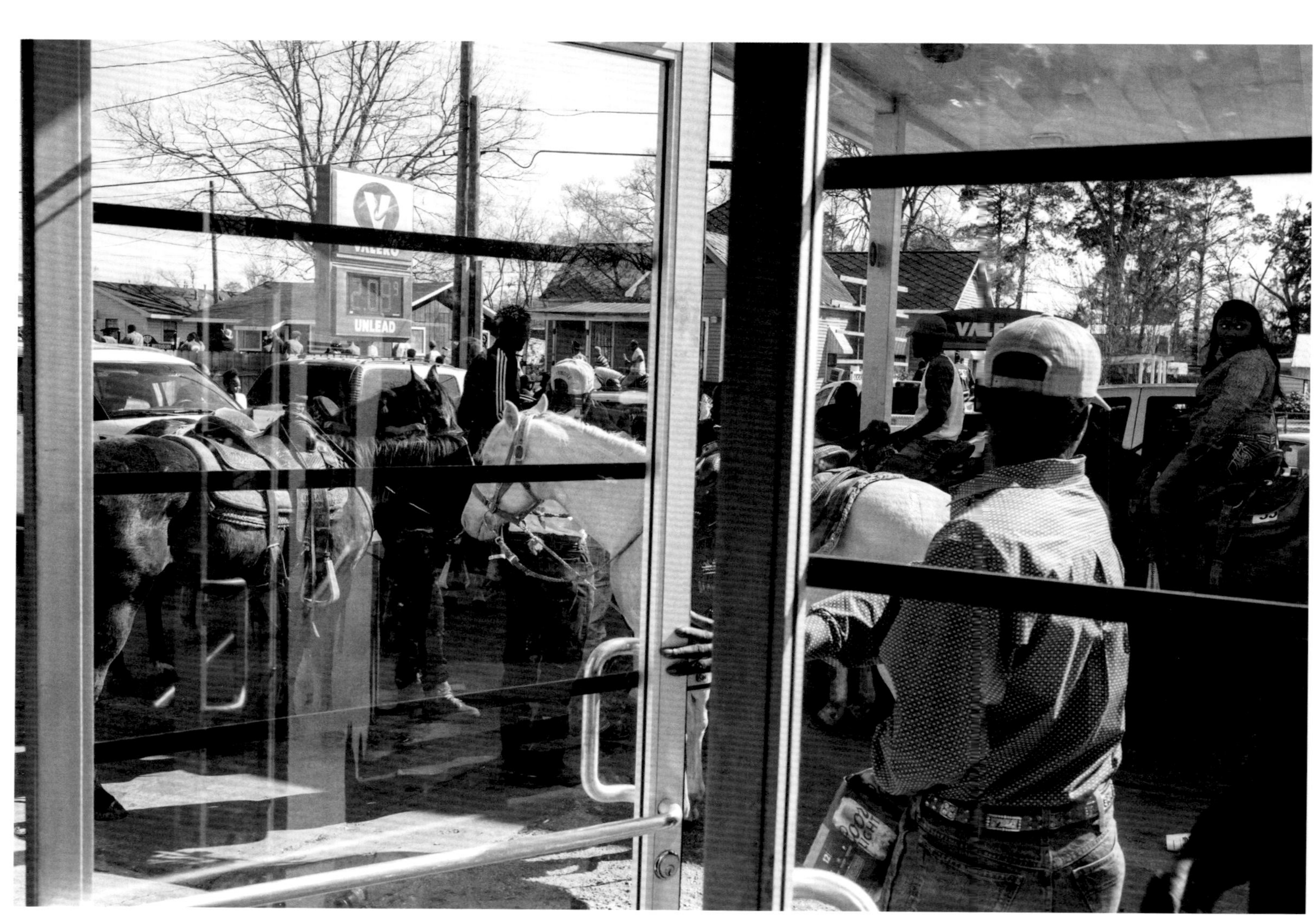
VALERO
UNLEAD

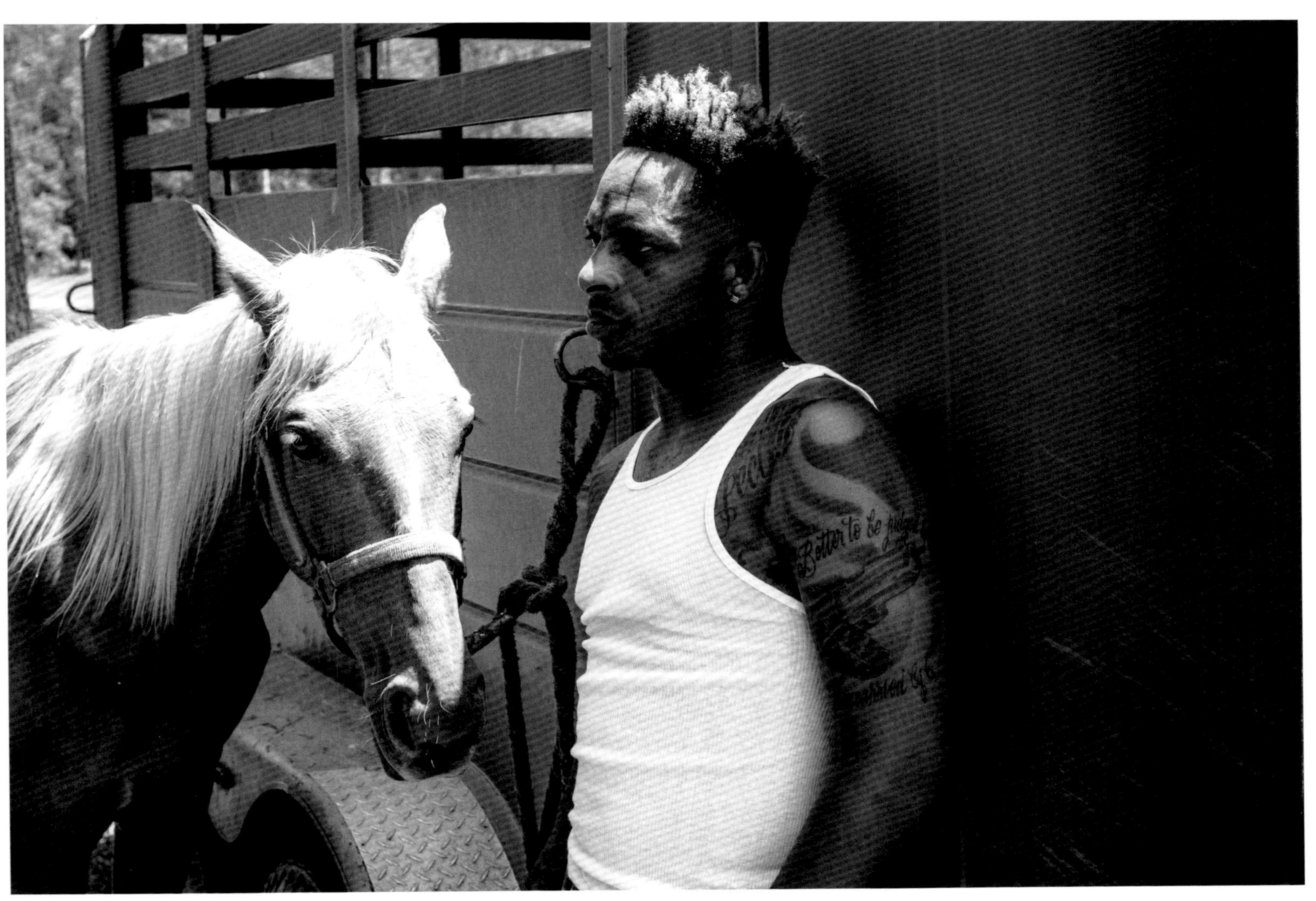
Better to be

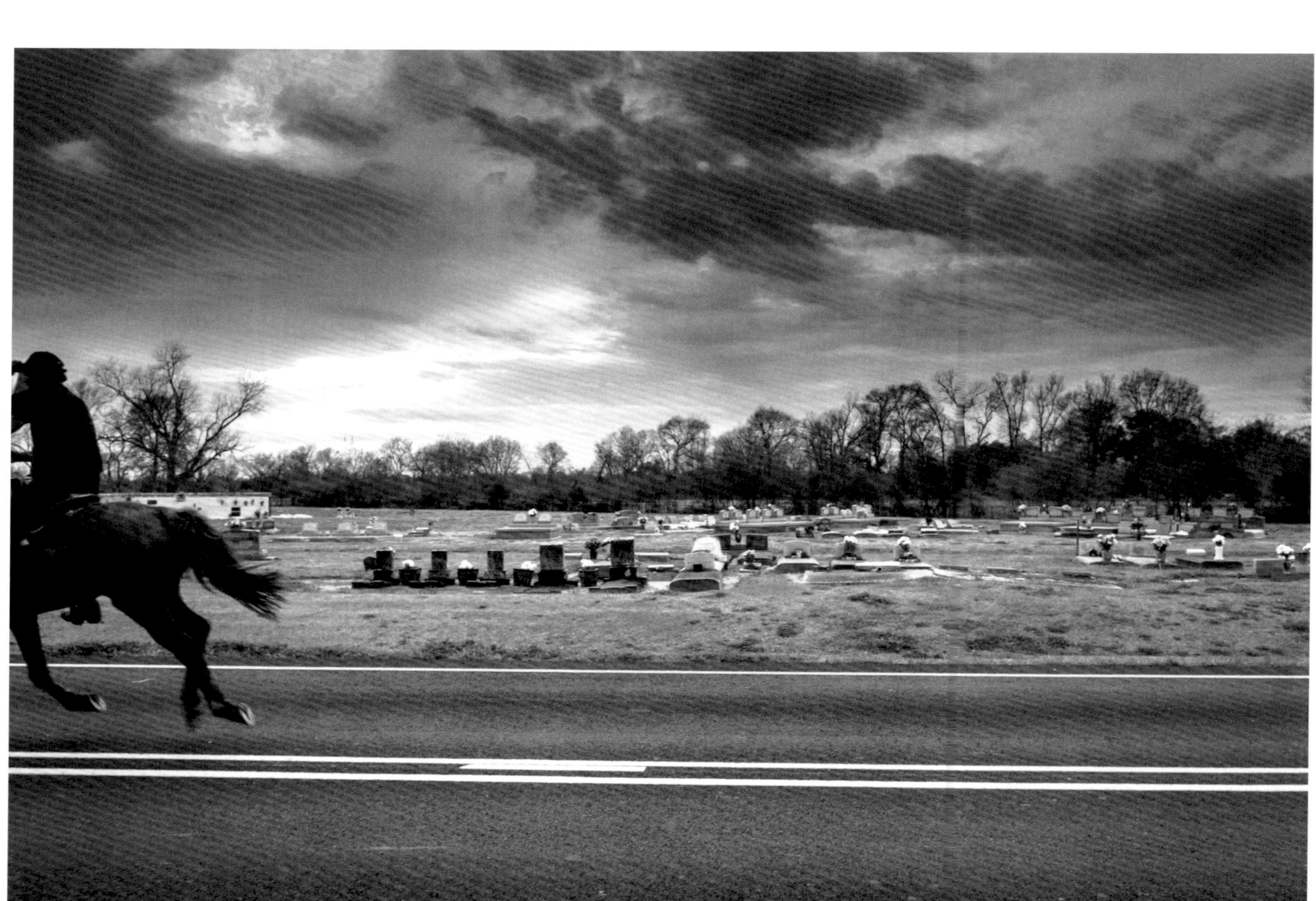

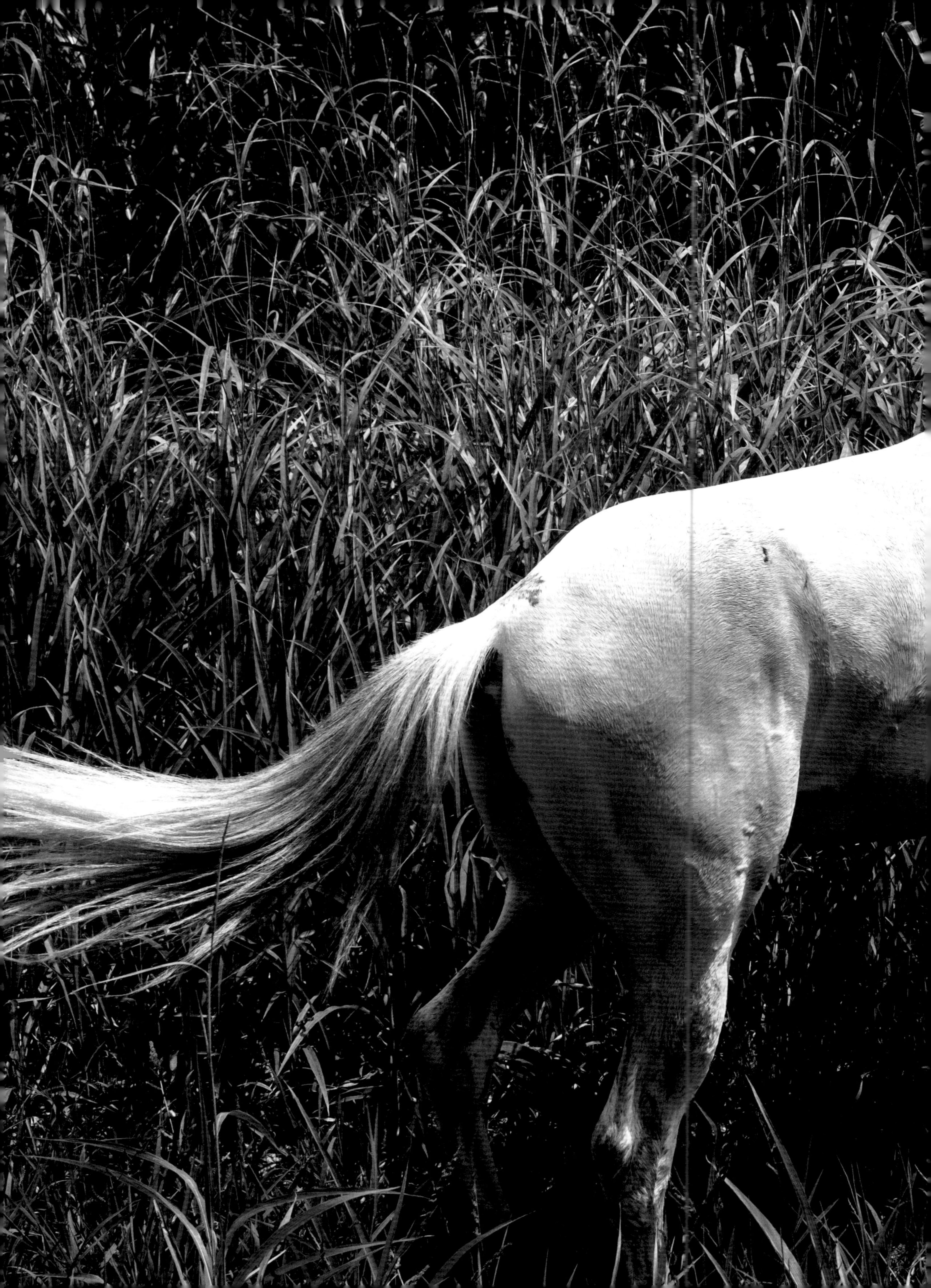

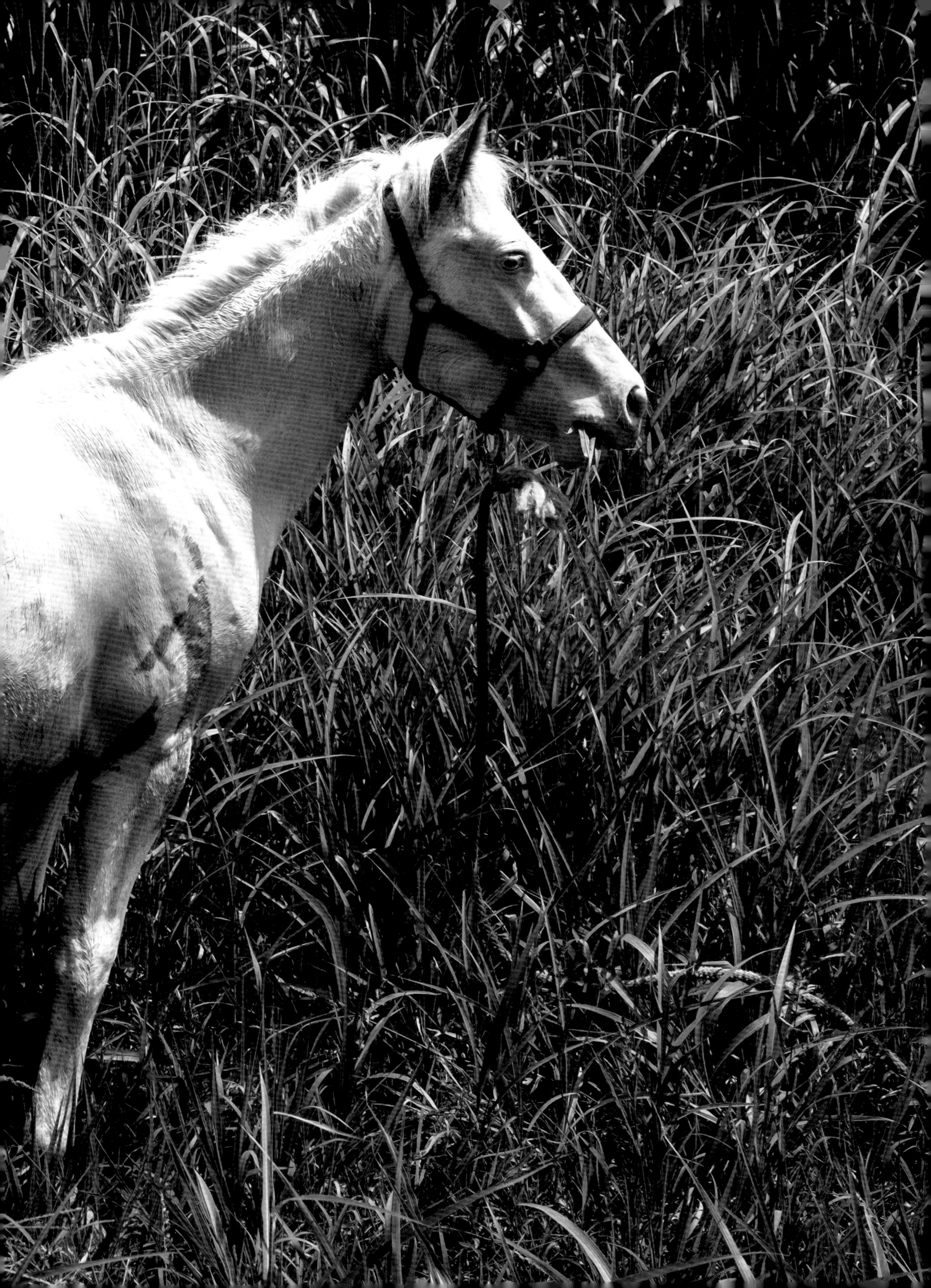

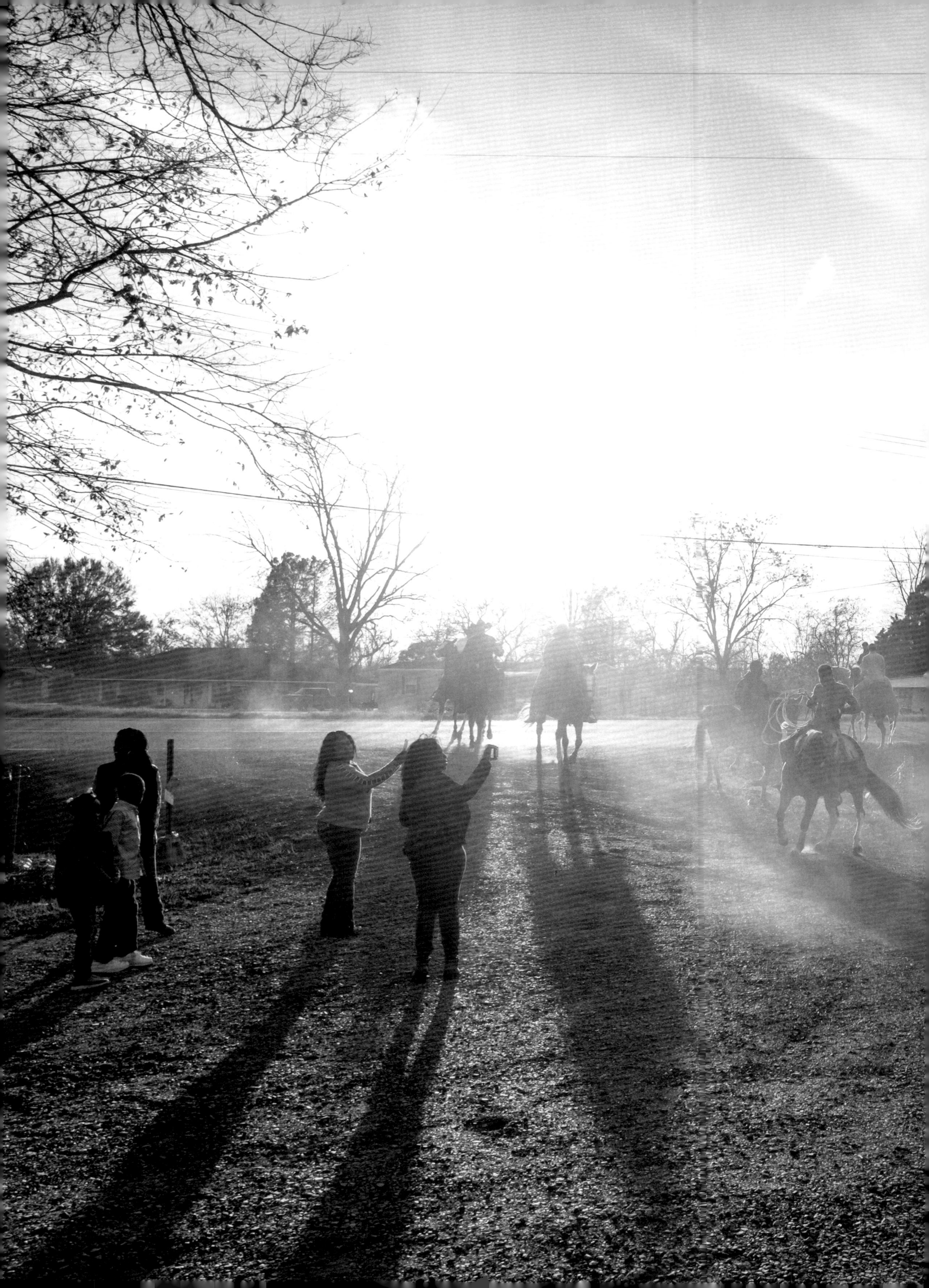

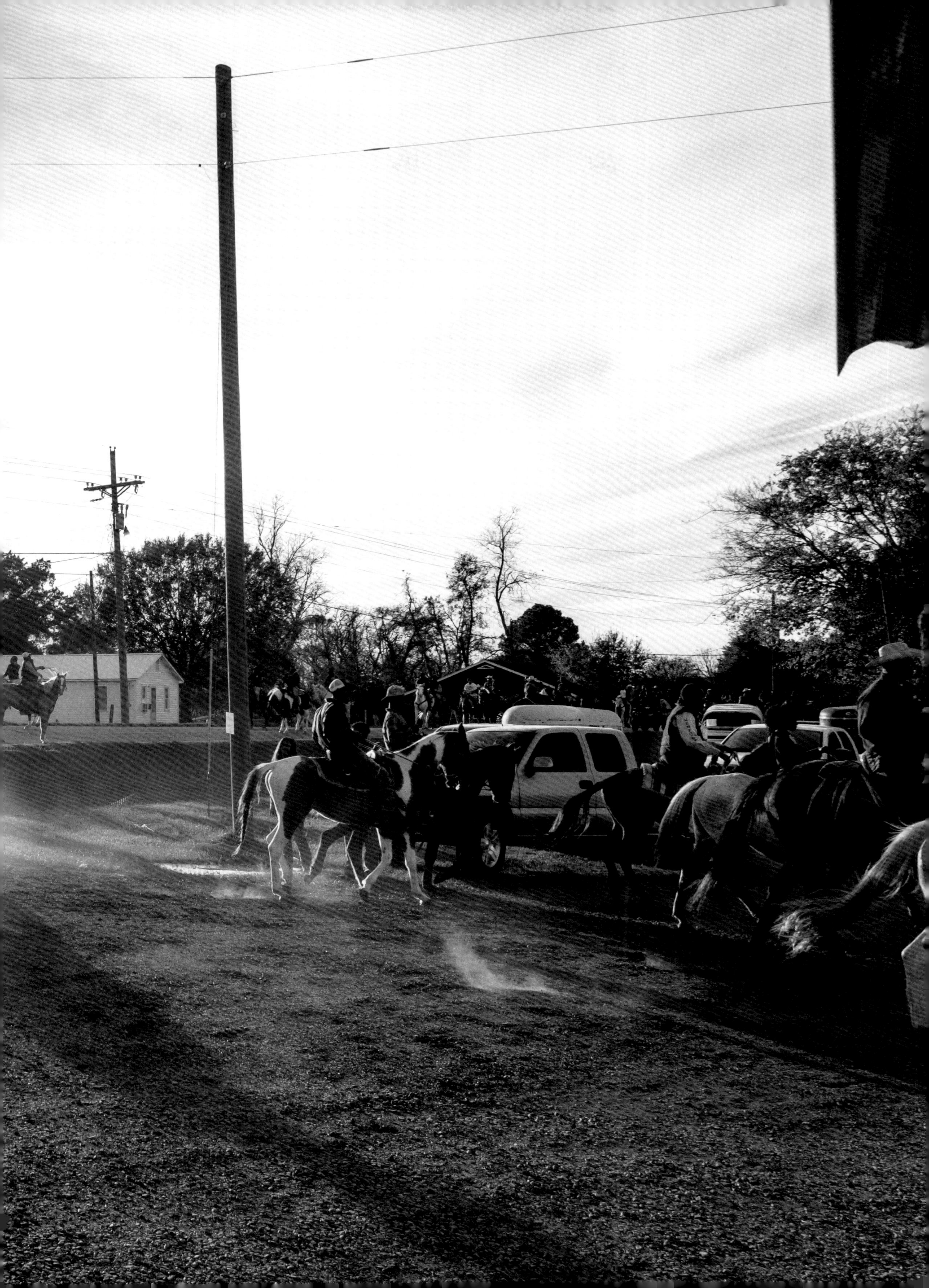

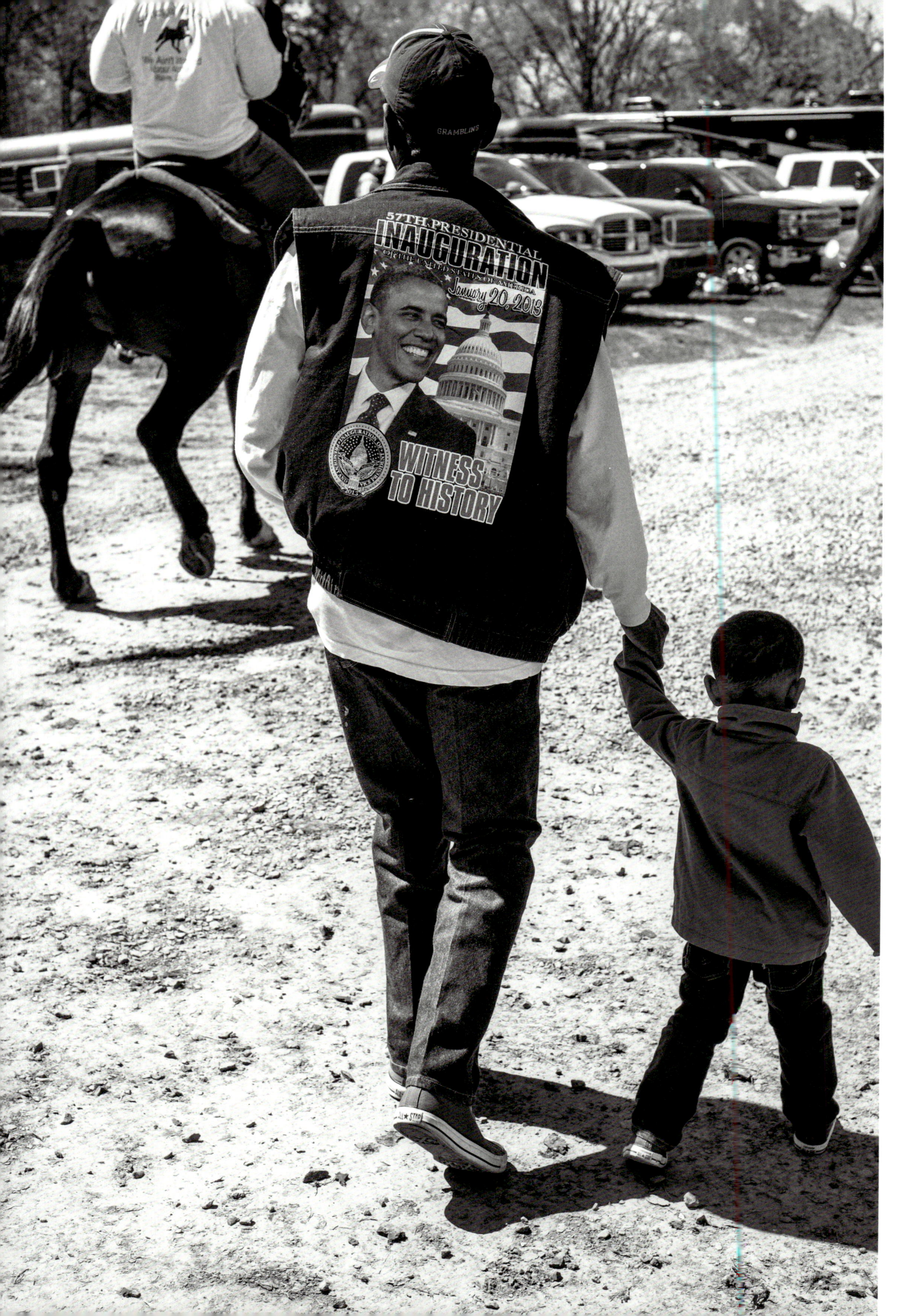
GRAMBLING
57TH PRESIDENTIAL
INAUGURATION
January 20, 2013
WITNESS
TO HISTORY

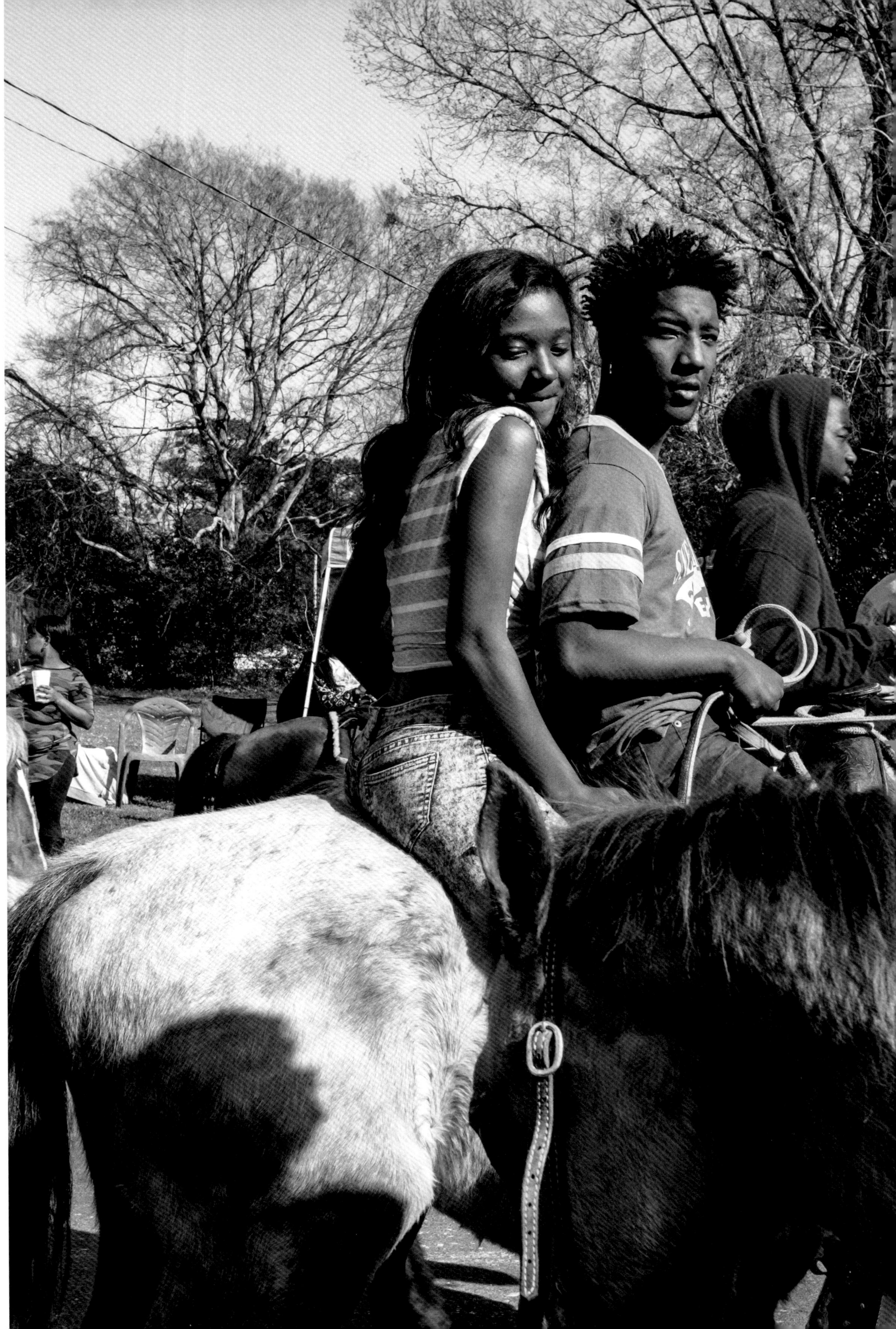

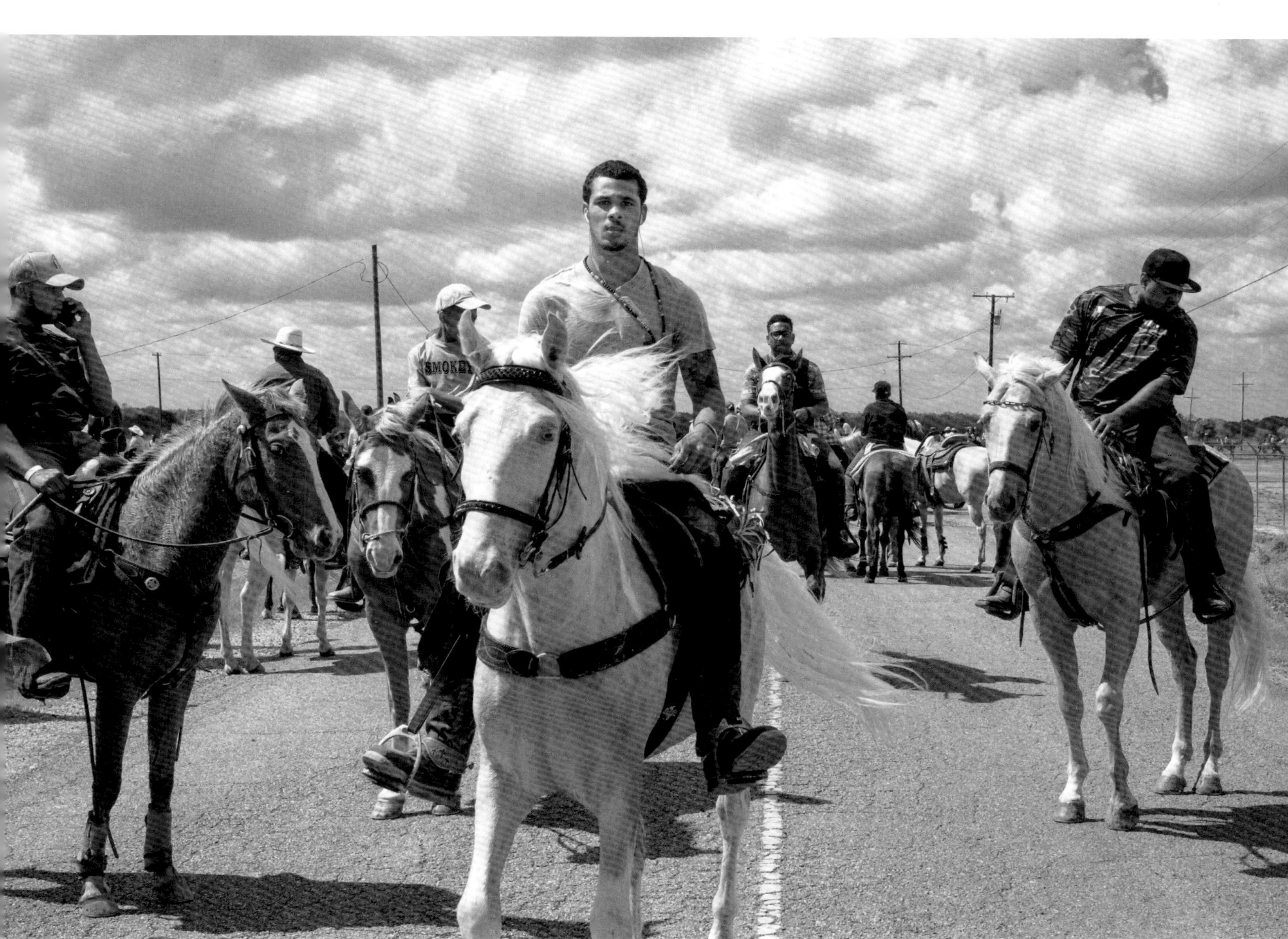

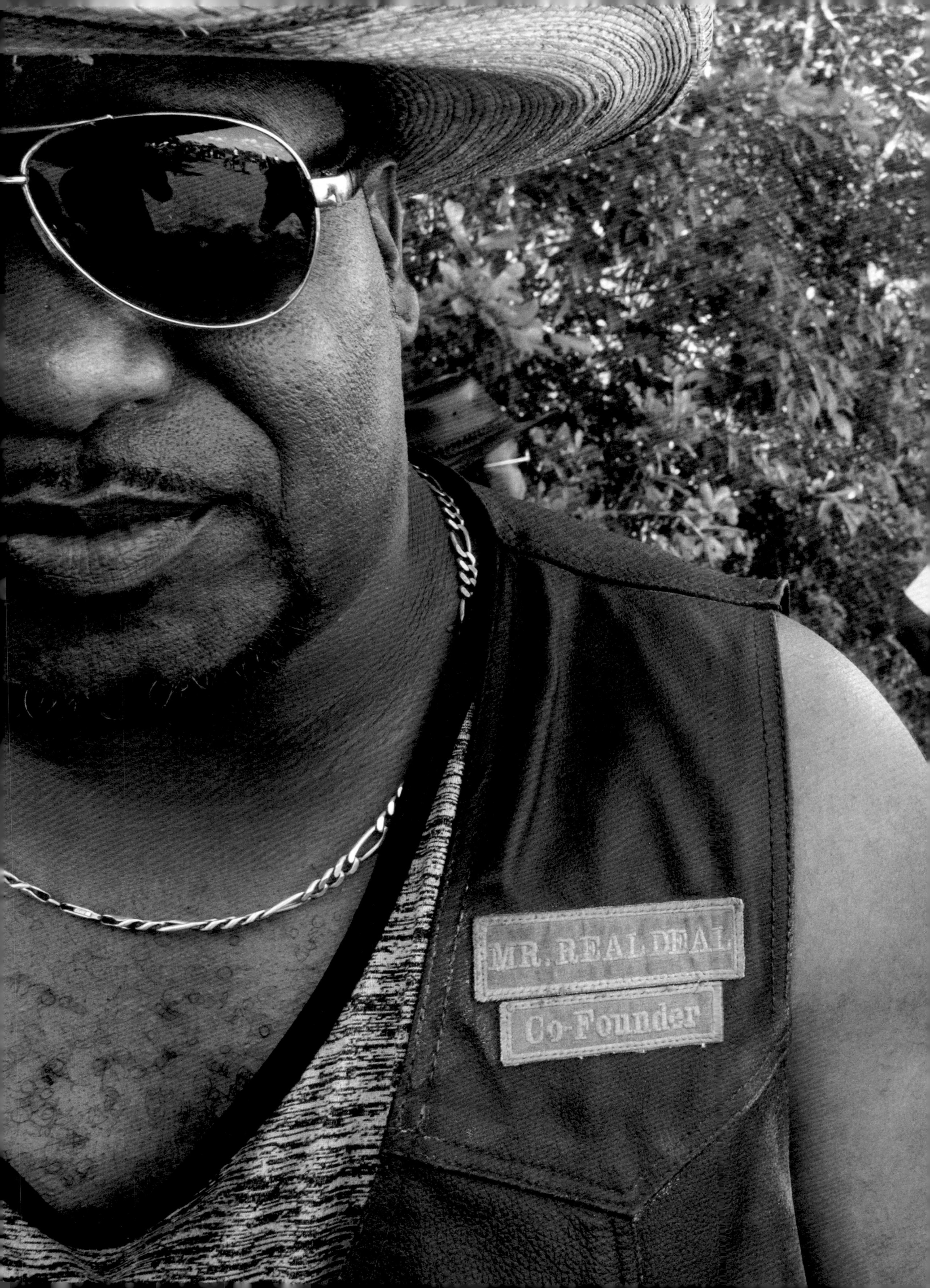
MR. REAL DEAL
Co-Founder

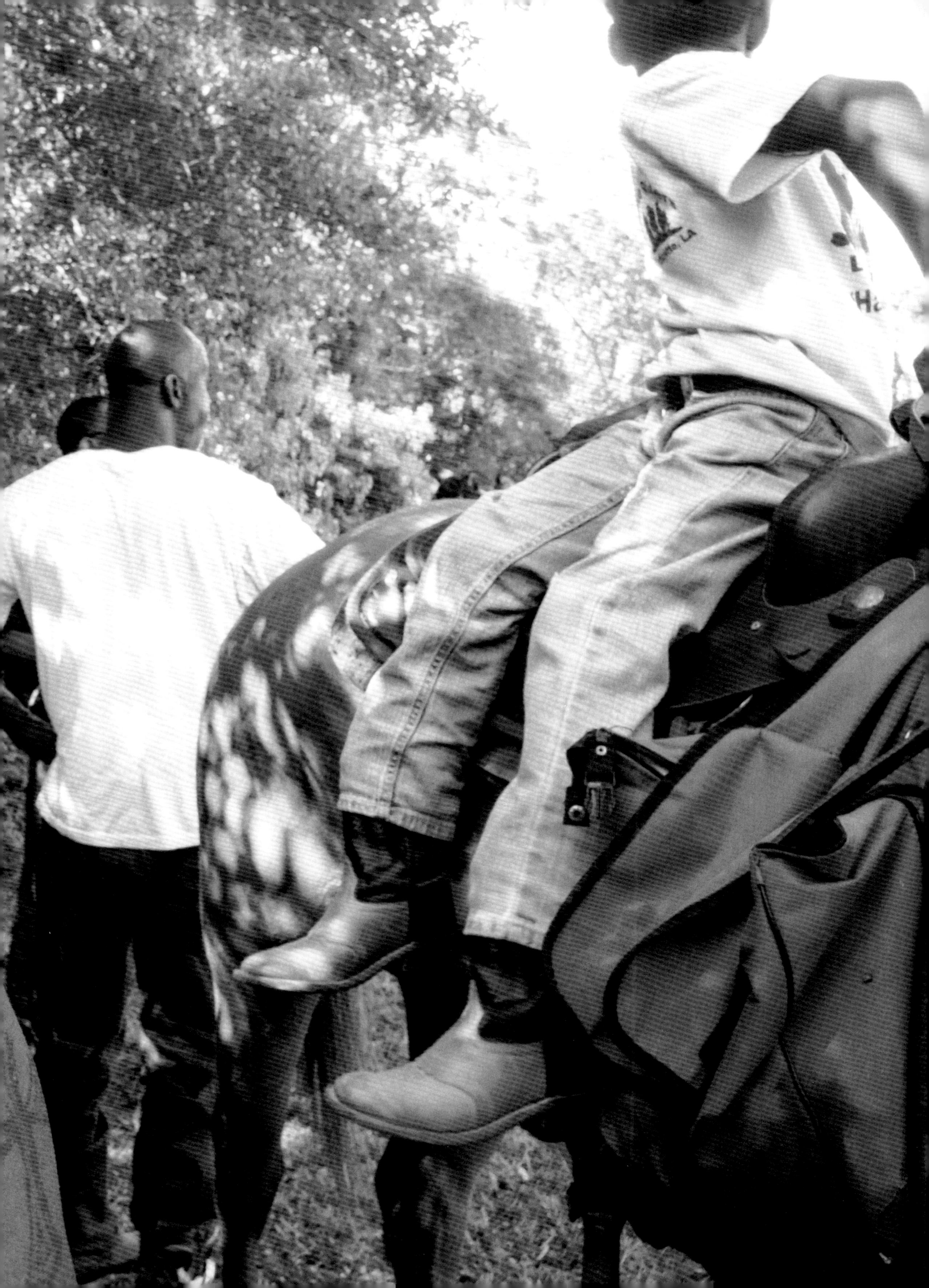

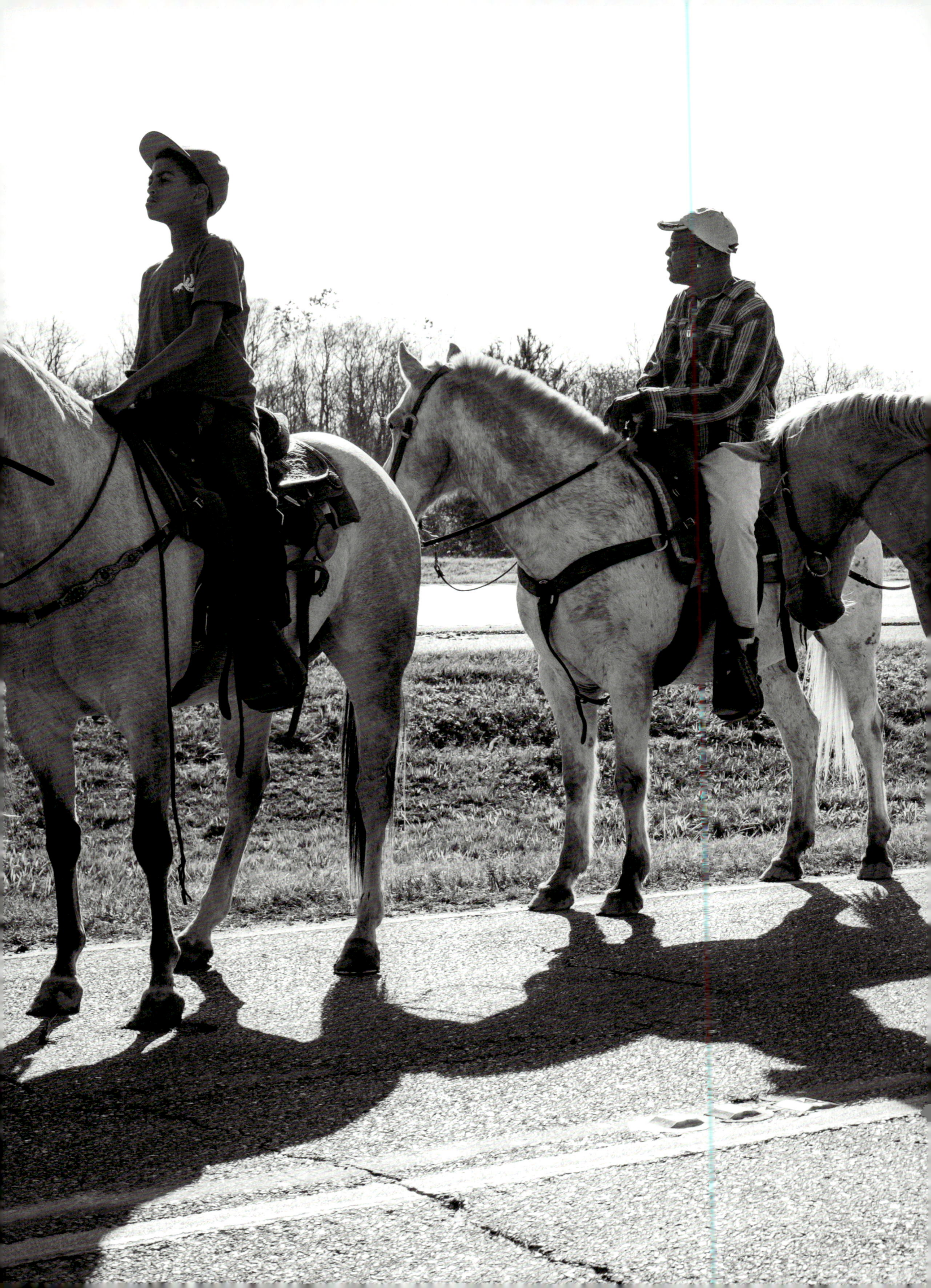

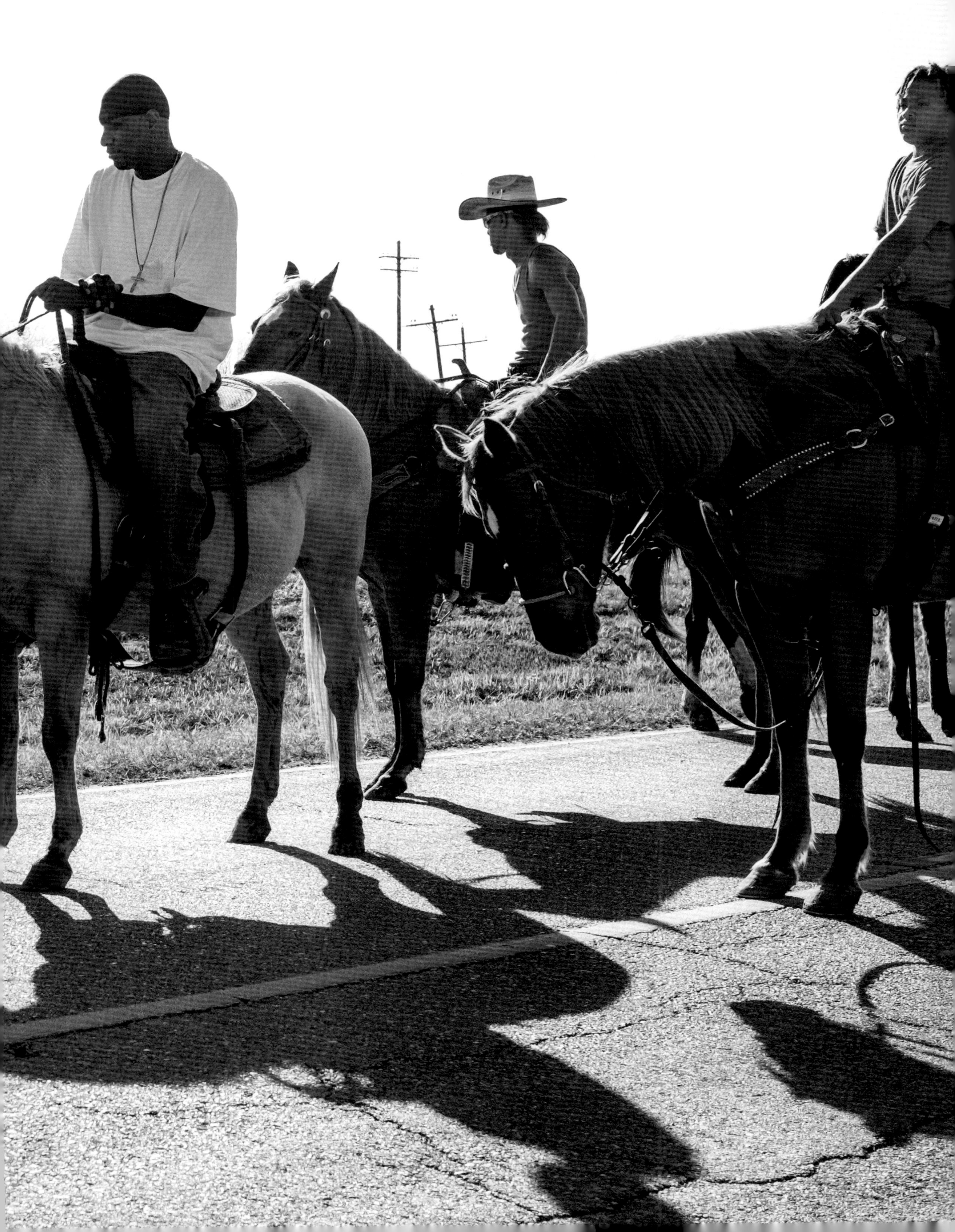

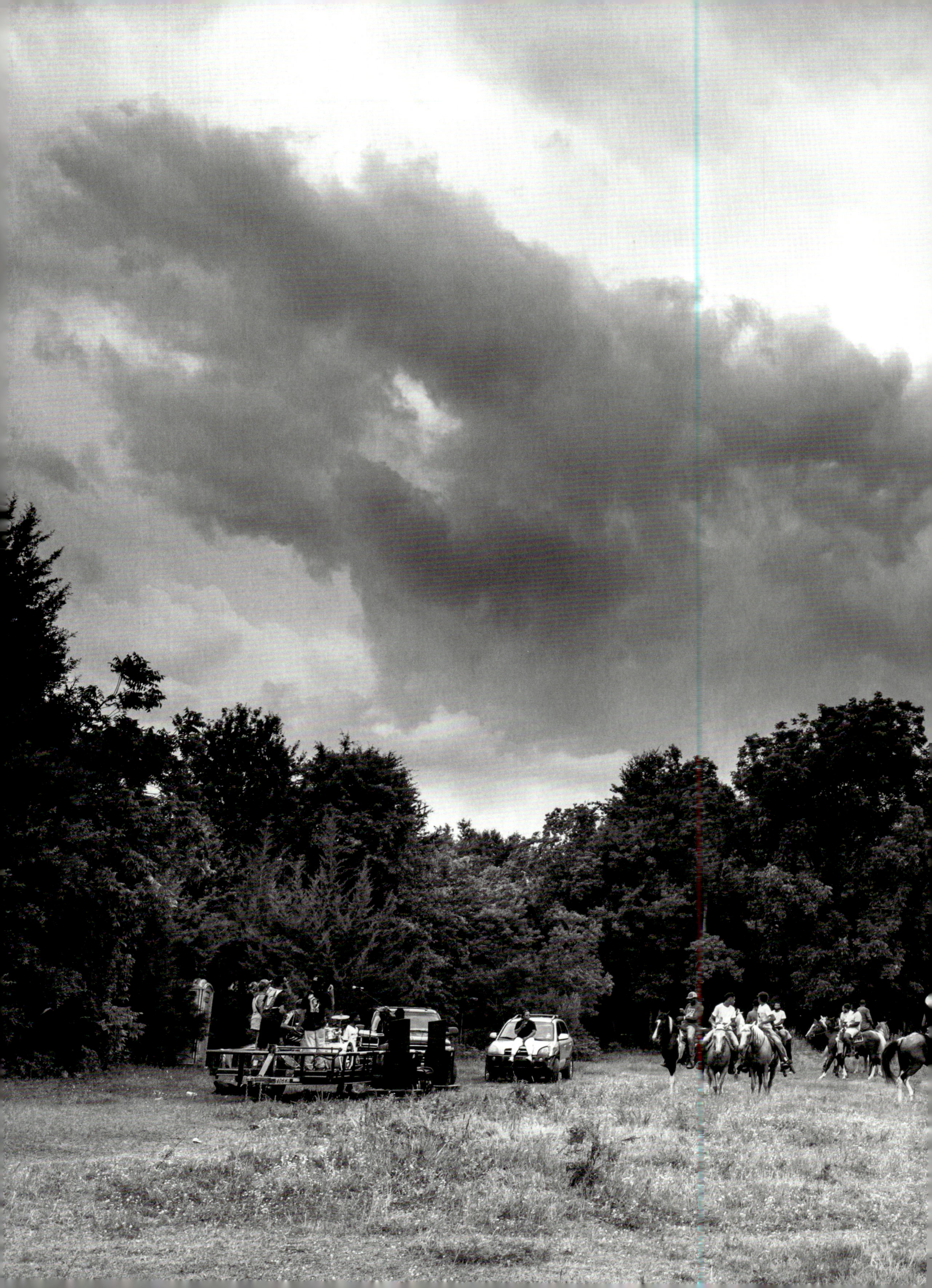

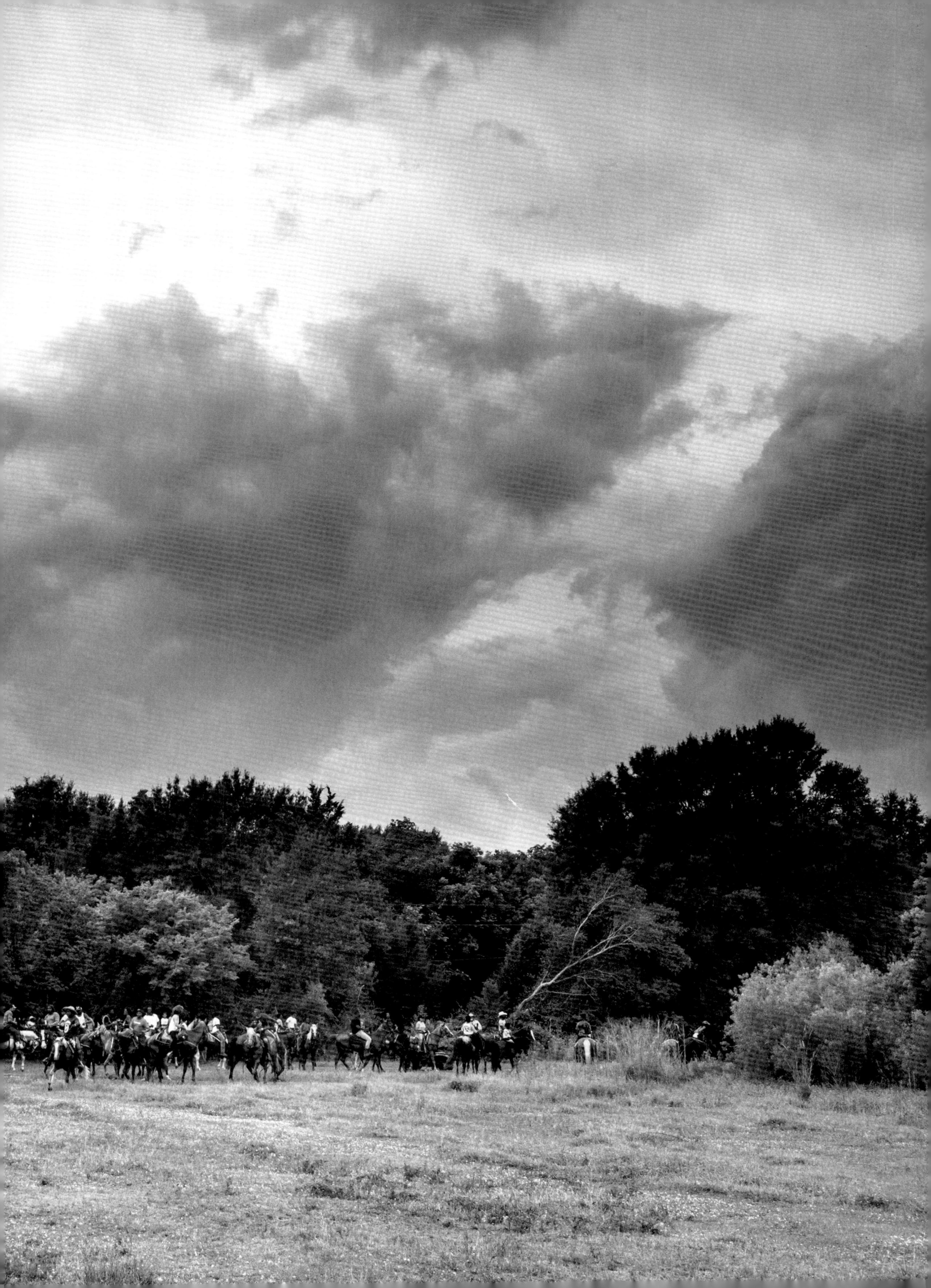

LOUISIANA STEPPERS | 5 STAR FILLIES | THUG RIDAZ | BAD AZZ FILLIES | LOCK & LOAD | BUFFALO SOLDIERS | STEP-PING IN STYLE RIDING CLUB | KOUN-TRY BUNNIES | STEP- N- STRUT RIDERS | GOOD OL' BOYZ | SWAGGED OUT RID-ERZ | RIDE OR DIE RIDERS | BLINGED OUT RIDERS | LET IT RIP RIDERS | YOUNG STUD OUTLAWZ | EUNICE EASY RIDERS | HUSTLE HARD RIDERS | WESTSIDE RID-ERS | WATCH YA SELF RIDERS | CUTTIN' UP RIDERS | STEADY STEPPIN RIDERS | COUNTRY BY NATURE | TOP NOTCH RID-ERZ | BOUNCE BACK RIDERS | BECK CITY BAD BOYS | REGULATOR RIDAZ | STEP-PIN' WIT STYLE | MALVEAUX CAVALIERS | DOUBLE A RIDERS | NO LIMIT POSSE | I-49 RIDERS | COUNTRY BOYZ RIDING CLUB | MIDNIGHT RIDERS | THE APACHE RIDERS | CRESCENT CITY COWBOYS | CRAZY HAT RIDERS | EZ RIDERS | AVENUE RIDERS | TRUE LOVER RIDERS | SHUGA SHACK RIDERS | YOUNG STUD RIDERS | BLINGED OUT RIDERS | PINEYWOODS RIDERS | DIRTY TRAIL RIDERS | 504 GIRLZ |

NUSTEP STALLIONZ | TRU 2DA GAME RIDERS | SENEGAL RIDERS | HIP-HOP GHETTO RIDERS | BUCKWILD RIDERS | SOLOSLABRIDERS|BAYOUBOYZ|COUNTRY RIDERZ | KENFOLK RIDERS | KEEP'N IT REAL RIDERS | BACKYARD RIDERS | "WHO DAT" RIDERS | LEESVILLE RIDERS | GUTTA GURLS RIDIN DIRTY | RUDE BOYZ | BAYOU RIDERS | DESPERADOS | 2 STEP RIDING CLUB | AVENUE RIDERS | SOUTHERNCROSS RIDERS | FIRED UP RIDAZ | SELF MADE OUTLAWZ | 1-90 TRAIL RIDERS | THE REAL DEAL RIDING CLUB | OBERLIN RAMBLERS | TOMBSTONE DIVAS AND DEBOS | FREE RIDERS | LA JEWELS AND GENTS | OAKDALE O.G. RIDERS | GREENSBURG POSSE | 5TH WARD ROUGH RIDERS | BARNYARD POSSE TRAIL RIDERS | CAMPTOWN RIDDAHZ | HERITAGE RIDERS | COUNTRY GIRL RIDERS | BAD WEATHER STABLES | STEPPIN DIVAS | DIRTY TRAIL RIDERS | CONCEITEDLY CLASSIE | SADDLE TRAPS | STUD-R-US RIDERS | INDEPENDENT RIDERS | LAST OF A DYING BREED |

Louisiana's Black Trail Riders: A Living History

Alexandra Giancarlo

Convening in often-secluded fields and riding on country lanes, trail rides brings generations of black riders together nearly every weekend. Syncopated rhythms of zydeco music announce the riders' passing. At a designated resting place, they'll pause to enjoy pork-steak sandwiches and some shade and water for their horses. Before long, the sea of matching t-shirts and colorful button-downs, adorned with evocative names such as the Pineywoods Riders and Barnyard Posse Trail Riders, gallops to life again. These riders gather to honor the path-breaking journeys of their ancestors, many of whom count themselves as among the first cattlepeople in the nation, to experience the vibrancy of their present-day culture in all its complexity, and to "pass a good time" with friends, neighbors, and children—the next generation of riders.

Crystal Davis of the trail riding group The Kountry Bunnies shared indelible memories of growing up attending trail rides held in conjunction with cookouts, campouts, and zydeco concerts: "I can remember my grandfather and my grandmother starched down in their pants and their shirts and I was following right behind 'em: 'Let's go!'"

Southern Louisiana has three or four major associations that serve as the organizing entities for their respective dozen or so trail riding groups. Each hosts an annual ride. Facilities range from rustic with homemade food for sale, to slick, large-scale productions that attract out-of-state vendors and thousands of sponsorship dollars. Regardless of the size of the event, for Neil Bob, former president of the Rainbow Trail Ride Association, "We are all like one big family. Some of them are the ones who are real close and we talk, we call each other in the morning to just see how you are doing and what's up for the weekend." Robert Phillips of the Crazy Hat Riders—who rode for more than a half-century before his passing in 2017—explained, "It's a hobby that I love. I feel 100 percent when I am riding my horse."

Trail riding is a particularly embedded tradition for those Louisianans who identify as "Creole"—mixed-race French heritage people who reside in the southwestern part of the state. The term "creole" was used centuries ago to describe people born in the new colony to parents who hailed from the "Old World." Both Europeans and enslaved peoples qualified under this definition; the crucial distinction was not race, but birth, and it differentiated the local-born from newcomers. "Creole" has undergone a multitude of geographic and period specific changes since. Today, it's most often employed to identify people of at least partial black ancestry (usually in combination with European and Native American lineage). Creoles are likely to have cultural attributes such as Catholic religious faith, region-specific culinary traditions, and an affinity for accordion-driven zydeco music, a synthesis of traditional Creole music called "la-la," African-American musical traditions like R&B, blues, and—more recently—hip hop, with influences from Cajun music as well. A connection to agricultural life through rural land ownership, livestock raising, horsemanship, and, more rarely today, cattle ranching, are also strong cultural identifiers.

That free Creoles of color and enslaved peoples (both of whom were ancestors of today's Creoles) in the antebellum period were heavily involved in the establishment and perpetuation of the area's cattle ranching ecology helps to explain the association of these communities with horseman/horsewoman-ship. In fact, when Governor O'Reilly issued an ordinance in 1770 in New Orleans regarding the distribution of land grants, of which many newly arrived Acadians availed themselves, a settler was required to prove that "he owns one hundred domesticated head of cattle, some horses and sheep, and that he has two slaves to tend to them." Indeed, the land claimants were not required to establish residence on the frontier. As a result, many sent their sons along with the property (animals and slaves) required by the terms of the ordinance. It appears that some male slave owners sent their enslaved mixed-race sons to the Opelousas Post; these sons were promised freedom and stock provisions to establish themselves on the frontier. There, "(o)nce the claim was established the (enslaved sons) remained with the herd on the prairie where they worked under a minimum of supervision" write Oubre and Leonard.[1] Historian James Dormon explains, "The popularity of the trail rides suggests the historic association of the Prairie Creoles with cattle ranching. Many of their forebears were, in fact, cowboys."[2]

Trail rides, it seems, morphed into their modern form about thirty years ago. Such little documentation on the practice exists that the voices collected here might constitute the most authoritative history of the tradition. Although black horsemanship exists throughout the country, trail riding as a formalized cultural event tends to be confined to southern Louisiana, particularly the southwestern region, and eastern Texas, though black Mississippians are increasingly connecting with the practice. An important difference between today's rides and rides of the past is that, formerly, it was more common for the horseback ride to be held on actual trails or to meander through pastures, whereas today they are typically held on public roadways. Many other foundational elements endure. On Friday, a free "cowboy stew" is on offer for attendees (rice and mixed meat with gravy, Creole-style), with a DJ and dancing in the evening. Saturday features cooking and visiting amongst attendees—many of who come with an RV or camper—with possibly a short horseback ride, followed by a DJ or band in the evening. Sunday, a longer horseback ride with a designated resting place halfway along the route is the main focus, followed by one or two bands in the late afternoon/early evening. One element present in Louisiana trail rides of the past rarely seen in their present incarnation is a multi-day ride, such as that described by Ulysses Charles that involved an eighteen to twenty mile ride from Cecilia to Leonville.[3] Or, as former rider Linus Jordan explained: "If it was a long weekend, it might be a two or three day trail ride. . . . And every stop overnight you'd have bands playing—Cajun music, zydeco music—(and) people barbecuing."

Trail riding as a recreational activity likely has overlapping origins: as a fundraiser for local Catholic churches or community centers, as a family outing that evolved from an era when horses were used for transportation and everyday life on the farm (as cultural activist Dustin Cravins put it, "It was really just a social gathering, something to do in the middle of nowhere!"), and as an homage to ancestral black cattlemen and women. John Broussard, co-host of the zydeco radio show *Zydeco Est Pas Salé*, summarized his understanding of the history of trail rides:

> As you very well know, the first cowboy happened to be black. And that was a means of travel. And also it was a means of entertainment, getting together. . . . It represented what was a culture or an activity, a means of survival, travelling from one location to another, was through trail rides on horse, wagons, and all of that. But trail rides are just a reenactment of what took place many years ago, and the belief of the importance of a horse.

Other less common origins offered were that formalized trail-riding, similar to what is seen today with an admission fee, began due to the expense of caring for horses. Kenneth Wayne Bellard of the Eunice Easy Riders suggested that going to trail-riding events to support each other helped to offset the costs of feeding and caring for animals. Neil Bob asserted that recreational trail-riding grew out of rural Creole Mardi Gras events, which involves a begging ritual on horseback to gather ingredients for a communal celebratory gumbo. Other community members tie the practice more explicitly to labor, explaining that they began as get-togethers in the early twentieth century for those who had little disposable income; participants would gather with their horses, contribute ingredients for a communal meal, and camp overnight.[4]

Today one can "trail ride" *sans* horse, especially at the large-scale festival-like trail rides, such as Step-N-Strut, that boast thousands of attendees who come to enjoy bands and food vendors, to camp and cook, and to catch up with friends. For those who don't have a horse but wish to participate in the ride itself, it's possible to borrow one from a friend or to ride on a party wagon decorated with the group's colors and logo.

By most accounts, in the earlier days of trail-riding, a stronger gender divide existed than at present, though women on horseback is still a relatively rare sight. In the nineties, Rex and Yvonne Mills, interviewed for a folklife series published by LSU-Eunice, noted that female riders were becoming

1. Claude F. Oubre and Roscoe Leonard, "Free and Proud: St. Landry's *gens de couleur*," in *Louisiana Tapestry: The Ethnic Weave of St. Landry Parish*, eds. V. Baker and J. T. Kreamer (Lafayette: Center for Louisiana Studies, University of Southwestern Louisiana, 1983).

2. James H. Dormon, "Ethnicity and Identity: Creoles of Color in Twentieth-Century South Louisiana, in *Creoles of Color of the Gulf South*, ed. J. H. Dormon (Knoxville: University of Tennessee Press, 1996).

3. Sherry T. Broussard, *Louisiana's Zydeco: Images of America* (Charleston, S.C.: Arcadia Publishing, 2013).

4. Tissa Porter, "A Zydeco What?," *Creole Magazine*, 1991, 5-9.

more common than in the early days of trail-riding.[5] Mary M. Milton-Fontenot of the Buckwild Divas was pleased to share that she grew up a part of her mother's trail-riding group, the Opelousas Lady Trail Riders, which held the first women's trail ride. Today, a handful of groups are segmented into subgroups for their male and female riders, though they usually participate in trail rides as one large group. The Phenomenal Katz are the female counterpart to the Palamino Riders while the Buckwild Riders are the male counterpart to the all-women Buckwild Divas. The bulk of duties of the hosting group are shared across genders, although on the ride it is usually a male who is the flagperson (the association representative who leads the riders and keeps order on the route). Men will also more commonly drive the trucks with the wagons attached during the ride. Acynthia Villery, who has Creole roots in Louisiana and is president of the Texas trail-riding group The Bill Pickett Trail Riders, insisted that all responsibilities for the ride are shared:

> Anything from organizing, setting up the vendors, to getting the tent set up, to all the press and everything else prior, going out to [get] whatever type of license I need to obtain, to getting there, to picking up trash, to parking, to dealing with issues . . . the gate and everything else. It's not gender. It's not.

Many trail riders boast a strong affiliation with Creole roots and French ethnic heritage evident on the one hand and an awareness of and connection to the experiences and challenges of mainstream black American life on the other. This hybridity mirrors the increasing infusion of hip-hop into zydeco music, which has led to debate within the Creole community about the role of hip-hop music in attracting a "bad element" to trail rides. Indeed, one of the most striking elements of trail ride culture is the blend of black American aesthetics with rural motifs, seemingly to little controversy or contradiction. "Because we are people of color, people tend to adopt the urban trends. . . . The hip-hop culture in trail rides is getting to be really big," describes Charles Cravins, co-host of the radio show *Zydeco Extravaganza*, in capturing this convergence of identities. In general an affection for or identification with black America or "urban" culture does not require a disavowing of rural roots, or vice versa. Zydeco great Keith Frank has released a number of double albums whose cover art demonstrates two "sides" of his persona. One CD contains more hardline traditional zydeco tunes and the other features a contemporary zydeco sound with influences from other genres; one of his biggest hits, a version of his song "Haterz," features a guest verse by Baton Rouge rapper Boozie Badazz (formerly Lil'Boosie). Anthropologist Sara Le Menestrel explains that "despite these obvious intermingling of styles, Frank makes a point . . . to link his contemporary style to an overarching tradition." She also notes a generational shift towards an urban style that, she suggests, "is not necessarily at odds with the image of the cowboy, which maintains its aura and continues to be celebrated by a younger generation of zydeco fans, whether they are of rural origin or urbanites."[6]

Creoles have overcome incredible odds: the horrors of slavery, Jim Crow, and ongoing racial prejudice, as well as language and cultural denigration. And while trail rides are far from the only cultural tradition to endure, they are a striking one with particular relevance for the broader community and for the next generation. Acynthia Villery noted that horsemanship has had a positive effect on youth in her area: "There are some people that have been in the streets that have said, if it wasn't for this [trail riding] life there is no telling where I'd be. So now I have a responsibility. If I want to ride, I gotta stay out of trouble. I have to take care of my horse." Shane Boagni, president of Barnyard Posse Trail Riders, concurs, and explained that his role was to "[keep] the youngsters into it, just keeping the culture going."

For many Creoles, trail rides exemplify a proud and little-known history of black horsemanship, one to pass on to their youth, as well as constitute a support network. Mary M. Milton-Fontenot of the Buckwild Divas describes how "It's just like if you get in trouble, they have your back. . . . We always look out for each other." For others, galloping along the backroads of southwestern Louisiana to the strains of zydeco music is the highlight of their week. Either way, trail riding is more than a horseback ride; it's a practice with deep cultural and familial resonance, a living history.

5. Linda Langley, Susan G. LeJeune, and Claude F Oubre, "Le reveil des fetes: Revitalized Celebrations and Performance Traditions," in *Louisiana State University at Eunice FolkLife Series* (Eunice: Louisiana State University at Eunice, 1997)

6. Sara Le Menestrel, *Negotiating Difference in French Louisiana Music: Categories, Stereotypes, and Identifications* (Jackson: University Press of Mississippi, 2015).

Image Captions

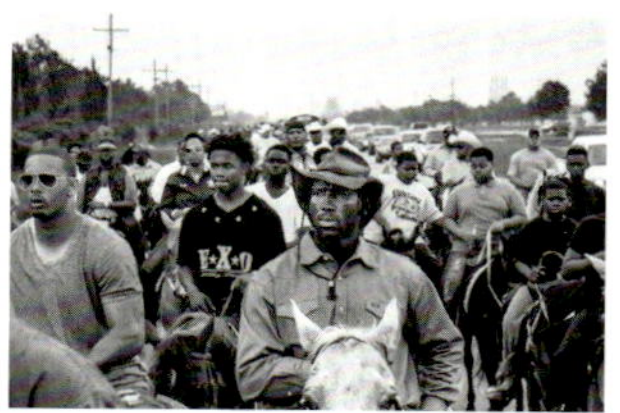

1. Riding Down LA 27,
(Calcasieu Parish) 2015

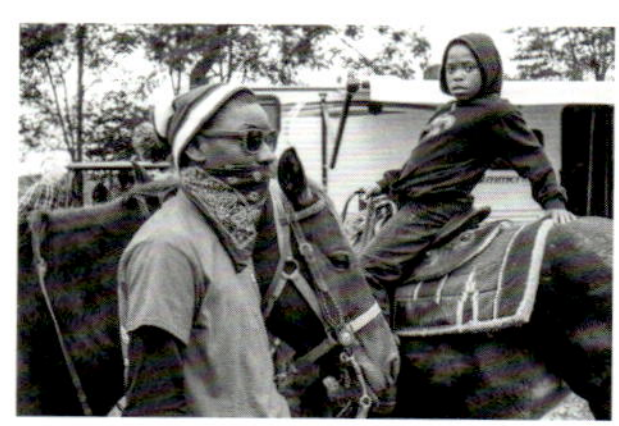

2. "Lil' Joe" (right) and
"Bowinkle,"
(Iberville Parish) 2014

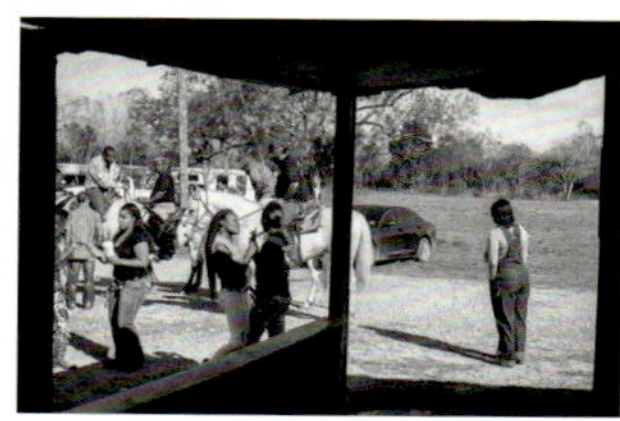

3. Before the Ride,
(Welsh) 2015

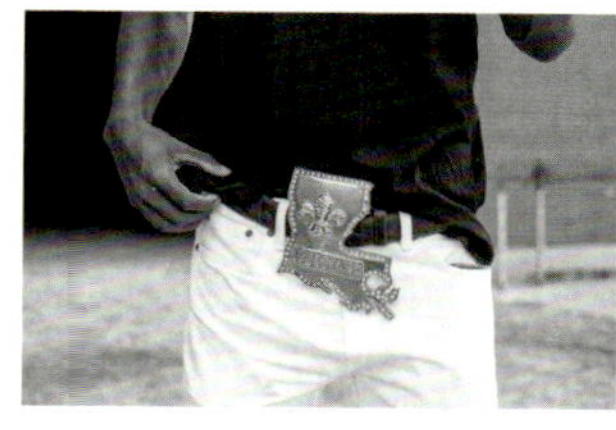

4. Louisiana Buckle,
(Sulphur) 2015

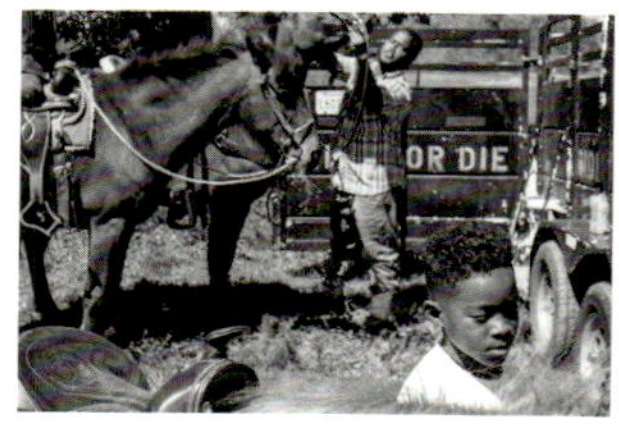

5. Jock (rear) and Gavin (front)
Saddle Horses,
(Opelousas) 2016

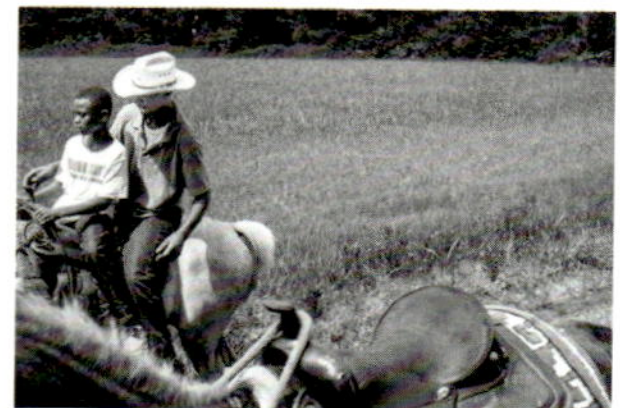

6. Father and Son,
(Cecilia) 2015

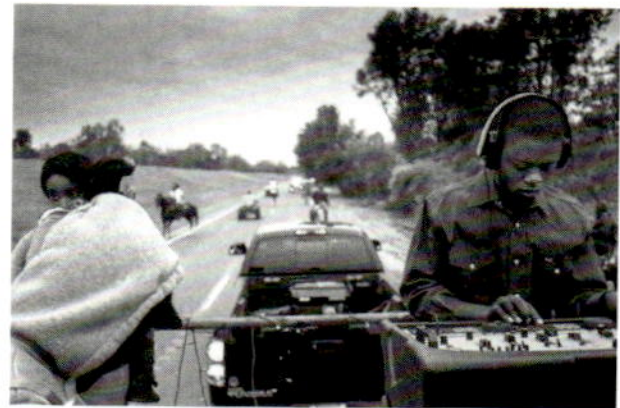

7. DJ, (River Road,
Iberville Parish) 2015

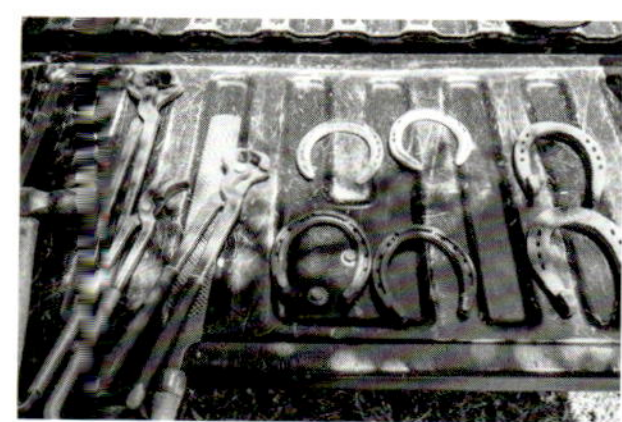

8. Tools belonging to
"Shelton the Shoe Man,"
(Evangeline Parish) 2017

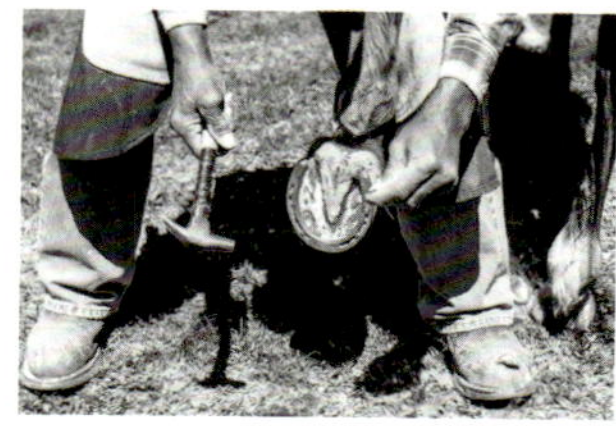

9. Jared Nailing a Horseshoe,
(Opelousas) 2016

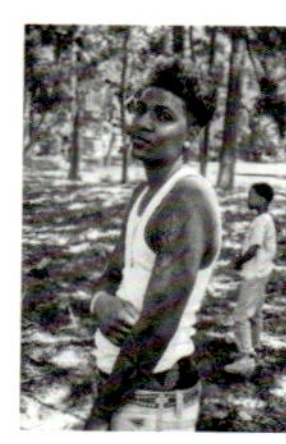

10. Jimmy,
(Kinder) 2015

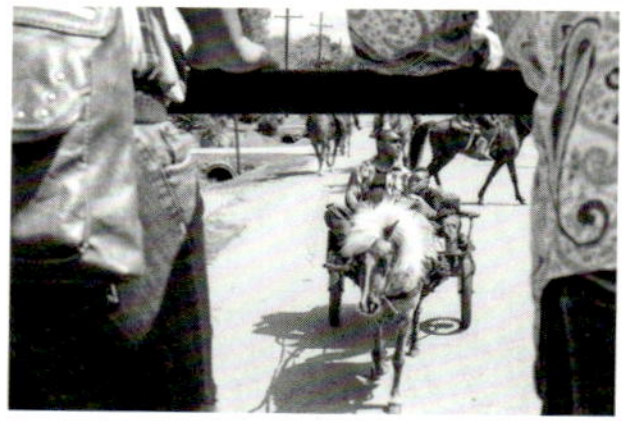

11. Father and Son on Chariot,
(Jeanerette) 2015

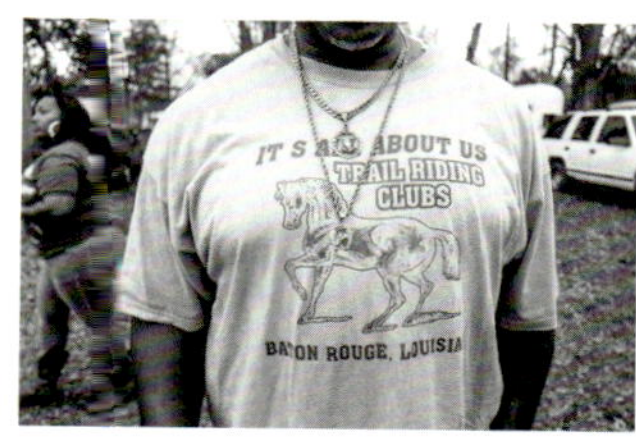

12. It's All About Us,
(Iberville Parish) 2014

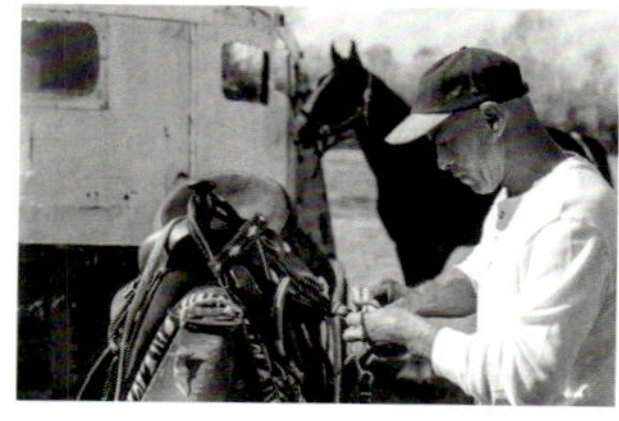

13. Gary,
(Welsh) 2015

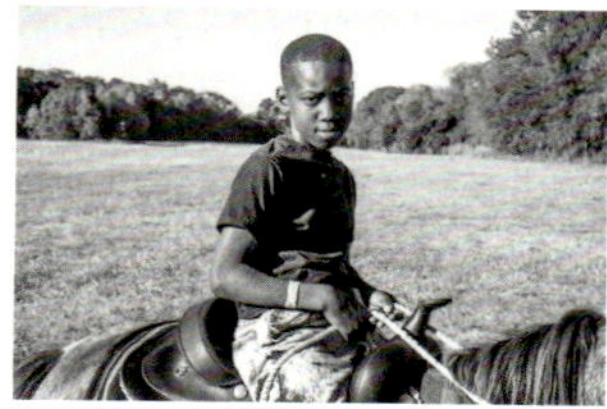

14. Biran,
(St Landry Parish) 2015

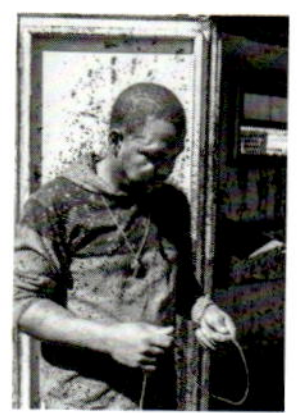

15. Derrick,
(Opelousas) 2017

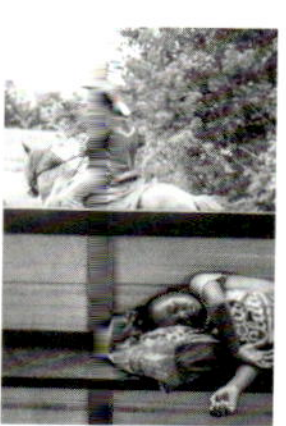

16. Sleeping Boy,
(St. Landry Parish) 2017

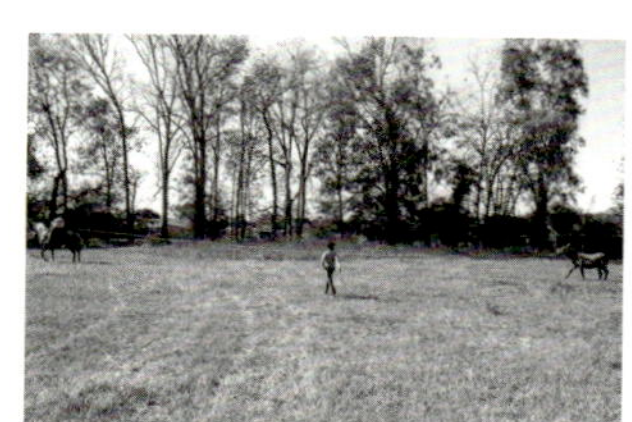

17. Pulling a Mule,
(St. Landry Parish) 2017

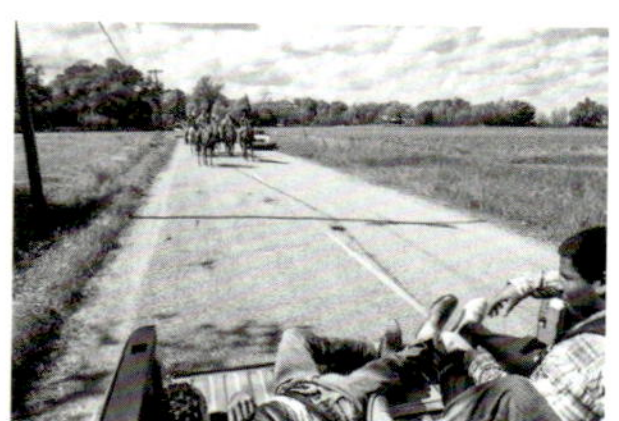

18. View from Tailgate,
(Iberia Parish) 2015

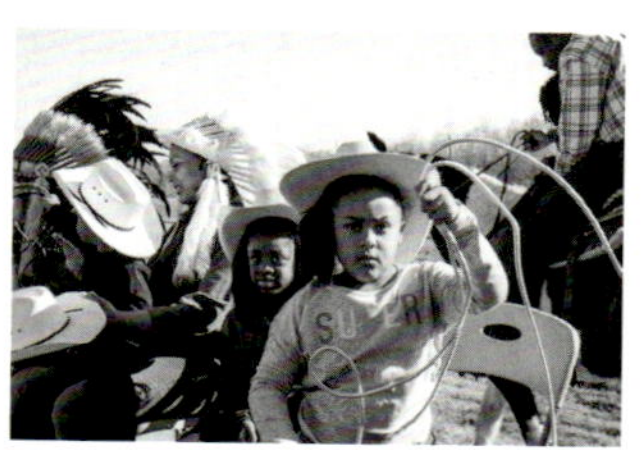

19. Apache Riders,
(Welsh) 2015

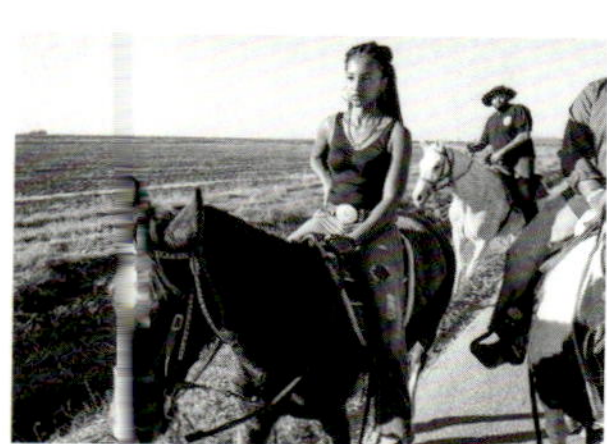

20. Amy,
(Jefferson Davis Parish) 2015

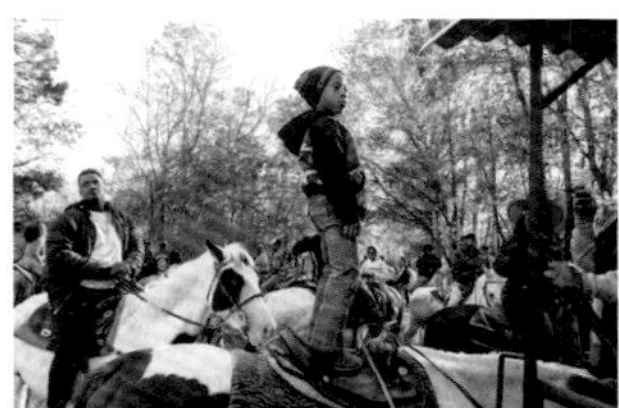

21. Mason Standing on Horse,
(St. Landry Parish) 2017

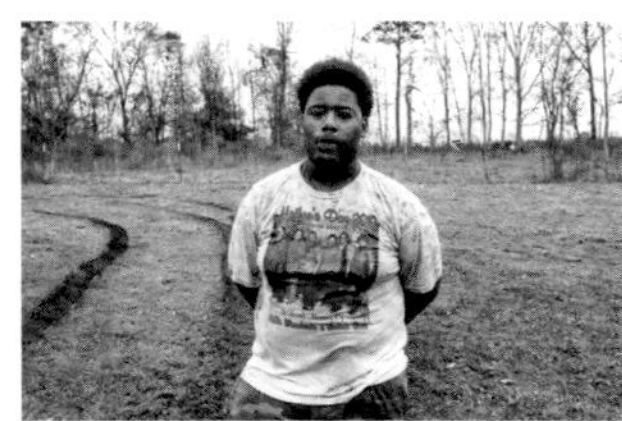

22. "KC",
(St. Mary Parish) 2015

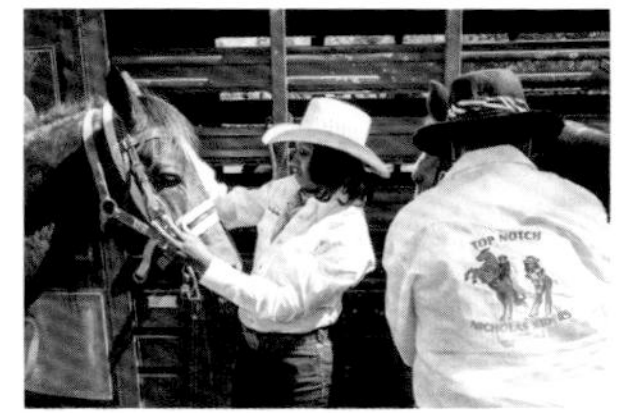

23. Top Notch Riders,
(Opelousas) 2017

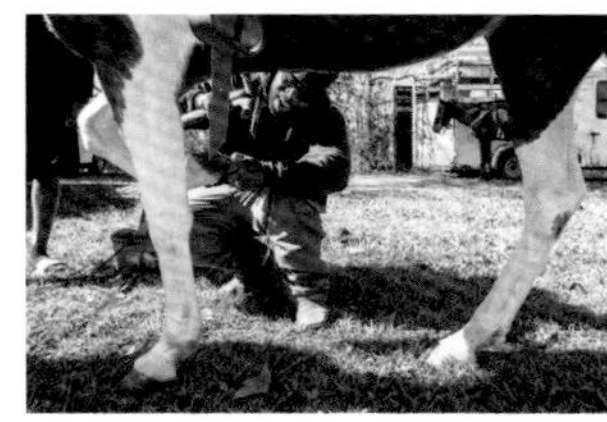

24. "Trouble Child"
Shoeing a Horse,
(St. Landry Parish) 2017

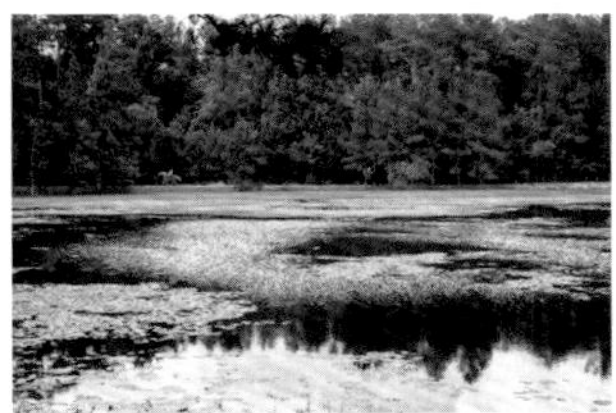

25. Louisiana Landscape,
(St. Landry Parish) 2016

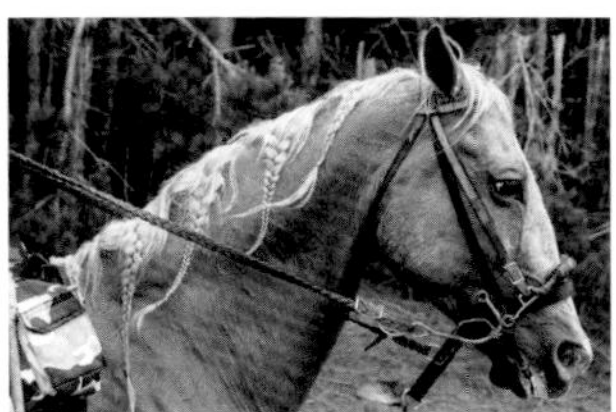

26. Horse,
(Calcasieu Parish) 2015

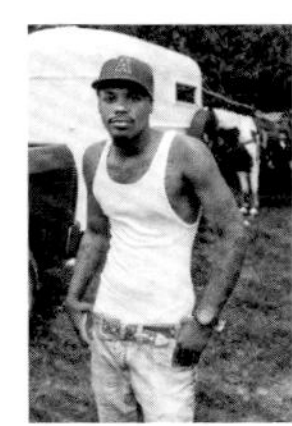

27. Gake,
(Jeanerette) 2015

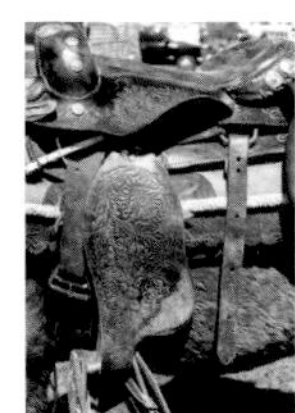

28. Saddle,
(Opelousas) 2016

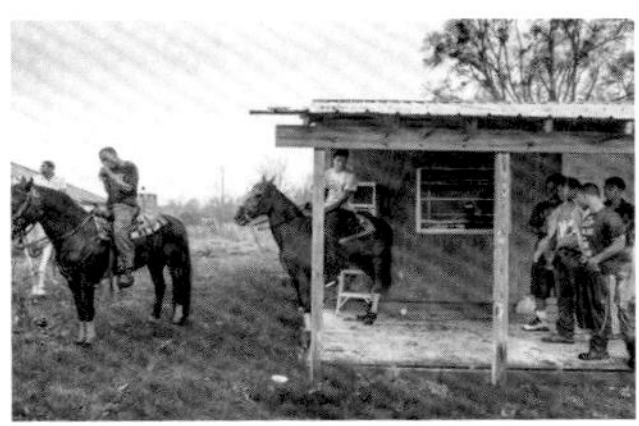

29. Afternoon Rain,
(East Feliciana Parish) 2015

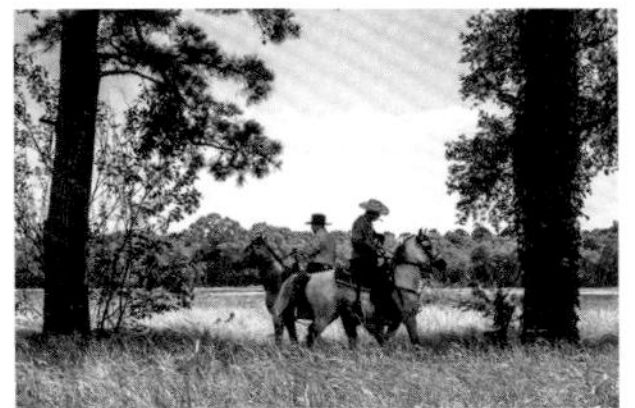

30. Riders in Field,
(Evangeline Parish) 2017

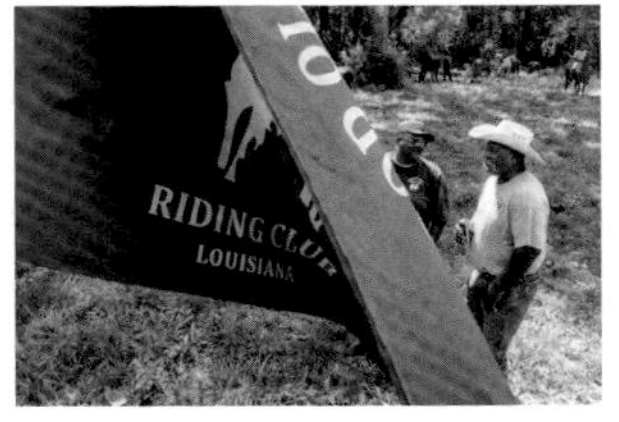

31. Aaron (left)
and Jimmy (right),
(Kinder) 2015

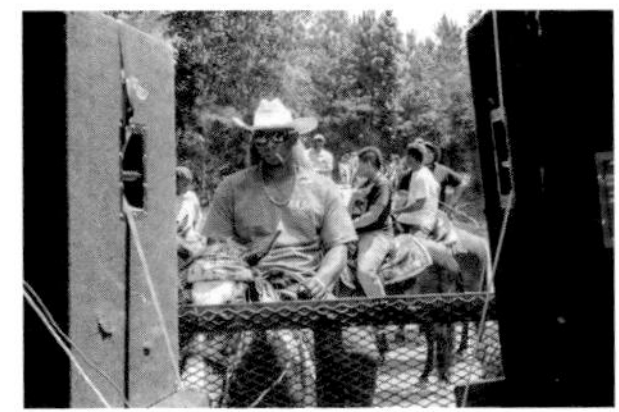

32. Troy,
(Allen Parish) 2015

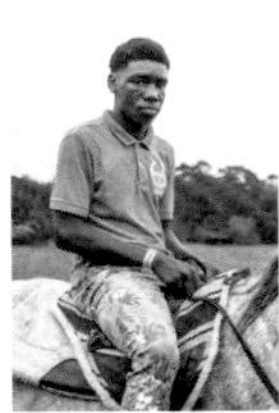

33. Jermaine,
(St. Landry Parish) 2017

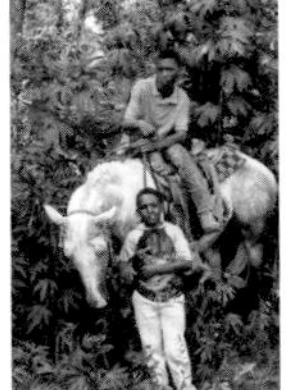

34. "Dutt" (horseback)
and Jamaire,
(St. Martin Parish) 2015

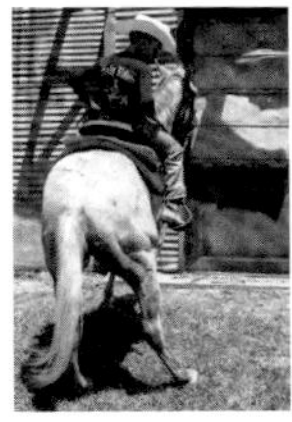

35. Darion,
(Opelousas) 2017

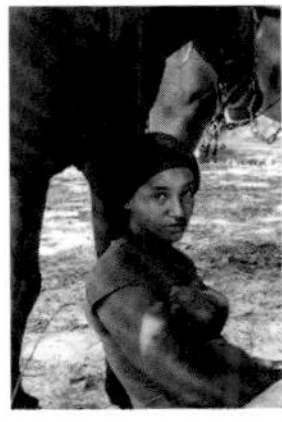

36. Amy,
(St. Landry
Parish) 2017

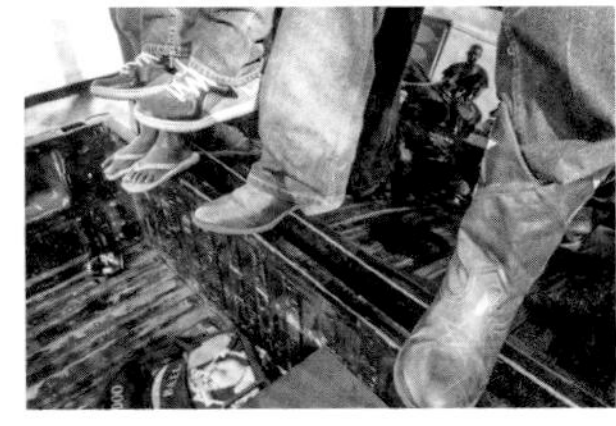

37. Kids on Truck,
(Iberia Parish) 2015

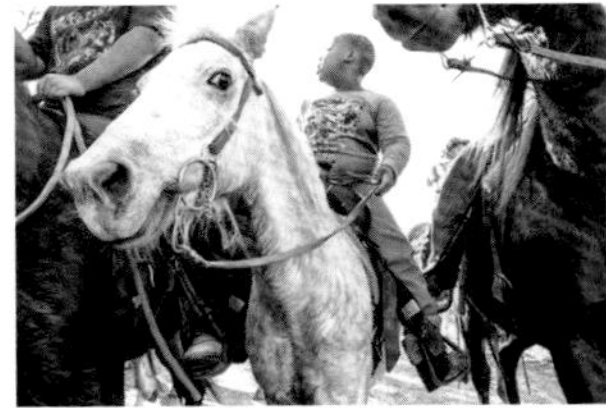

38. Zack Riding his
Horse Shuga,
(Jefferson Davis Parish) 2015

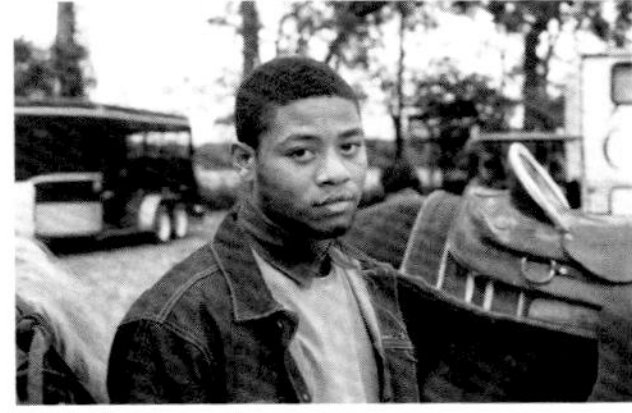

39. Jamire,
(Iberville Parish) 2014

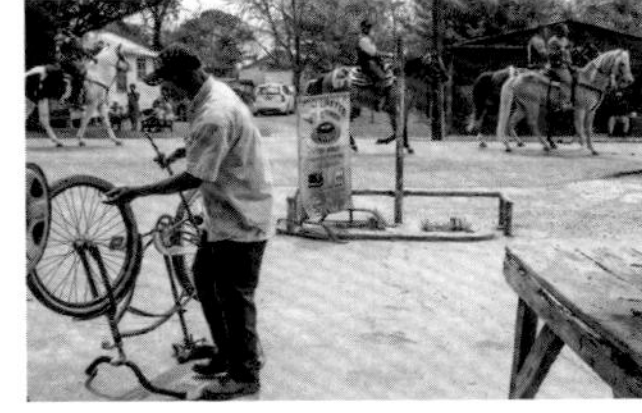

40. Riding Through Jeanerette,
(Jeanerette) 2015

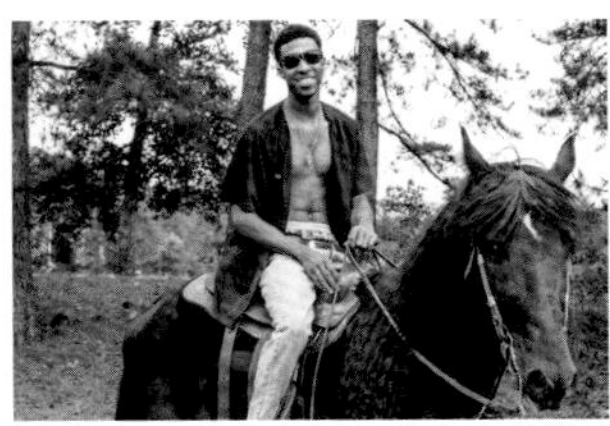

41. Bryan,
(Allen Parish) 2015

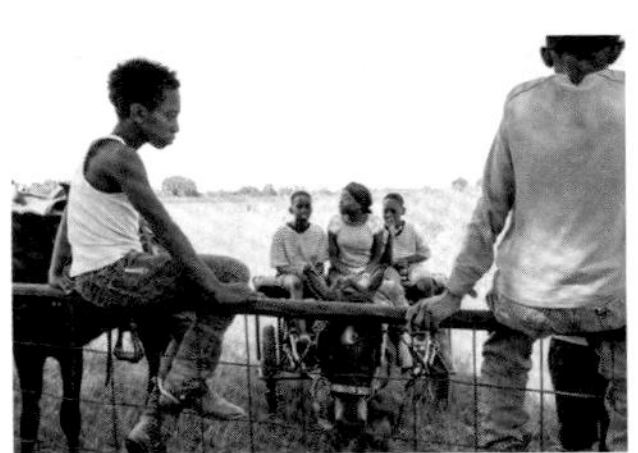

42. Steady Steppin' Trail Ride,
(Evangeline Parish) 2017

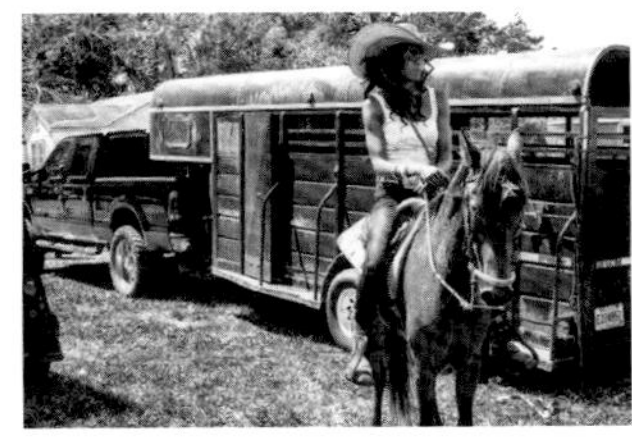

43. Latoya,
(Jeanerette) 2015

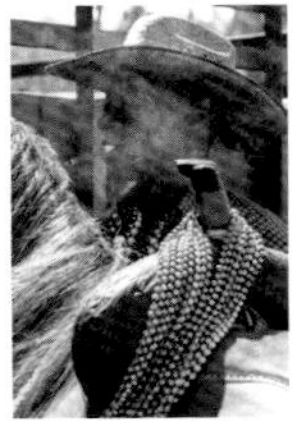

44. Troy,
(Opelousas) 2017

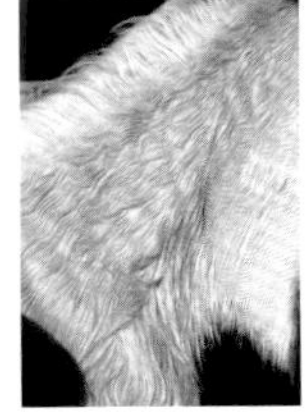

45. Horse (detail),
(Welsh) 2015

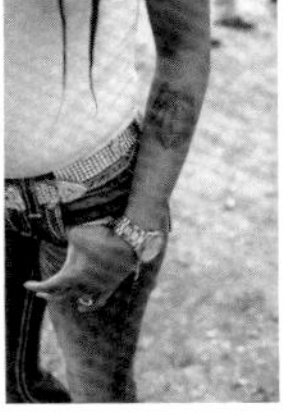

46. Megan,
(Welsh) 2015

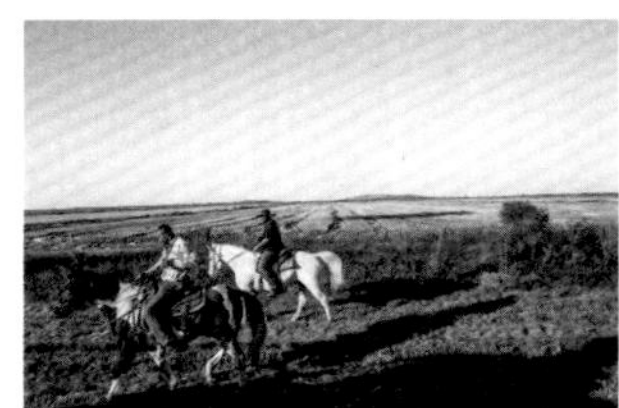

47. Chris (left) and Andre (right)
(Jefferson Davis Parish) 2015

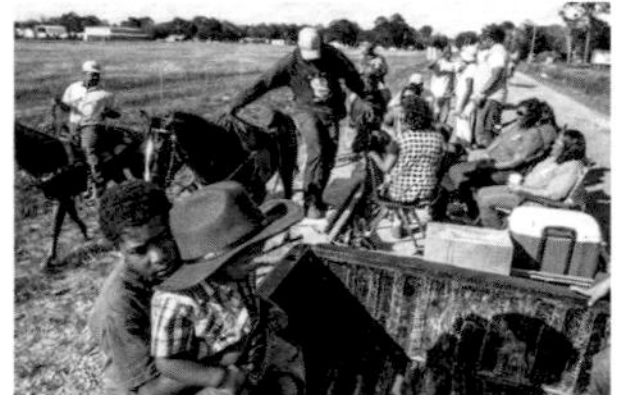

48. Double L Ryderz,
(Iberia Parish) 2015

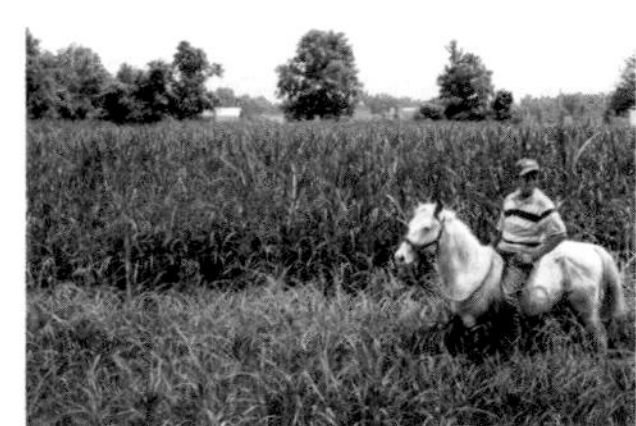

49. Bryson,
(St. Martin Parish) 2015

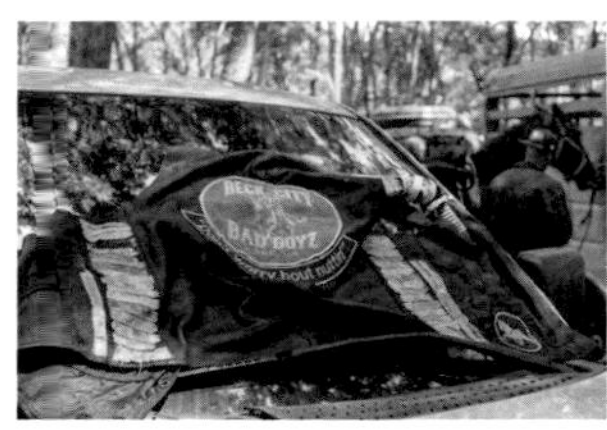

50. Beck City Bad Boyz,
(Jeanerette) 2015

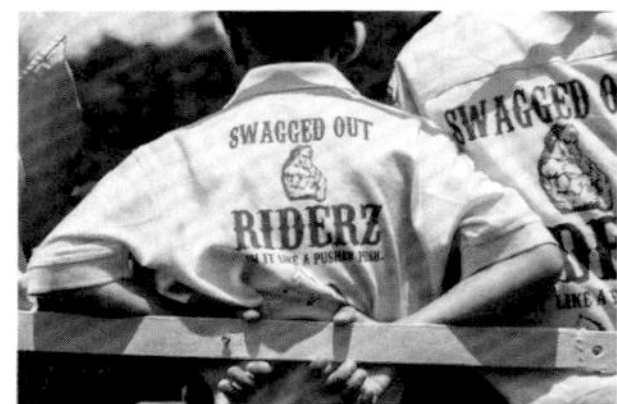

51. Swagged Out Riderz,
(Kinder) 2015

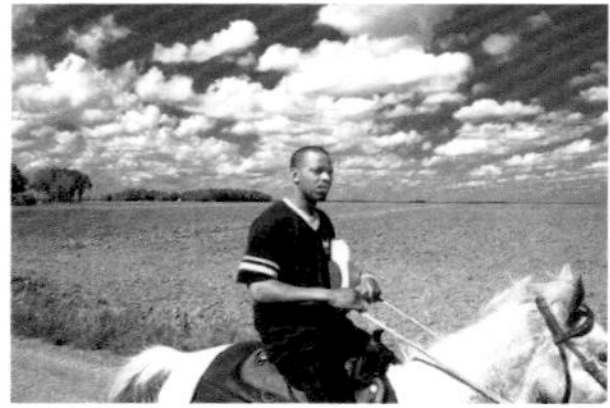

52. Unidentified Rider,
(Iberia Parish) 2015

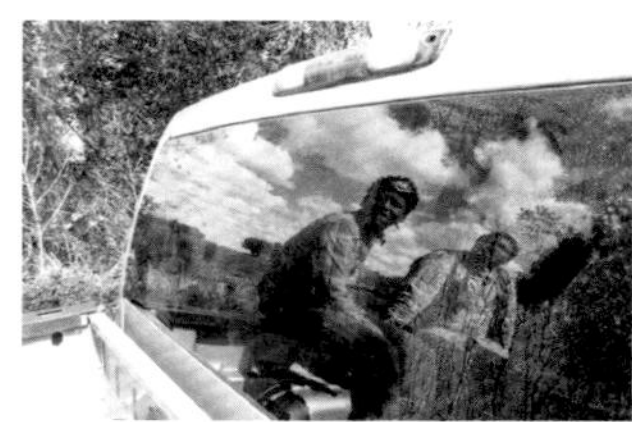

53. Rear Truck Window View,
(Iberia Parish) 2015

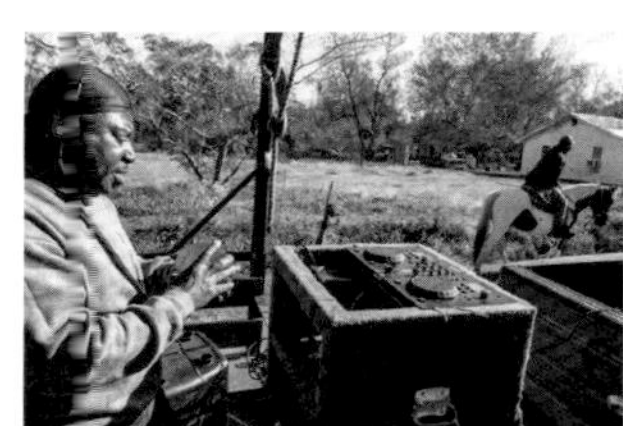

54. Arthur,
(St. Landry Parish) 2017

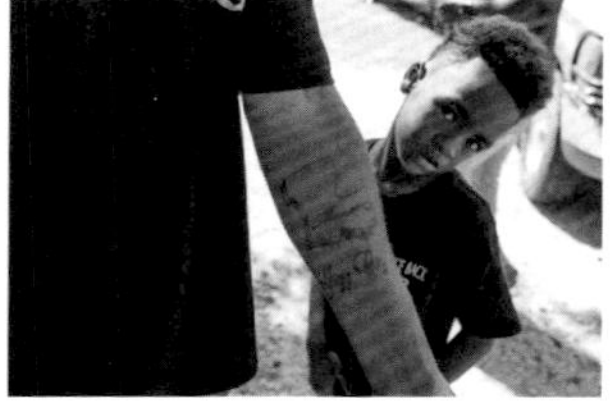

55. Josh and Son Logan,
(Evangeline Parish) 2017

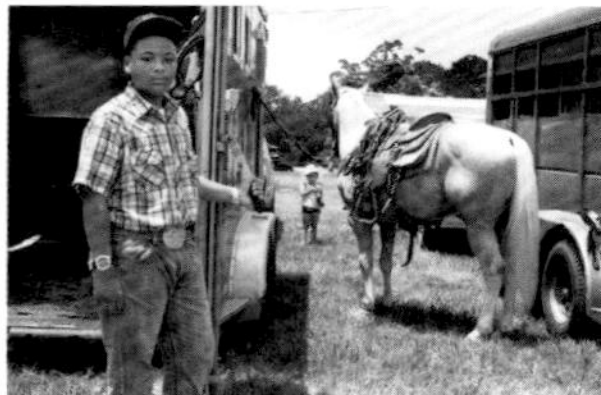

56. Young Riders,
(Cecilia) 2015

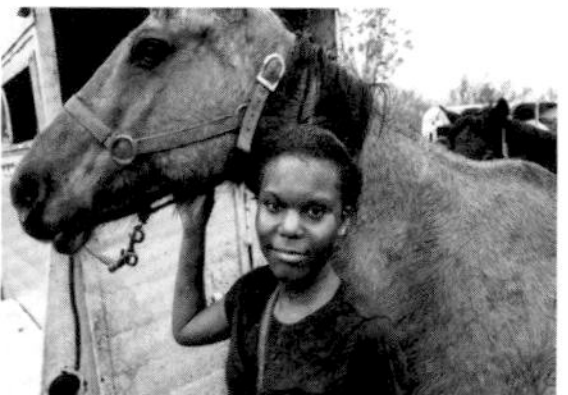

57. Unidentified Rider,
(St. Mary Parish) 2015

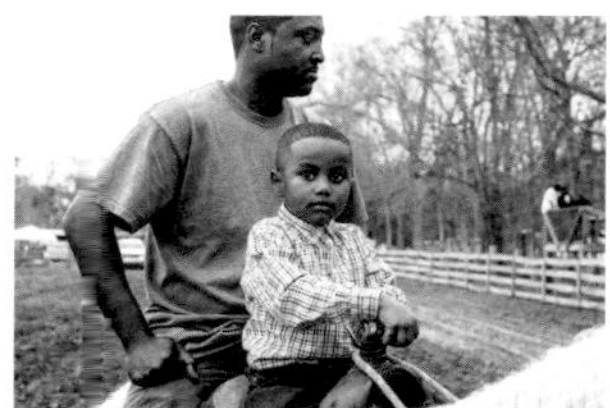

58. "Lil' Buck" and
Son on Horse,
(Iberville Parish) 2014

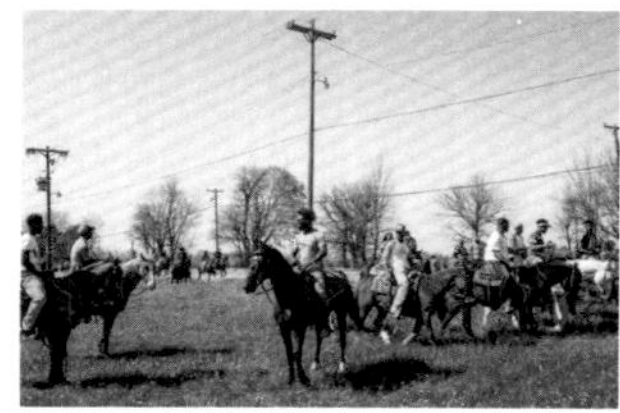

59. Along Ronald Reagan
Highway, (Opelousas) 2017

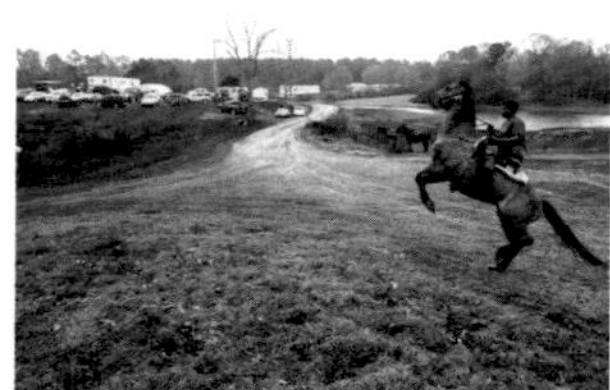

60. Riding in the Rain,
(East Feliciana Parish) 2015

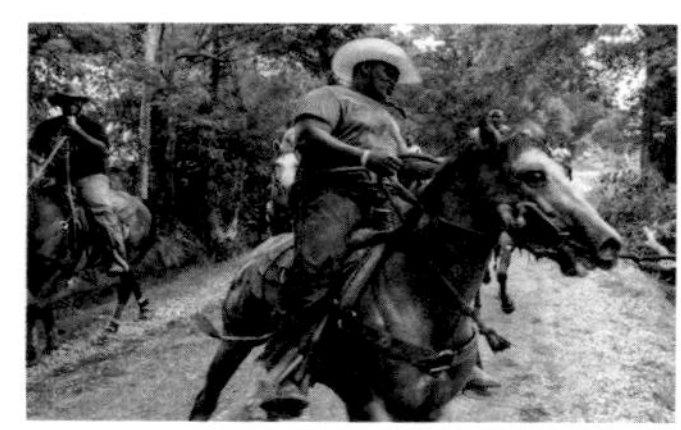

61. Reining Spin,
(St. Landry Parish) 2017

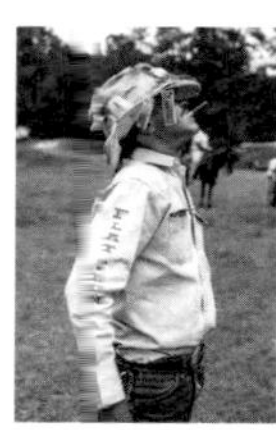

62. Flat Iron,
(Kinder) 2015

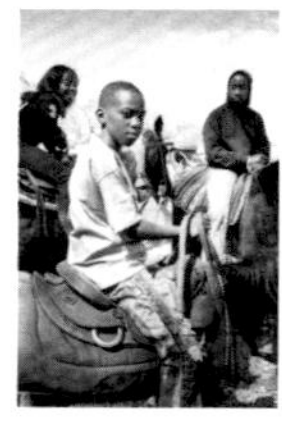

63. Biran and
Fellow Riders,
(Opelousas) 2017

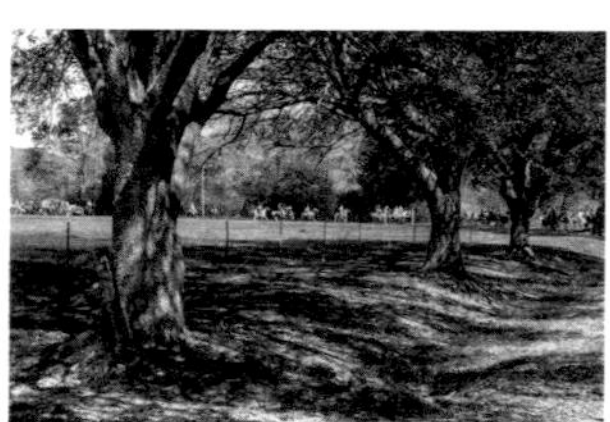

64. Trail Ride,
(St. Landry Parish) 2016

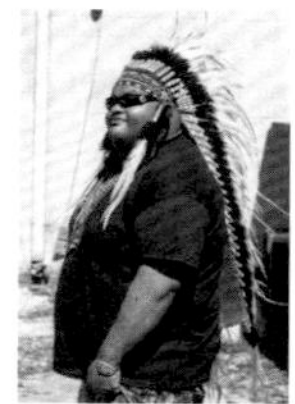

65. Quincy,
(Opelousas) 2017

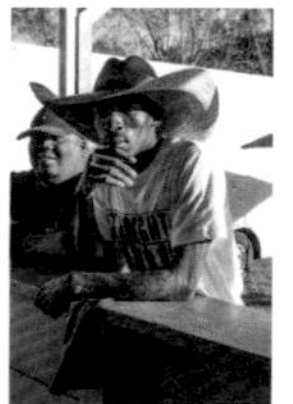

66. Jarrette,
(Leonville) 2015

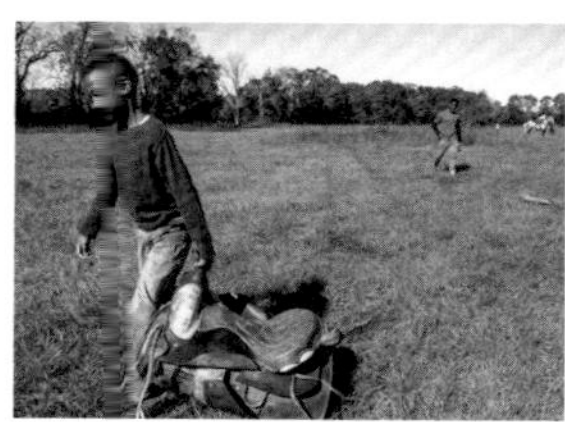

67. Boy with Saddle,
(St. Landry Parish) 2017

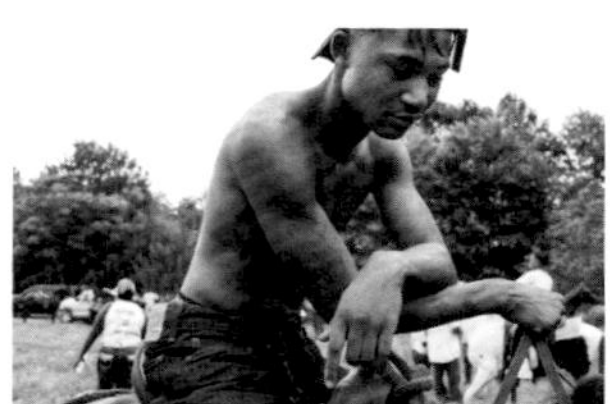

68. Phil,
(St. Landry Parish) 2017

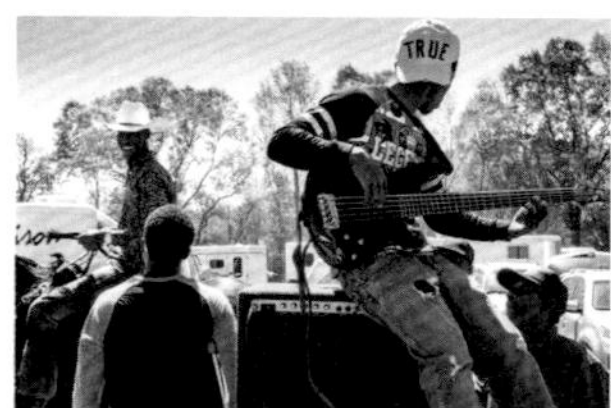

69. Musician on Trailer,
(Opelousas) 2016

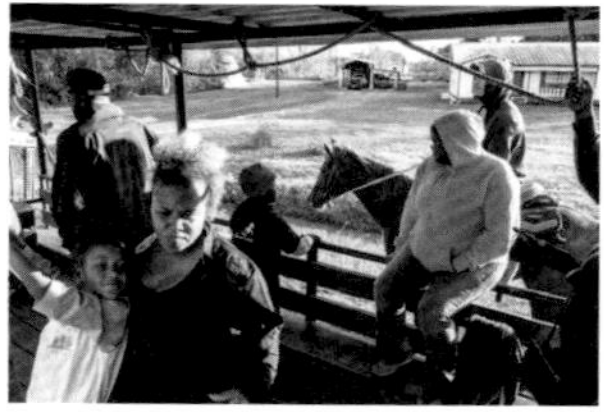

70. Shuga Shack Riders
Party Wagon,
(St. Landry Parish) 2017

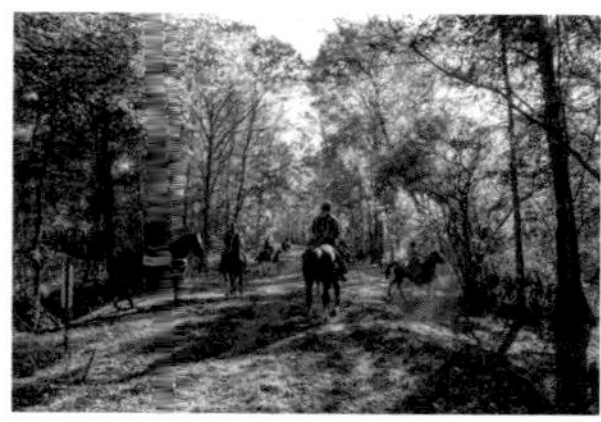

71. Merrick Road,
(St. Landry Parish) 2017

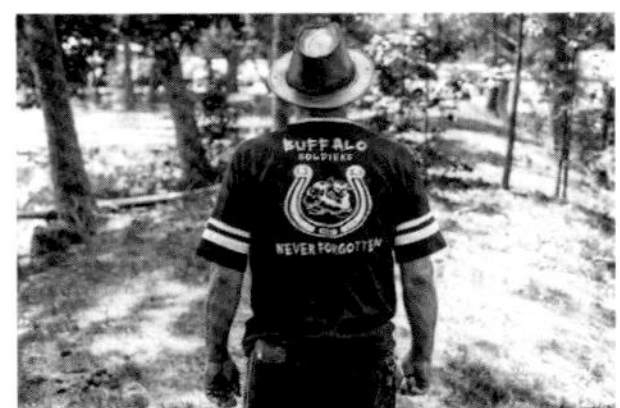

72. Buffalo Soldiers,
(Kinder) 2015

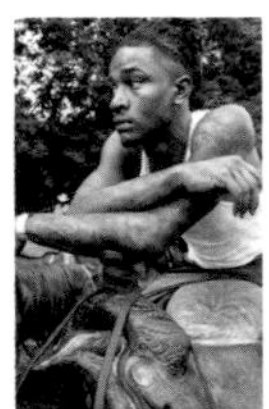

73. Decourion,
(St. Landry Parish) 2017

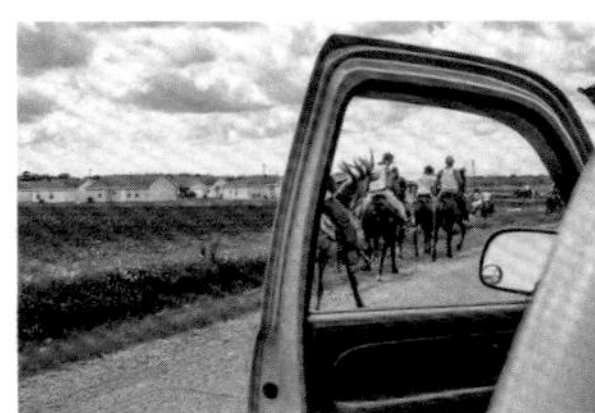

74. Window View,
(Iberia Parish) 2015

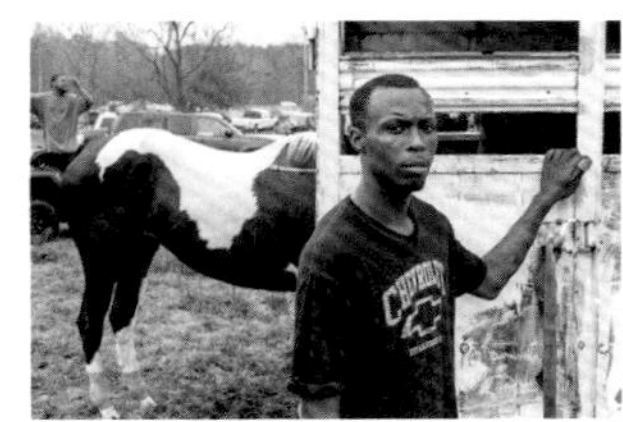

75. Tommi,
(St. Mary Parish) 2015

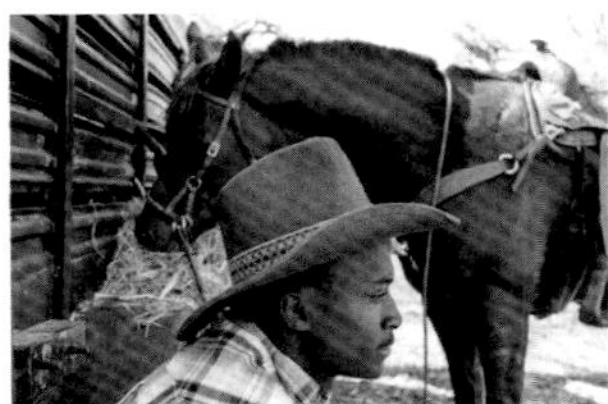

76. Keith,
(Opelousas) 2017

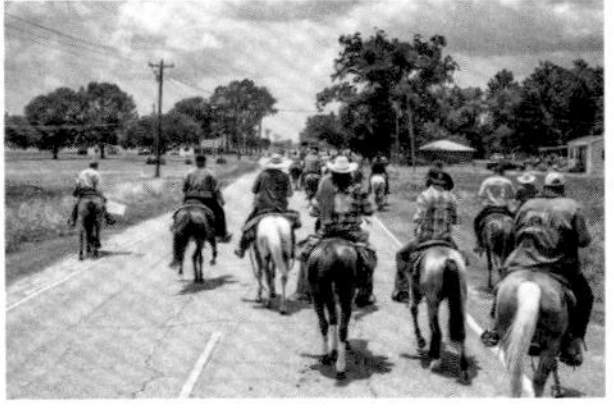

77. Procession,
(Cecilia) 2015

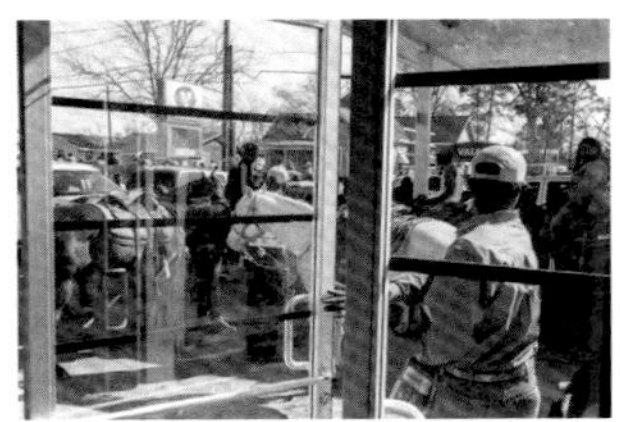

78. Valero Station,
(Opelousas) 2017

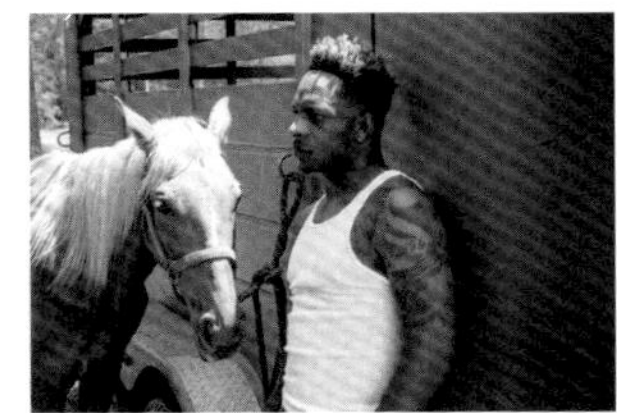

79. Shelton,
(Allen Parish) 2015

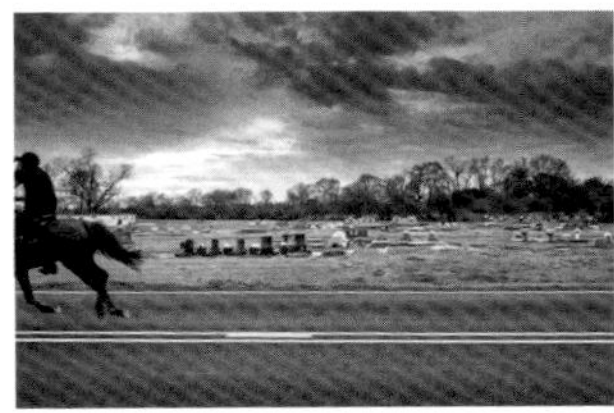

80. St. Joseph Cemetery,
Highway 77,
(Iberville Parish) 2014

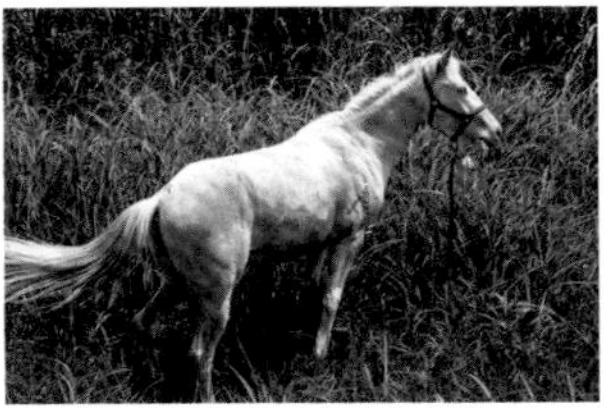

81. Horse in Sugar Cane Field,
(St. Martin Parish) 2015

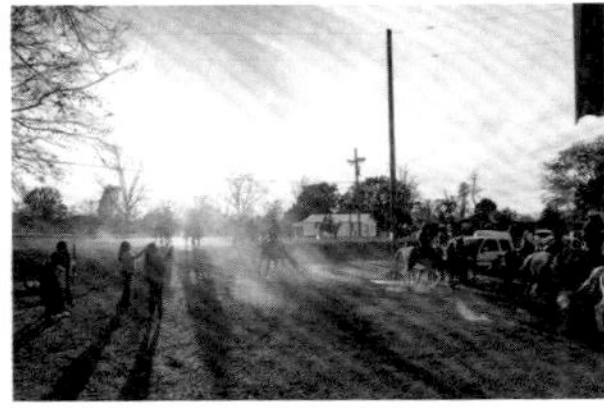

82. End of the Ride,
(St. Landry Parish) 2017

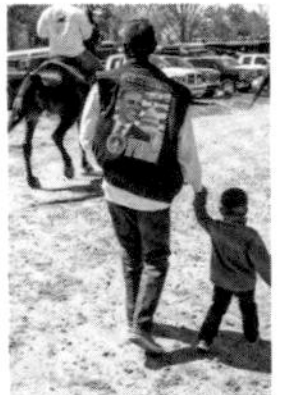

83. Witness to History,
(Opelousas) 2016

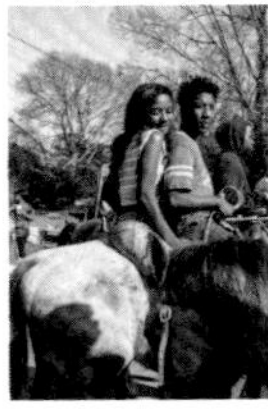

84. Young Riders,
(Opelousas) 2017

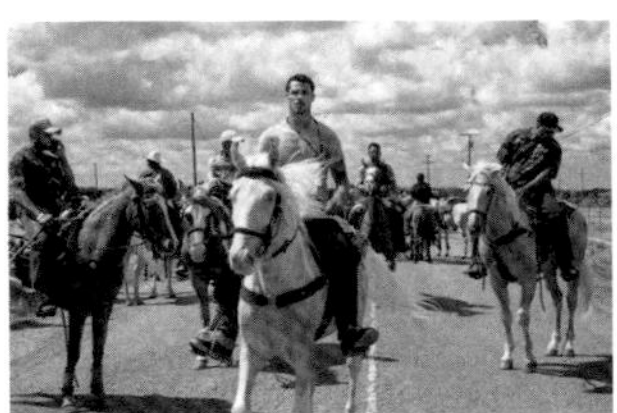

85. Homer (center) and Riders,
(Jeanerette) 2015

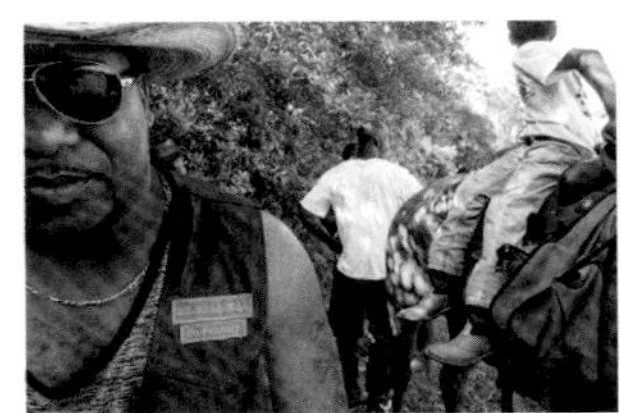

86. "Mr. Real Deal,"
(Iberia Parish) 2015

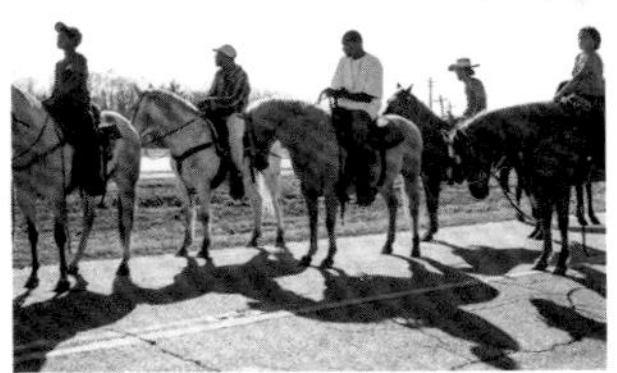

87. Silhouetted Riders,
(Jefferson Davis Parish) 2015

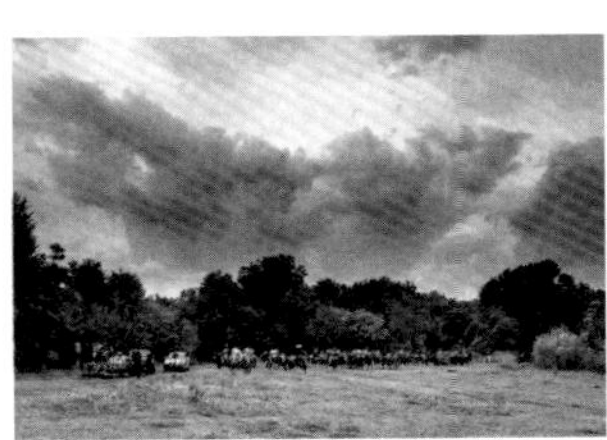

88. Zydeco Musicians in Field,
(St. Landry Parish) 2017

Acknowledgments

I am grateful to my mother for teaching me to ride a motorcycle and imparting in me the spirit of wonder and adventure that is at the root of this work. These pictures wouldn't be possible without you. I'm part of a creative community that includes friends and colleagues who inspire and challenge me, and whose opinions I deeply value. They have, directly and indirectly, helped shaped this project. I'm indebted to you. I would like to acknowledge and thank the Louisiana Endowment for the Humanities and South Arts, organizations promoting artists and scholars in the South. I'm appreciative to Billy Reid, who hails from Louisiana and is a proponent of southern culture, who first brought exposure to the work. Thank you to James Wilson at UL Press who shared my enthusiasm in bringing this project to publication. I am grateful to have encountered Alexandra Giancarlo's research into the riding clubs while beginning the book and am appreciative of her accompanying essay that helps us better understand the rich heritage of the trail rides.

I am especially thankful to Henry Jackson, who on my first chance encounter with a trail ride, encouraged me to join the passing procession. He was also kind enough to introduce me to fellow riders, opening the door for me to pursue the photographs you find here. Thanks to all the people who allowed me to ride with and photograph them, those who invited me into the back of their pick-up trucks, onto their trailers and party wagons, as well the DJs and musicians who never let the music stop. These photographs celebrate and honor you. To the riders that remain unidentified at the time of publication, I hope to attribute your participation in this community as the project moves forward. The trail riders I have come to know over the past few years have radically shifted my sense of how a cowboy can be defined and are reminders that black equestrian culture stems from a time when Louisiana Territory was in fact the American West. In the writing of the American story, many have been overlooked. With this project I hope to share one history that has largely remained untold.

J.A.
Baton Rouge
March 2018

ISBN 13: 978-1-946160-22-5

http://ulpress.org
University of Louisiana at Lafayette Press
P.O. Box 43558
Lafayette, LA 70504-3558

Printed in Canada on acid-free paper.

Library of Congress Cataloging-in-Publication Data

Names: Ariaz, Jeremiah, author.
Title: Louisiana trail riders / Jeremiah Ariaz.
Description: Lafayette, LA : University of Louisiana at Lafayette Press, 2018.
Identifiers: LCCN 2018006280 | ISBN 9781946160225 (paper : alk. paper)
Subjects: LCSH: Trail riding--Louisiana--Photographs.
Classification: LCC SF309.28 .A75 2018 | DDC 798.2/309763--dc23
LC record available at https://lccn.loc.gov/2018006280